CRITICAL ESSAYS IN APPLIED SPORT PSYCHOLOGY

DAVID GILBOURNE, PHD

Editor

University of Wales Institute, Cardiff, United Kingdom

MARK B. ANDERSEN, PHD

Editor

Victoria University, Australia

Human Kinetics

Library of Congress Cataloging-in-Publication Data

Gilbourne, David.
  Critical essays in applied sport psychology / David Gilbourne, Mark
Andersen.
        p. cm.
  Includes bibliographical references and index.
  ISBN-13: 978-0-7360-7885-6 (hardcover)
  ISBN-10: 0-7360-7885-1 (hardcover)
  1. Sports--Psychological aspects. I. Andersen, Mark B., 1951- II. Title.
  GV706.4.G549 2011
  796.01--dc22

                                                    2010039264

ISBN-10: 0-7360-7885-1
ISBN-13: 978-0-7360-7885-6

The Web addresses cited in this text were current as of March 2011, unless otherwise noted.

Acquisitions Editor: Myles Schrag, **Managing Editor:** Anne Cole, **Copyeditor:** Tom Tiller, **Indexer:** Dan Connolly, **Permission Manager:** Martha Gullo, **Graphic Designer:** Joe Buck, **Graphic Artist:** Kathleen Boudreau-Fuoss, **Cover Designer:** Bob Reuther, **Printer:** Sheridan Books

Printed in the United States of America   10 9 8 7 6 5 4 3 2 1

The paper in this book is certified under a sustainable forestry program.

Human Kinetics
Web site: www.HumanKinetics.com

United States: Human Kinetics
P.O. Box 5076
Champaign, IL 61825-5076
800-747-4457
e-mail: humank@hkusa.com

Canada: Human Kinetics
475 Devonshire Road Unit 100
Windsor, ON N8Y 2L5
800-465-7301 (in Canada only)
e-mail: info@hkcanada.com

Europe: Human Kinetics
107 Bradford Road
Stanningley
Leeds LS28 6AT, United Kingdom
+44 (0) 113 255 5665
e-mail: hk@hkeurope.com

Australia: Human Kinetics
57A Price Avenue
Lower Mitcham, South Australia
5062
08 8372 0999
e-mail: info@hkaustralia.com

New Zealand: Human Kinetics
P.O. Box 80
Torrens Park, South Australia 5062
0800 222 062
e-mail: info@hknewzealand.com

CONTENTS

Contributors   ix ❙ Preface   xi ❙ Introduction   xiii

Introduction: David Gilbourne   xiii ❙ Introduction: Mark Andersen   xvii
Our Motivations   xix ❙ The Abuse of Language   xxi
Closing Thoughts   xxiii ❙ References xxiv

PART I   Methodologies and Inquiries in Research and Practice   1

ESSAY 1: A Narrative Perspective: Identity, Well-Being, and Trauma in Professional Sport 3

Kitrina Douglas
University of Bristol, United Kingdom

David Carless
Leeds Metropolitan University, United Kingdom

Introduction   3 ❙ The Potential of Narrative Inquiry   6 ❙ Identifying Sport Narratives   8 ❙ Silencing Alternative Narrative Types in Sport   10 ❙ Consequences of the Performance Narrative   15 ❙ Conclusion   17 ❙ Ideas for Reflection and Debate   19 ❙ References   19

ESSAY 2: Representing Applied Research Experiences Through Performance: Extending Beyond Text 23

David Llewellyn
Liverpool John Moores University, United Kingdom

David Gilbourne
University of Wales Institute, Cardiff, United Kingdom

Carmel Triggs
University of Chester, United Kingdom

Introduction   24 ❙ Ethnodrama and Theater   24 ❙ Sport-Based Ethnodrama Examples   29 ❙ Conclusion   36 ❙ Ideas for Reflection and Debate   37 ❙ References   37

ESSAY 3: In Praise of Quantitative Methods: How Numbers Can Change Culture 39

Harriet D. Speed
Victoria University, Australia

Mark B. Andersen
Victoria University, Australia

> Introduction 40 ▌ Background: The Sport 43 ▌ The Research 45 ▌ The Research Outcomes 46 ▌ Interpreting the Numbers 52 ▌ Recommendations 53 ▌ Response to the Research Outcomes and Recommendations 54 ▌ Conclusion 56 ▌ Ideas for Reflection and Debate 56 ▌ References 57

ESSAY 4: Critical Reflections on Doing Reflective Practice and Writing Reflective Texts 59

Zoe Knowles
Liverpool John Moores University, United Kingdom

David Gilbourne
University of Wales Institute, Cardiff, United Kingdom

Ailsa Niven
Herriot-Watt University, United Kingdom

> Introduction 59 ▌ Current Reflective Practice Studies 62 ▌ Expanding the Boundaries of Reflective Writing 65 ▌ Conclusion 68 ▌ Ideas for Reflection and Debate 69 ▌ References 69

ESSAY 5: Representing Multilayered Lives: Embracing Context Through the Storied Self 73

David Gilbourne
University of Wales Institute, Cardiff, United Kingdom

David Llewellyn
Liverpool John Moores University, United Kingdom

> Introduction 73 ▌ The Emergence of New Epistemologies 75 ▌ A Fracture in Convention 77 ▌ Autoethnography: A New Form of Writing 78 ▌ Autoethnographic Illustrations: Personal Selections 80 ▌ Conclusion 84 ▌ Ideas for Reflection and Debate 84 ▌ References 85

ESSAY 6: The Practitioner and Client as Storytellers: Metaphors and Folktales in Applied Sport Psychology Practice 87

Mark B. Andersen
Victoria University, Australia

Harriet D. Speed
Victoria University, Australia

Introduction   88 I The Power of Metaphors and Folktales   88 I The Wise Fool: Mullah Nasruddin   91 I Metaphors in Popular Media   93 I An Attachment Metaphor: Two Monks, a River, and a Lady   96 I A Story of Attachment: Hungry Ghosts   96 I A Story of Self-Protection: Hermit Crabs   97 I Hearing and Listening to Others and Ourselves   99 I A Final Metaphor   101 I Conclusion   102 I Ideas for Reflection and Debate   102 I References   103

PART II   Issues in Professional Delivery   105

ESSAY 7: Collaborative Practice: Multidisciplinary Support Alongside Multiagency Engagement 107

Dearbhla McCullough
Roehampton University, United Kingdom

Michael Korzinski
Private practice, United Kingdom

Introduction   107 I K's History   109 I Psychotherapy Support: Michael Korzinski   112 I Sport Psychology Support: Dearbhla McCullough   120 I Conclusion   124 I Ideas for Reflection and Debate   125 I References   126

ESSAY 8: Playful Deviance 129

William B. Strean
University of Alberta, Canada

DJ Williams
Idaho State University, United States

Introduction   129 I Playful Research Deviance   130 I What BDSM Can Teach Us About Sport Psychology   132 I Applied Practice   136 I Lessons Learned from Social Work, Forensics, and Playing With Bad Guys   137 I Labeling and Other Insanity From Dr. Deviant   139 I Conclusion   140 I Ideas for Reflection and Debate   140 I References   141 I

ESSAY 9: Sport Psychology Services Are Multicultural Encounters: Differences as Strengths in Therapeutic Relationships 145

Stephanie J. Hanrahan
University of Queensland, Australia

Introduction   145 ❘ Cultural Awareness: Self and Other   146 ❘ Relationships: Multicultural at the Micro-Level   150 ❘ Developing Cultural Awareness   151 ❘ Adapting Behaviors to Suit the Cultural Context   154 ❘ Conclusion   155 ❘ Ideas for Reflection and Debate   155 ❘ References   156

ESSAY 10: Problems in Reflective Practice: Self-Bootstrapping Versus Therapeutic Supervision 157

Jack C. Watson
West Virginia University, United States

John R. Lubker
West Texas A&M University, United States

Judy Van Raalte
Springfield College, United States

Introduction   158 ❘ Self-Reflection   158 ❘ Supervision   161 ❘ Self-Reflection vs. Supervision   165 ❘ Future of Supervision   167 ❘ Conclusion   169 ❘ Ideas for Reflection and Debate   169 ❘ References   170

ESSAY 11: If You Meet the Buddha on the Football Field, Tackle Him! 173

Mark B. Andersen
Victoria University, Australia

Joe Mannion
Private practice, St. Louis, Missouri, United States

Introduction   174 ❘ Buddhism's Role in Sport Psychology   175 ❘ Two Tales From Our Practice   185 ❘ Conclusion   188 ❘ Ideas for Reflection and Debate   189 ❘ References   190

ESSAY 12: Taming the Wild West: Training and Supervision in Applied Sport Psychology 193

David Tod
Aberystwyth University, United Kingdom

David Lavallee
Aberystwyth University, United Kingdom

Introduction   194 ❙ The Current State of Applied Sport Psychology Practice   196 ❙ Overemphasis on the PST Approach   198 ❙ Underemphasis on Process-Oriented Issues   200 ❙ Supervision During Training   203 ❙ Supervision After Training   205 ❙ Disconnected Staff   206 ❙ Conclusion   209 ❙ Ideas for Reflection and Debate   210 ❙ References   210

ESSAY 13: Epiphanies and Learning: A Rejection of Performance-Based Myopia 217

David Gilbourne
University of Wales Institute, Cardiff, United Kingdom

David Priestley
Private practice, London, United Kingdom

Introduction   217 ❙ Qualitative Methodology and Applied Thinking: The Rationale for My Challenge   219 ❙ Some Storytelling   220 ❙ The Value of Stories   228 ❙ Conclusion   228 ❙ Ideas for Reflection and Debate   230 ❙ References   230

PART III   Issues in Sport Psychology Practice   231

ESSAY 14: Making Your Way in the Game: Boundary Situations in England's Professional Football World 233

Mark Nesti
Liverpool John Moores University, United Kingdom

Martin Littlewood
Liverpool John Moores University, United Kingdom

Introduction   233 ❙ The Football Environment   234 ❙ Transition and Identity   236 ❙ Existential Psychology   238 ❙ Existential Psychology and Transition in Sport   239 ❙ A Narrative: Trusting Yourself in Critical Moments   241 ❙ Conclusion   246 ❙ Ideas for Reflection and Debate   246 ❙ References   247

ESSAY 15: Safeguarding Child Athletes From Abuse in
Elite Sport Systems: The Role of the Sport Psychologist 251

Trisha Leahy
Hong Kong Sports Institute

Introduction   252 I Issues of Safeguarding   252 I The Biopsychoso-
cial Model   253 I Sexual Abuse in Sport   255 I Implications for Sport
Psychology Practice   260 I Conclusion   263 I Ideas for Reflection and
Debate   263 I References   264

ESSAY 16: Negotiating Expectations in Football's Complex
Social Culture. 267

Robyn L. Jones
University of Wales Institute, Cardiff, United Kingdom

Kieran Kingston
University of Wales Institute, Cardiff, United Kingdom

Carly Stewart
University of Wales Institute, Cardiff, United Kingdom

Introduction   268 I Writing and Engaging With Creative Coaching
Scenarios   268 I A Personalized Story: The Social Rules of Coaching
Practice   271 I Dealing With the Complexity: An Applied Psychology
Approach   277 I Outlining a Framework: A Multitheoretical Per-
spective   278 I Complexity Theory and Orchestration: Recognizing
and Manipulating Context   282 I Conclusion   285 I Ideas for
Reflection and Debate   285 I References   286

Index   289

About the Editors   294

CONTRIBUTORS

David Carless
Leeds Metropolitan University, United Kingdom

Kitrina Douglas
University of Bristol, United Kingdom

Stephanie J. Hanrahan
University of Queensland, Australia

Robyn L. Jones
University of Wales Institute, Cardiff, United Kingdom

Kieran Kingston
University of Wales Institute, Cardiff, United Kingdom

Zoe Knowles
Liverpool John Moores University, United Kingdom

Michael Korzinski
Private practice, United Kingdom

David Lavallee
Aberystwyth University, United Kingdom

Trisha Leahy
Hong Kong Sports Institute

Martin Littlewood
Liverpool John Moores University, United Kingdom

David Llewellyn
Liverpool John Moores University, United Kingdom

John R. Lubker
West Texas A&M University, United States

Joe Mannion
Private practice, St. Louis, Missouri, United States

Dearbhla McCullough
Roehampton University, United Kingdom

Mark Nesti
Liverpool John Moores University, United Kingdom

Ailsa Niven
Herriot-Watt University, United Kingdom

David Priestley
Private practice, London, United Kingdom

Harriet D. Speed
Victoria University, Australia

Carly Stewart
University of Wales Institute, Cardiff, United Kingdom

William B. Strean
University of Alberta, Canada

David Tod
Aberystwyth University, United Kingdom

Carmel Triggs
University of Chester, United Kingdom

Judy Van Raalte
Springfield College, United States

Jack C. Watson
West Virginia University, United States

DJ Williams
Idaho State University, United States

PREFACE

Researchers, academics, and practitioners with connections to sport and exercise psychology are found in a wide range of disciplines: mainstream psychology and counseling, philosophy, rehabilitation, education, coaching science, leisure and tourism, cultural studies, social science, and health. This breadth of interest in sport and exercise psychology suggested to us that the audience for this book might be extensive and wide ranging, and we hope that the essays included here fit well with a diverse audience. The authors of these essays come from a number of disciplines and persuasions and offer insights into the intoxicating yet sometimes dark cultures of professional, elite, and sub-elite sport. The essays draw from a broad-based menu of applied practice—for example, how to disseminate applied qualitative research through performance art; provide the chance to see alternative interpretations of people's lives through the lenses of differing counseling traditions; question the underlying ethics of practice; and examine the value, potential pitfalls, and challenges of reflection. In this regard, the book takes on sufficient academic scope and critical challenge to influence pedagogical practices, research approaches, and applied training in sport psychology service delivery curricula and research directions across a range of interrelated disciplines.

We have brought together critical thinkers who offer differing points of view and promote alternative perspectives. The book is intended for those who teach, mentor, and practice in and around the field of sport and exercise psychology, but it extends beyond the traditional boundaries of applied sport psychology to reach interested clinical psychologists, psychotherapists, and research psychologists from a range of training and academic persuasions. The essays are grounded in the domain of applied practice and methodology, and we hope that they serve as valuable resources for people who work alongside, manage, or employ those who offer applied psychology support (e.g., coaches, professional sport administrators, player welfare officers, physical therapists). Each essay offers a distinct perspective on applied sport psychology practice, and we hope that together they stimulate applied debate, encourage diverse thinking about applied research directions, address applied training requirements and practices, and contest the status quo in a variety of ways.

In pedagogic terms, we also hope that this book helps students in and around the field of sport psychology to think and write critically. In order to write critically, students must refer (and sometimes defer) to the academic literature, yet examples of applied critique are relatively rare. We believe that this book provides a resource for contemporary ideas, illustrates critical thinking in action, and offers new ways of uncovering and representing applied knowledge. Finally, we hope that these essays, as a collected body of critical thinking, challenge, provoke, disturb, and excite practitioners, as well as encourage reflection and open a critical space in which researchers, practitioners, and teachers might be stimulated by new approaches and feel motivated to reevaluate their own developmental needs.

The contributors to this volume are recognized nationally and internationally for their applied thinking, and the body of critical essays presented here gets us beyond the limitations imposed when challenging ideas are spread across different journals, books, and book chapters—and across time. The authors purposefully attempt to move readers onto new landscapes, offer them different ideas, and extend the boundaries of what might be considered interesting, valuable, and relevant to professional practice and research. We feel that these essays have the capacity to influence how sport and exercise psychologists think about their own practice and research. The essays are eclectic in both style and content and, as editors, we want each essay to represent independent, not necessarily interconnected, viewpoints. Several essays, however, do share interweaving threads. Organizationally, we have divided the book into three sections, but there is no particular ordered way in which to approach this collection; readers can start anywhere. Part I covers diverse methods and inquiry in research and practice. The essays in part II engage with issues in professional service delivery, and part III addresses specific topics in sport psychology practice. One reader might wish to start with familiar topics, then progress into foreign territory. Another reader might prefer to jump right into the more iconoclastic essays. Whatever the approach, pick an essay and dive in. We hope readers find these essays engaging, infuriating, thought provoking, and entertaining. We certainly did!

INTRODUCTION

David Gilbourne

University of Wales Institute, Cardiff, United Kingdom

Mark B. Andersen

Victoria University, Melbourne, Australia

INTRODUCTION: DAVID GILBOURNE

As editors, Mark and I warmly welcome all readers to this text. Given what is to follow, it seems important from the onset to stress that we both believe that applied sport psychology is a central facet of athlete support, and we would defend this view to the last. With the same vigor, we also suggest that the profession risks failing those who might be most in need of help (winners and losers alike). We could rationalize this statement through any number of critical observations (and many of these are sketched out in the present book), but the positioning of applied sport psychology lies at the core of our dissatisfaction, and many other critiques stem from a disquietude over sport psychology's history and application. Through the various contributions and observations contained in this volume, we warn that an emerging profession that delimits its client base and intervention options by emphasizing performance before people is setting itself on a path that encourages practitioners to focus on behaviors and renders many professionals inadequately equipped to treat athletes.

Convincing Mark that we should think seriously about working on the critical essays project was not at all difficult. We had both recognized a need for an applied text that contained something different. I found Mark's support particularly gratifying because, over the years, moments when other colleagues have openly shared my concerns or appreciated my sense of genuine alarm and worry have been rare. With little evidence of support, I have sometimes wondered whether my critique of the profession, the one I once practiced and taught, as so far off the beam that no one *could* support it. I had begun to see my critique as somehow unacceptable, something others viewed as plain wrong.

Since we began this project, however, I have come to understand that many other applied practitioners, scholars, and commentators share a critical view of applied sport psychology (their critiques manifest in different ways and are articulated in different approaches). Later in this opening essay, Mark and I comment on the disparate nature of critique—how it often appeared, only to be lost in the primacy (and comfort) of the status quo. On reflection, and possibly as a consequence of the present project, I have come to see my past critique in more opaque and incomplete terms, as partial, implicit, even covert, and as a critique that might be easily missed or misinterpreted. In truth, my unease, and any critique that leaked out from this discomfort, was often shrouded in dry asides and questioning observations that tended to fade as the cadence of my sentences fell away. Therefore, I know that my critique was easily missed. However ineffectual I was at conveying critical messages, it was, nonetheless, a very real iceberg for many years (more beneath the surface than visible above it).

The world of pedagogy in applied sport psychology that I inhabited for 15 or more years offers a good example of my critical subterfuge. I taught the typical applied sport psychology curriculum to generations of students while at the same time feeling uneasy with the way psychological skills training (PST) had dominated the applied landscape for so long. One day (and deep down, I had always known such a day would arrive) I had to face the consequences of teaching one thing and thinking another.

"You lied to me," said the postgraduate student; she was standing in the doorway of my office. We had known each other for several years, first as undergraduate student and lecturer, and later as PhD candidate and supervisor. Though a little taken aback, I instantly took her point; I had lived a lie of sorts for some time. If pushed, I would now say that for years I had spoken to a flawed applied agenda, one that I had failed to challenge—a failure based on critical omission. The motivation behind the present book can be traced back to that moment. My student made it clear that there is little merit in thinking critically and saying nothing.

In the minutes that followed, she made me ponder; she made me confront a need to talk more openly about what applied work entailed, and I thank her for that. I tried to explain that I hadn't really lied. I was, however, culpable, and I said as much. My case was that I had demonstrated professional weakness by not challenging the status quo. I also admitted that, in the past, I had failed to fully confront my misgivings about the utility of theory and the dominance of PST, and, over those years (during my procrastination born of professional anxieties and the usual worries over promotion and the like), she had listened to my neat lectures and responded by writing equally neat essays. Now living and researching in the messy, uneven, emotive, unpredictable, multilayered, unforgiving world of professional sport, she began to test me with stories: an athlete with an eating disorder, a parent taking money from a young player, a player and a coach on the edge of a physical confrontation, an unwanted pregnancy. . . . The tales went on. As she told the stories, I now see that she waited, in vain, for some reaction, maybe some sense of shock. When she realized I was not at all surprised by her tales, she concluded that I had withheld this reality from her and her fellow students. In short, I had knowingly misled by omission and failed to articulate the most important part of the applied world (ergo, I had lied). But to do so would have undermined the very theories and models that I was charged with explaining (and that the students were expected to write about), while also breaking a pedagogical contract between established learning outcomes and lecture content.

This excuse is hardly a defensible one, but I hope she understood my dilemma. Her stories provided contextually framed, culturally charged examples of human existence and illustrated what much of the academic applied sport psychology literature had failed to confront and articulate. Sometimes I retell elements of these stories to audiences at conferences and workshops. At one such event, a delegate referred to the story that I will present later in this essay and asked, "Why do you always focus on the negative aspects of sport?" I was reminded then that sport is good and that the goodness of sport is a truism. I would paraphrase the tone of the question as "and if you don't think it's good then you are *not* one of us." I realized then that I was (at last) happy to be outside gazing in but also disappointed that it had taken me so long to take the plunge. Later that evening, I wondered how many others are resigned (de facto) to reinforcing myths regardless of whether they have started to have doubts. When there is no constituency for genuine challenge, speaking out becomes risky. Anyway, here is the story, the one perceived by the delegate as being negative. An odd take on matters, for, to my mind, it's a rather beautiful story, one that speaks volumes about trust and care and so opens another window onto applied practice. I have partly fictionalized the tale to make it more accessible, but it is founded on an applied sport psychologist's account of an actual consultation (the same sport psychologist who stood in my doorway several years ago):

> I'm just sat up in bed . . . reading . . . and then the phone goes. . . . it's this player: "Can I talk?" I said, "No worries." . . . He's never once spoken to me before so this all felt a bit weird . . . then he tells me that his girlfriend's pregnant, and the club can't get to know . . . his dad said.
>
> So like I'm just reacting . . . and I say, "We need to meet up. . . . don't do anything or say anything till we meet, all right?". . . He said, "okay." . . . We talk a bit more, then (just before the call's over) I say, "Can your girlfriend come to the meeting, can she come?" He said, "I'll ask." . . . Should I have done that? Was that right, asking his girlfriend to come along?
>
> Anyway, we met in a coffee shop—me, the player, and his girlfriend. She's really pretty and seems really quiet. . . . she cried loads in the meeting, just cried loads. . . . she kept saying, "What a mess" and stuff. He kept looking at her: "Don't cry," he said. . . . I'd never seen him like that, being nice and gentle. Football doesn't allow him to be that way.
>
> We made some plans. . . .
>
> Next day I saw him at the training ground. He stood next to me but at a distance so others wouldn't think he was talking to me, and then without looking towards me he said, "My girlfriend told me to say thanks . . . for yesterday . . . for wanting to meet her. . . . she said for me to say 'thanks.'"

The story suggests to me that "being there" is not just an athlete thing; it might also relate to influential others who share the athlete's life. I sometimes wonder how the player got hold of my former student's phone number, and I wonder why he opted to call her at such a difficult time of day. I imagine him maybe asking another player for help, and maybe that player recommended he contact someone who has listened to and helped others in the past, someone who has gained trust and respect within the player's group. I also imagine the player's angst before he made the phone call and the vulnerability he felt during the coffee shop meeting. But most of all, as I recount the tale, I am always moved by his words as he passed on the gratitude of his girlfriend; moreover, and in the broad fabric of this short tale, I see much for the profession of applied sport psychology to be proud of.

INTRODUCTION: MARK ANDERSEN

I have had a long and difficult relationship with sport and physical education. Being a hand-eye motor moron, I was constantly chosen last for sport teams throughout primary and secondary school. Luckily, my father moved me toward sports in which I could enjoy some degree of success (e.g., swimming, skiing, sailing). In these sports, I was not required to catch, throw, or bounce anything. Since those times, and now stalking sport psychology as an avenging demon, I have sought to paint a different picture of sport, one that allows for the possibility that participation might damage or hurt. In terms of intervention, I have sought to right the wrongs of abusive practices and so shift the focus from performance to people and to look at the individual in the sport context as being far more complex and convoluted than has been portrayed in many applied sport psychology texts.

To help establish the germ of my own critical perspective on applied sport psychology I have decided to draw on ideas that I discussed in a lecture at Aberystwyth University on March 3, 2009. There I outlined a series of critical points, and I have selected a few extracts here:

> *Taking the performance enhancement approach to sport and exercise psychology service delivery is like a house painter who is more than happy to paint your home, but only if you want it one specific shade of blue. Athletes' and coaches' lives are not blue; their concerns cover a great deal of the visible spectrum. Their lives also delve into the usually unexamined infrared and ultraviolet realms of hidden fears, desires, abuse, trauma, and shattered dreams. I think we need to address the full spectrum of the issues psychologists, counselors, and consultants encounter when they focus on working with people, and not just when they dip their brushes into blue paint. I don't want to bag performance enhancement per se . . . Oh hell, yes I do, but it's not because I think such interventions are unimportant; I think they can be of tremendous value. What's a rainbow without some blue in it? But what are we to make of the rest of the spectrum? The full range of what may be encountered when we look at whole people rather than specific behaviors? Even when we focus on performance, we have to see how sport behavior fits, or doesn't fit, in the lives of those we serve. An 800-meter run does not take place in a vacuum.*

All the relaxation exercises in the world will probably have little effect on competition anxiety if those fears are tied to some dire imagined or real consequences of failure, such as parental psychological abuse, the withdrawal of love, or feelings of worthlessness and emptiness.

I question the conventional mantra that "sport is good, and participation in sport is good for you," and so my critique tends to drift (temporarily) away from the athlete and toward questions about how these positive views of sport might have negative consequences, both generally for the ways in which sport psychologists approach sporting environments and more specifically for how they work with athletes who reside within those environments. Here is another brief fictional narrative, again taken from the Aberystwyth presentation:

I believe sport is a good thing; I believe improving performance is a good thing. I believe athletes coming to me are interested in improving performance. I believe it is my job to help them improve. Then an athlete arrives at my door and talks about his performance anxiety and his fears of disappointing his coach and how that coach will go ballistic if the athlete makes an error. I have seen the coach in action and do not like his verbally and psychologically abusive style. He yells; he demeans athletes, and then he lavishes praise on good performance. His relationships with his athletes are chaotic, and his charges walk on eggshells around him. To serve this athlete, I teach him some cognitive skills and relaxation exercises to help with the anxiety he has about performance and to cope with the coach's psychologically abusive practices. His anxiety response is exactly the sort of reaction that will nearly ensure that what he fears most will happen, does happen (he makes an error, and the coach starts screaming). So I help him out with that anxiety problem. He is a psychologically abused young man, and the abuse is ongoing. His sport environment is toxic, and his coach is a bully, but I still think sport is good, and I have colluded in helping him stay in his sport with this manipulative and horrible coach and continue to be abused. The athlete may see me as a really nice guy, but I am also part of the problem. I stand by and watch the abuse continue. It is odd that many people tolerate their children being yelled at and demeaned by coaches, but if those same coach behaviors were brought into a child's classroom with a psychologically demeaning and abusive teacher, then parents would be calling for the teacher's head. Sport is good, and we stand by and watch abuse. I help the athlete change his anxiety response, but for how long? In the face of continued abuse, I have applied a band-aid to a deep (and possibly infected) wound. I have, by my action and my inaction, contributed to the continued abuse of someone in my care by not seriously asking the ethical question, "What is the right thing to do?" Such moral questions about what it is to "do the right thing" are difficult but need to be asked. But if sport is ultimately a good thing, such questions may never get asked, and abuse will continue.

As a helping profession, applied sport psychology seems in some ways to be moribund. It has not kept up with other sport professions that developed during the time when it was emerging as a sport science and an applied practice (Andersen, 2009; see also chapter 12 in this book). Signs of hope are coming from many researchers and practitioners who are carving new pathways and territories of service, but one begins to despair when articles appear in the literature with titles such as "At an Elite Level the Role of a Sport Psychologist Is Entirely About Performance Enhancement" (Brady & Maynard, 2010). I wonder if performance enhancement will ever give up the ghost of primacy and take a secondary or tertiary position behind an overarching agenda of the health, happiness, and welfare of athletes and coaches. Toward that end, we want this book to help expand the debate on the depth and breadth of potential service, and in the remainder of this introduction we discuss (in a kind of split-screen, talking heads manner) our motivations and our hopes for this profession we have been intimately involved with for decades.

OUR MOTIVATIONS

David (D): Some might say we are aging, angry, cranky old men (Mark's older, but he argues that I'm crankier by some margin). Well, we have certainly been in and around the business of academic and applied sport psychology for more years than we care to reveal and through that time have developed critical (some might say cynical) eyes on the field of applied sport psychology, both as practiced and as researched.

Mark (M): I have talked with David many times over many years, and I can say without hesitation that he can be extremely grumpy. That observation aside, David's applied critique resonates with many facets of my own experiences, so I have learned to listen carefully to his grumblings. As we sit and talk, it is clear that we approach the critical agenda from the constraints and possibilities offered through our own history and training. For example, David, as he emphasized earlier in this introduction, gets very agitated when our conversation moves toward the dominance of mental training techniques (PST). His own experiences, the experiences of his PhD students, and many of his applied contacts across the spectrum of sport convinced him long ago that PST should *not* be the cornerstone, or the primary focus, or the core challenge of applied practice. As Shane Murphy (2000), the former head of sport sciences at the U.S. Olympic Training Center in Colorado Springs, once wrote:

> *The sport psychology literature is filled with texts that describe techniques and interventions. Although many of these works are excellent, they leave the lingering impression that sport psychology is the sum of such interventions as goal setting, visualization, and attention-control training. Yet the practicing sport psychologist realizes that knowledge of such techniques is but the first step in a long journey toward gaining proficiency in actually being able to help athletes. . . . [R]eflect[ing] on my own work with elite athletes, . . . [I notice] how infrequently I ever do straightforward interventions such as those we see studied so often in our journals.* (pp. 275–276)

According to old grumpy, Shane's observation offers an optimistic view of the applied practitioner, and David remains unconvinced that the research or pedagogy of the UK sport psychology system demonstrates much, if any, evidence of the progressions Shane suggested. For David, "getting critical" is a kind of default setting. In one exchange, at the 2007 meeting of FEPSAC (the European Federation of Sport Psychology), he argued that sport psychology training and practice had developed an inward and uncritical quality, one typified by the narrow and predictable application of a small number of unconnected social-cognitive theories compounded by (often unconnected) PST-based interventions. As he spoke, I'm sure I could hear tumbleweeds rolling; that is, as David suggested earlier, one-off asides often get missed, so perhaps the audience was just thinking about the coffee and muffins to follow. The moment came and went and, we both feel, made little impression. We do not wish, however, to set up a PST straw man and take potshots at him. David's experiences in the UK differ greatly from mine in Australia. In the Land Down Under, sport psychology training and practice have taken a decidedly different path than the ones in North America and the UK. In Australia, the education, training, and supervision of sport psychologists are all housed within the parent discipline of psychology. We train sport psychologists to be *psychologists* first, and PST is just one small part in the education of our graduate students on their paths to becoming fully registered psychologists. PST is not the dominant paradigm in the Australian context, and our graduates often go on to careers as psychologists in many areas outside of sport. I am fortunate to live in a country where applied sport psychology is much more about individuals' lives than it is about their performances. Performance enhancement is not our raison d'être; people are.

THE ABUSE OF LANGUAGE

(D): Both Mark and I have a thing about language. I love to see it being used creatively, and we both see language as a medium that might help us capture, and so possibly understand, the experience of being. Language and the opening of discourses and discourse media emerge as underlying themes throughout this book. That said, we both go ballistic when we hear language used in a way that creates popular but suspect attributes (e.g., mental toughness). Our reading of the history of academic applied sport psychology finds that false gods are all too easily created and that, once established, they morph into truisms that make the resulting prejudices and biases legitimate, almost corporeal. For example, early in the 1970s and 1980s, many sport psychologists conducted research into personality and success in sport. Because all sorts of successful athletes have all sorts of personalities, personality is not a good predictor of sporting prowess, and this line of research did not greatly advance knowledge about psychology and sport. This line of research, however, has not faded away, and one personality-like disposition, mental toughness, is currently all the rage in research. The "toughness" part of mental toughness is what really gets Mark and me. It reeks of much that is bad in sport. We wonder whether applied sport psychologists have much stomach for the dark side; we wonder whether researchers want to tread paths that might highlight pain and disturbance and get under the skin of the glamour, the medals, the championships, and the other adornments of sport that capture the headlines. When we hear the phrases "I want to be tough" from a 14-year-old boy or "I'm a winner" from a 15-year-old girl, we begin to worry about language and labels.

(M): As part of my brief stay in the UK to work on this book, David invited me to his own institution, the University of Wales Institute, Cardiff, to deliver a symposium on applied practice. Here is a short extract from that presentation to help illustrate my own concern about how language might be manipulated dangerously:

> *So … if you are not "tough," then you are "soft"—just about the worst thing you can say about someone in sport. Toughness smacks of "no pain, no gain," "play with pain," "play when injured," "don't be a girl," "don't be a sissy," and all that other macho bullshit that permeates the hypermasculine world of sport. So when sport psychologists become pushers of mental toughness, we begin to worry that they are also part of the problem.*

Like me, David is suspicious of the mental toughness agenda, and he shares my concerns about the connotations of the word *tough,* one that is easily twisted and abused. He worries about whether, in the wrong hands, the notion of toughness might be used to justify dubious applied practices. To his way of thinking, toughness speak is getting out of control, and he has little faith in the term being applied sensibly. Some might wave their hands and dismiss such views as little more than a rant, but I believe his worry is thoughtful and held with a degree of passion. He also hates the word *tough.* He often asks me to imagine the lifelong consequences of being told, explicitly or implicitly, "You are not mentally tough enough." David knows a good number of applied sport psychologists; he has great affection for many of them as people, and he respects the important work they do. He also knows that although they all acknowledge the challenges of consistency in high-level sport, none of them would use the "T" word when working with their clients.

(D): It may be harsh for us to illustrate our worries over language by focusing on mental toughness because sport psychology has become hostage to a range of "I'm tough" terms, and they are all connected to the same agenda—the agenda of being a winner and selling the efficacy of practice as a process that leads to winning). We should also recognize and acknowledge the genuine research that has taken place in this area. Unfortunately, sport psychology seems to be considered a self-confessed, performance-focused profession in many countries, which is interesting because only a few people win but many fall short. At a recent world congress on science and football in Turkey, I told the audience that because about 96% of elite young football players are no longer playing the game by the time they reach the age of 24, it might be more apt to refer to sport psychology as a failure profession. Then came more asides, more tumbleweed, and little effect. . . .

The drive toward making sport psychology a performance profession brings it close to being a "winning" profession. In the UK, athletes who fall short have been depicted as "debris" (my essay in chapter 13 explores those sentiments in greater detail). Such comments make both Mark and me angry and, in our view, house a potentially dark and dangerous agenda. We see sport psychology as a people profession, one that should embrace notions of care as readily as it embraces performance. We hope the profession will help develop new generations of applied practitioners capable of supporting most all athletes, going beyond false dichotomies such as winners and losers, task and ego orientations, mental "toughness" and mental "weakness," and intrinsic and extrinsic motivations.

CLOSING THOUGHTS

(D): Psychologists often study themselves. For example, my PhD thesis returned me to the field of sport injury (my own football career was blighted by repeated knee surgery), and Mark's doctoral dissertation addressed the psychosocial and attentional precursors that constitute risk factors for future injury. It seems, then, that we are both intrigued by the notion of damage. My autoethnographic writing has opened up the possibility of understanding the difficulties that might be experienced by others (in the present) through a critical and literary exploration of my own past, whereas Mark's focus addresses the prevention of damage, whether it is due to injury, pathogenic coaching and training practices, or other factors.

(M): In terms of career, David and I have negotiated different scholarly pathways and so have traveled divergently. My journey includes the study of mainstream psychology and psychodynamic psychotherapy. David, in contrast, has spent time in professional sport participation, in physical and outdoor education, in applied sport psychology, and, more recently, in qualitative inquiry. Despite these diverse routes, our journeys have, in recent years, intersected in a coalescing and shared sense of dissatisfaction with some of applied sport psychology's directions, as well as a mutual desire to promote alternative perspectives that might influence pedagogy, applied training, and practice. We hope this book contributes to the debate and to the changes that we both believe need to happen.

REFERENCES

Andersen, M.B. (2009). Performance enhancement as a bad start and a dead end: A parenthetical comment on Mellalieu and Lane. *The Sport and Exercise Scientist,* (20), 12–14.

Brady, A., & Maynard, I. (2010). At an elite level the role of a sport psychologist is entirely about performance enhancement. *Sport and Exercise Psychology Review, 6,* 59–66.

Murphy, S.M. (2000). Afterword. In M.B. Andersen (Ed.), *Doing sport psychology* (pp. 275–279). Champaign, IL: Human Kinetics.

PART I

METHODOLOGIES AND INQUIRIES IN RESEARCH AND PRACTICE

The third essay in this opening part illustrates that quantitative research data can serve as powerful tools to help bring about practice-based change. This essay is a lone and welcome quantitative contribution in an opening section otherwise dominated by the nuances of qualitative inquiry. This emphasis arguably reflects a contemporary research environment in which the range of methodologies that applied sport psychology researchers might deploy and the ways they might present and represent research and applied findings have expanded to embrace all the colors and shades of the qualitative dimension.

The authors in many of the essays included in this opening part reflect on the expansive and sometimes creative possibilities afforded by qualitative inquiry into applied practice. These authors explore different ways of thinking, different ways of writing, and thus different ways of telling. The authors of the opening essay use issues relating to narrative inquiry to build a case for alternative interpretations of athletic lives. Essays 2 and 5, respectively, involve philosophical and technical explorations of ethnodrama and autoethnography in considering how personal experiences can be presented both in text and, in a physical sense, on stage. Essay 4 is concerned with various ways of undertaking reflective practice (technical, practical, or critical), and the authors of essay 6 use storytelling, with an emphasis on the power of metaphor and folktales, to consider other ways of engaging clients in the therapeutic process. These more qualitative contributions may help readers critically explore and examine how stories of self and others can help us all to reflect on and appreciate the contextualized complexity of people's lives both inside and outside of sport.

A NARRATIVE PERSPECTIVE:
Identity, Well-Being, and Trauma in Professional Sport

Kitrina Douglas
University of Bristol, United Kingdom

David Carless
Leeds Metropolitan University, United Kingdom

In this essay, Kitrina and David draw on the life stories, gathered during a 6-year research project, of female professional golfers. The authors present three narrative types: performance, discovery, and relational. The first-person stories establish the existence of different routes to success in professional sport and provide insights into athletes' diverse biographies, motives, beliefs, and expectations. The essay explores the consequences of these narratives for women's psychological well-being throughout their careers, and shows how the different ways in which the women talked about their lives in golf shaped or constricted their experiences of retirement. Finally, the essay takes an applied turn and uses the narratives as a platform for reinforcing the importance of long-term well-being alongside the pursuit of excellence. The chapter's conclusion explores how such ideals might be embraced by means of a broadly conceived, person-focused approach to practice.

INTRODUCTION

Norman Denzin (2003) suggests that an ethical choice of research focus is one that lies close to home—within our own backyards—yet relates to culturally and politically relevant issues of our time. For him, there is an ethical imperative that social science researchers direct their endeavors toward the intersection of culture, politics, and personal biography. In sport, Andrew Sparkes has exemplified this approach in his explorations of narratives of the self in relation to masculinity and the experience of career-ending injury (1996, 2003). Sparkes (1996, p. 466) suggests that this work can provide "rich and dramatic insights" because the researcher-athlete, who is part to what he or she describes, is a "feeling and emotional insider, rather than detached (but interested) outsider." Thus a degree of reflexivity is necessary for any researcher to become aware of where her personal biography intersects with contemporary issues in sport culture.

For Kitrina, a successful professional tournament golfer, subscribing to this ethical position has meant conducting research among high-performance athletes. Her experience in professional golf led Kitrina to became aware of a gap between, on one hand, sport psychology theory and practice and, on the other hand, what she observed and experienced during 20 years in elite sport. Similar tensions were evident in the transcripts of the life history interviews that Kitrina conducted for her doctoral research with nine of Europe's most successful golfers. As an outsider and critical friend, David read these transcripts and found that the stories were not what he expected to hear. The participants did not portray life in elite sport as the media portray it, nor did they portray life as it is represented in sport psychology and sociology textbooks and journal articles. Through the combination of Kitrina's lived experience of professional golf *and* our analysis of the life histories, we began to wonder how important issues had come to be absent from existing literature and research. We now understand that one answer to this question relates to broader concerns about the way research has oversimplified and exaggerated the similarities between athletes, while giving less attention to their differences. As a result, alternative ways of being in elite and professional sport have often been masked.

Todd Crosset's (1995) ethnography of American women's golf is an example of how female athletes can be homogenized. Describing members of the tour, Crosset suggests these women are physically isolated by the relentless travel and insulated from the everyday reality of mainstream society by the all-consuming nature of their profession, and that players lack control and responsibility for themselves (p. 23). The "all-consuming" portrait painted too often results in athletes' being described as fixed, focused, and entrenched in an athletic identity and a glorified, aggrandized self (Alder & Alder, 1989). From such a perspective, there seems to be an underlying belief that the top professional athlete has, and *must* have, such a narrow focus on achieving optimal performance that "it is *impossible* for him (or her) to be much else" (Werthner & Orlick, 1986, p. 337, emphasis added).

Through our ongoing research (Douglas & Carless, 2006, 2008a, 2008b, 2008c, 2009a, 2009b; Sparkes & Douglas, 2007; Carless & Douglas, 2009; Douglas, 2009), we have become aware that an absolutist perspective can be damaging to the individual when it silences alternative life stories and ways of being. Our concern about how some stories have been silenced frames this chapter as we strive to provide some pointers toward alternative thinking, approaches, and practices within sport psychology theory and practice. Central to our work is a belief that in the human and social sciences at this time, as Arthur Frank (2000, p. 363) puts it,

> *More knowledge may be less important than a clearer sense of value. . . . [P]ut another way, the old faith was that more facts and better theories would render ethical dilemmas moot; the new realization is that knowledge only increases the density of ethical dilemmas. . . . Deciding what to do about what we know requires having an ethical standpoint. The challenge for intellectuals is to help people make policy, clinical, corporate, and personal decisions in a milieu of profound dislocation.*

Our view is that we must prioritize research that has the potential to help sport psychologists make ethically and morally informed decisions if our field is to develop in ways that promise beneficial, adaptive, healthful, and helpful support to athletes. Like Smith and Sparkes (2009), we have found that narrative inquiry allows us to move toward meeting the ethical and moral requirements of our research. In addition to honoring participants' stories, narrative approaches provide a theoretical perspective that makes sense and works in the context of our own lives *as well as* in the life stories of our participants. Because few narrative studies have been published in sport psychology, we begin here by summarizing the theoretical foundations that underpin this kind of work. We then illustrate theory in practice and provide some suggestions about how the theoretical insights and applied possibilities of narrative approaches may contribute to sport psychology.

THE POTENTIAL OF NARRATIVE INQUIRY

Narrative theorists have suggested that humans are storied beings and that our sense of self and identity is composed in part through the stories we tell (see, for example, Bruner, 1986; Somers, 1994). Stories can be created either when an individual performs a dialogue with the self or when an individual creates and shares accounts of her life with others. In the latter case, stories provide a means through which others come to know us (Lieblich, Tuval-Mashiach, & Zilber, 1998). For Neimeyer, Herrero, and Botella (2006), the importance of creating and telling stories about our lives goes beyond the need to know ourselves and be known by others; the processes of storying also provide a way to bring a degree of coherence and meaning to life by linking dissimilar and unconnected events. As Chase (2005) notes, "Narrative is a way of understanding one's own and others' actions, of organising events and objects into a meaningful whole, and of connecting and seeing the consequences of actions over time" (p. 656).

For Crossley (2000) and McAdams (1993), the ability to story and restory—to tell, retell, and share stories—is implicitly connected to mental health. These authors suggest that when an individual feels unable to tell her story or is impelled to silence, the result can be a number of emotional responses linked with depression and poor mental health. In contrast, when we have opportunity to share stories of our lives and be met with understanding, support, and empathy, telling stories can constitute an important aspect of mental health and personal development.

This practice, however, involves more than just inventing a story. Rather, storytellers create accounts of events that are based on their own experience *as they know it,* and typically present their stories in a socially acceptable form that others can understand. In McLeod's (1997) terms, "even when a teller is recounting a unique set of individual, personal events, he or she can only do so by drawing upon story structures and genres drawn from the narrative resources of a culture" (p. 94). In other words, a person's own story is shaped and constrained by the narrative types that are available within his sociocultural setting. For Frank (1995), a narrative type is "the most general storyline that can be recognized underlying the plot and tensions of particular stories" (p. 75). Frank argues that some narrative types—for example, the medical story of restitution that follows the plot yesterday I was healthy, today I'm sick, but tomorrow I'll be healthy again—are so powerful that they come to shape many people's personal stories. One problem with the restitution narrative, however, is that not all ill people live the story's projected future of a return to health: some remain chronically unwell, and some die. In this regard, the dominance of the restitution narrative, Frank suggests, denies such individuals alternative narrative scripts by which to story their own experience.

It is not just the storyteller who is immersed in the dominant narrative; such narratives also provide a template for others (e.g., family, friends, doctors) to follow. Frank (1995) shows how family members as well as the medical profession, through collectively expecting the "cure" that is implicit in the restitution narrative, may find it almost impossible to hear or accept an alternative story. Often without realizing it, friends and family commonly attempt to steer the sick person back toward the restitution story—to "never give up" and to expect a cure—even when restitution is impossible. This can result in tensions or trauma for the individual concerned, and it may rob some people of a chance to die with dignity or say goodbye in a way that is in keeping with their own life story (for more on this, see Frank, 1995).

According to McLeod (1997, p. 27),

> *The stories that, for the most part, construct our lives are "out there," they exist before we are born and continue after we die. The task of being a person in a culture involves creating a satisfactory-enough alignment between individual experience and "the story of which I find myself a part."*

The point McLeod clarifies is one that we have found helpful in our research in sport. Sport narratives, like illness narratives, are "out there." That is, as athletes, performance directors, psychologists, and even researchers, we enter a "stage" and take our part in a "play" that has a preexisting plot or narrative script. Stories told in sport teach us what is expected of each of us in our particular role, what types of stories are acceptable, and what a happy ending looks and feels like. We have narrative maps to show us what is valued and metaphors ready to help give color and expression to our tales. One example, according to Sparkes (2004), is the "hero" narrative, in which life is storied like the act of climbing a mountain: hurdles are overcome, and the athlete is disciplined, makes sacrifices, endures hardships, and emerges victorious. In this narrative map, winning is an emotional high that makes all the hard work worthwhile.

When McLeod (1997) discusses achieving "alignment," he draws attention to the fact that our experiences do not always match the story of which we are a part. He suggests that when a "satisfactory-enough alignment" can be created, we will likely experience psychological health and adaptive development. At other times, it may be impossible for an individual to create a personal story that links her experiences with the narrative of which she is a part; in these cases, the gulf between culture and experience is simply too wide. This circumstance, McLeod suggests, can render the individual unable to share his story, which, as research has shown, can lead in turn to anxiety, distress, and, in more extreme cases, trauma and serious mental health problems (see Crossley, 2000).

The potential of a dominant narrative to act as a guide or map offers both possibilities and problems. Because narratives provide both instruction and control, they help an individual find her way; however, because they are told in patriarchal systems, they can, as Richardson (1995) notes, become problematic: "If the available narrative is limiting or at odds with the actual life, people's lives end up being limited and textually disenfranchised" (p. 213). By limiting, Richardson refers to the narratives such as the one we mentioned earlier, in which a high-performance athlete cannot "be" much else. On this basis, Sparkes (2004) calls for alternatives to the dominant narrative to be made available in the public domain, and we believe these alternatives are urgently needed in the arena of sport. By providing a reservoir of culturally available narrative types, as opposed to relying on a single narrative, a variety of maps or templates become available through which to bring meaning and value to life.

IDENTIFYING SPORT NARRATIVES

Our first step toward understanding narrative theory as it relates to high-performance sport was to conduct an analysis of narrative (see Lieblich et al., 1998) from data gathered during life history interviews with nine female professional tournament golfers (Douglas, 2004). Through these processes, we explored how women brought meaning and coherence to their lives in sport. We identified three types of narratives that we term the *performance narrative*, *discovery narrative*, and *relational narrative* (see Douglas & Carless, 2006). Like Frank (1995), we accept that this list is neither exclusive nor exhaustive and that there may be additional narrative types in sport. Here is a summary of the three narrative types we worked with (for a full account of these types, see Douglas & Carless, 2006).

In the performance narrative, which was the most frequent type among our participants, performance-related concerns appear to infuse all areas of life. This is a story of single-minded dedication to sport performance to the exclusion of all other areas of life and self. It illustrates how and why, for some athletes, sport is life, and life is sport. The storyteller shows how personal beliefs align with the dominant cultural storyline through comments such as "I think for all of us, it [sport] becomes our whole life." It is, we have suggested (Carless & Douglas, 2009), a *monological* narrative in that all stories are told from the singular self-position of athlete. The plot of this narrative shows the fragile nature of self-worth when it comes to be dependent on sport performance—and how a glorified self and overriding athletic identity can become problematic during performance fluctuations or when the storyteller contemplates retirement.

In contrast, in the discovery narrative, the storyteller discovers and explores a diverse and multifaceted self and a life full of people, places, and experiences and uses sport as a conduit to achieve these aims. Absent are signs of an athletic identity or a glorified self; instead, the teller recounts achieving success in golf without prioritizing sport over other areas of life. The discovery narrative is dialogical in that its stories originate from multiple self-positions and roles and sustain diverse identities and interests such as travel, being a partner, or being a mother (Carless & Douglas, 2009). In this narrative type, self-worth does not depend on sport achievement but relates to negotiating and valuing multiple roles and activities. In contrast to the performance narrative, the future retirement is storied, not as a time of loss, but an opportunity for new exploration and discovery.

The third story type is the relational narrative, a story of complex interdependent connection between two people in which sport performance is essentially a byproduct. Although it could be said that all narratives are relational in that they exist within relations with others, we use the term here to highlight that for this storyteller the relationship is valued above all else. The teller of a relational story shows how "being with" (as in "I liked being with my dad") is more important than achievement in terms of tournament successes, trophies, and glory. The plot is dominated by altruistic rather than egoistic motivation as the storyteller places the perceived needs of others above the needs of the self: "His pleasure was enough." Like the discovery narrative, the relational narrative type explicitly challenges the assumptions of the performance narrative because the teller has achieved success at the highest level without subscribing to the values and behaviors scripted in the performance narrative.

We describe the discovery and relational narratives as alternative narratives because they go against what is expected in contemporary culture. These narratives show how it is not a foregone conclusion that at the highest level in sport an individual has to become consumed by glory and an athletic identity to the extent that alternative selves and identities are foreclosed. They show that sport success can be a conduit or a byproduct of other activities, motives, and selves that are more highly valued by the individual. For Frank (1995), the benefit of identifying alternative narrative types is that they act as "listening devices" (p. 24) that help us hear and accept diverse personal stories.

When used in this way, the performance, discovery, and relational narratives can sensitize sport psychologists (and others within sport environments) to the problems, difficulties, and possibilities associated with story types. It is not the case that we should try to fit ourselves or the athletes we work with into one type or another but that, by attending to the stories we ourselves tell and by listening carefully to the stories that athletes tell, we can more fully understand the type of story being developed and what its future unfolding may entail. With such an awareness, we are better placed to understand some of the narrative tensions that arise within a particular narrative type and therefore respond in a more effective and supportive manner. Through this awareness, we become empowered to stand outside our own individual narrative in order to observe how our own stories, like those of the athletes we hope to help, are influenced in profound ways by cultural scripts that permeate sport.

SILENCING ALTERNATIVE NARRATIVE TYPES IN SPORT

The performance narrative provides a script in which the athlete wants so much to win that he accepts discipline, sacrifice, and pain in the pursuit of glory. Being competitive is storied as "natural" as is the feelings of pain and shame that accompany failure. Losing hurts. As we have observed elsewhere (Douglas & Carless, 2006, 2008a, 2009a), this type of story is often expected of athletes and is assumed to fit the reality of all high-performance athletes. However, when the script of the performance narrative is applied to those who tell a relational or discovery narrative, it fails to fit the storyteller's experiences. Neither relational nor discovery storytellers, for example, feel shame and loss of self when they lose (Carless & Douglas, 2009; Douglas, 2009; Sparkes & Douglas, 2007).

McLeod (1997, p. 100) observes that

> *The culture we live in supplies us with stories that do not fit experience, and experience that does not live up to the story. It may also fail to supply us with appropriate arenas for narrating whatever story we have to tell. The common theme across all of these circumstances is the experience of silence, of living with a story that cannot be told. And, taking into account the fact that storytelling is a performance, an event that requires an audience, very often the existence of a personal "problem" can best be described as a response to silencing, the unwillingness of others to hear the story that in some sense "needs" to be told.*

We see both the discovery and the relational narratives being currently silenced in sport, yet they are stories that need to be told for two reasons. First, by silencing alternatives, as McLeod suggests, the mental health and well-being of those individuals who *do not* conform to the dominant narrative are threatened. Second, in silencing alternatives, we restrict and limit the identity and life options that are open to people in sport.

To a large extent, alternative stories are silenced as a result of others' unwillingness to hear them. An example was provided by one participant (Kandy), who referred to the trauma she experienced as a single parent in professional sport. In her words, "No one ever asked about my baby or how I was coping. The media only wanted good news. My problems did not interest them at all" (Carless & Douglas, 2009, p. 60). It is not only the interests of the media that silence alternative stories. Earlier in Kandy's story, when she described leaving university to get married, her decision was seen by others as "a disaster" and she as "a drop-out." We have documented a similar unwillingness to *hear* in research with professional coaches who provided written feedback on the narrative types (Douglas & Carless, 2008a). Despite the majority of coaches believing the performance narrative did not represent a healthy, balanced life, the story was recognized and accepted as depicting *the* way to get to the top in sport. In contrast, and mirroring Frank's (1995) research in medical contexts, most coaches found alternative narratives difficult to understand or believe. For example, one coach said, "I find it hard to believe you can reach the top of sport playing for someone else." Another questioned, "(She is) always trying to please and worry what someone else thinks: Why?" (Douglas & Carless, 2008a, p. 39). The alternative narratives, therefore, did not fit with the expectations of most coaches. In the case of the relational narrative, rather than question their own beliefs, coaches were more likely, as in the following quotation, to interpret the motives of the storyteller as questionable:

> *Shows how it's not a good idea to live your life for the benefit of someone else. It's surprising that she was a multiple tournament winner when she did not want to be there. A little sad. Lost sight of her own goals and ambitions. Played for her father when she should have played for herself. This caused her to see the game as only a job and lost sight of the true reasons behind playing the game. Grew to hate the game and as a pressure, it was the only way people saw her. However, she now has future opportunity.*

These quotes from various coaches at a professional development seminar illustrate how the values of the performance narrative can act as a benchmark by which others judge what the storyteller *should* have done. That is, for the storyteller referred to in the preceding coach's comment, to play golf for herself, not to think of the game as simply a job, not to lose sight of the "true" reasons for playing, and not to play golf for someone else. None of the coaches, however, considered the possibility that the storyteller was right to maintain an important relationship, none questioned how young people become enculturated to value winning in sport above interpersonal relationships, and few questioned the values implicit in the performance narrative. These responses illustrate the way that particular narrative types can lead others to believe a singular conception of what is ethically and morally acceptable. The coach quoted previously reveals his belief that there is one "true" reason for playing golf and that it is not—in his opinion—for someone else. We would ask, therefore, why it is that in a different arena—for example, motherhood—it is accepted that an individual sacrifices aspects of herself for another.

In her research into moral development, Carol Gilligan (1993) has written extensively on the ways in which women's voices and stories are silenced. For Gilligan, "the failure to hear the differences in their voices stems in part from the assumption that there is a single mode of social experience and interpretation" (p. 173). Likewise, McLeod (1997) critiques the assumption that individuals inhabit "a single monolithic culture" and suggests that "many people experience themselves as caught between different cultural systems" (p. 100). When these differing cultural systems are recognized, singular expectations of behavior and responses become untenable as an individual's life is understood as complex, contingent, and multidimensional.

In accepting that alternative modes of social experience are possible, Gilligan identifies some of the dangers inherent in two diverse approaches. One mode, which has traditionally been applied to masculine stories, sees danger in close personal affiliation arising from intimacy. Here, danger is storied as entrapment in a suffocating relationship or as being betrayed and humiliated by rejection. A second mode, traditionally associated with female stories, sees danger as the experience of isolation, being set apart through impersonal achievement situations that result from competition. These two modes relate very closely with the performance and relational narratives, respectively; the first is oriented toward the values of hierarchy, individuation, and competition, whereas the other is oriented toward communion, interpersonal relations, affiliation, and attachment.

Those who articulate a relational narrative construct a sense of self through their affiliations and relationships. Therefore, as Miller (1976, p. 83) warns, "the threat of disruption of an affiliation is perceived not just as a loss of a relationship but something closer to a total loss of self." This viewpoint makes it easier to understand the behaviors of people who tell relational stories and to appreciate, for instance, why throwing an event or cheating to get thrown out of a tournament can be a reasonable course of action that does not threaten the storyteller's sense of self. For the relational storyteller, the threat to be avoided is not the loss of a golf tournament—as it is for the performance storyteller—but the experience of isolation through a loss of intimacy or relationship. Miller, then, does not cast the relational narrative as psychopathology—which is how it is viewed from the perspective of the performance narrative—but as a psychic starting point that "contains the possibilities for an entirely different (and more advanced) approach to living and functioning . . . [in which] affiliation is valued as highly, or more highly . . . than self-enhancement" (Miller, 1976, cited in Gilligan, 1993, p.169). This perspective directly challenges the assumptions that underlie the performance narrative because "the suggestion that money, glory, and trophies cannot compare to a relationship is dynamite in a sporting world which promotes money, glory, and trophies as the ultimate satisfaction and interests of the self as paramount" (Douglas and Carless, 2006, p. 24).

It is not only coaches and the media who silence alternative narrative types; athletes themselves also advance performance narratives that are totalitarian. This point is illustrated by a quotation we shared earlier in the chapter: "I think for all of us, it [sport] becomes our whole life." The storyteller could have chosen to say, "It had to become my whole life." As told, however, her story reveals a belief—shared with all the women who told performance stories—that *all* high-performance athletes must story their lives this way. Such a statement draws on what is known *culturally,* not just what the athlete knows of herself; in this way, tellers of performance narratives align with the story that dominates elite sport culture. In doing so, they limit their own and others' identities and future options.

Sparkes and Smith (2002) suggest that researchers can also unwittingly sustain and reproduce culturally preferred narratives by failing to hear or recognize alternatives in participants' accounts. For Frank (1995), the challenge for those of us who use interview methods is "to hear not to steer" (p.101). That is, we must attend to how *our* story preferences influence participants' responses, and how *our* unease with some story topics may make it impossible for transgressive stories to be told. Many of the currently popular positivistic research methods used in sport psychology remove the possibility of exposing alternative narratives. For example, surveys, questionnaires, and structured interview schedules are unlikely to elicit complex, unexpected, or difficult-to-hear stories. In our research, all of the participants were known to Kitrina, and in each case they had an opportunity, over many years, to observe and come to know her. Some participants made clear that the stories they shared—which included accounts of cheating, self-harm, attempted suicide, sexual abuse, and depression—had never been voiced before and were told now through a bond of trust with Kitrina, not only as a researcher, but also as a member of a sisterhood of professional golfers. This bond of trust was exemplified when one participant, during a time of severe depression, contacted Kitrina for support in preference to the sport psychologist with whom she had been working before she retired. While the project provided us with some methodological challenges, we have learned that unless we as researchers are permitted to present accounts that illuminate the complexity of research relationships and the messiness of life in elite sport, then *our* stories—as well as those of our participants—will remain silenced in sport psychology research (Douglas & Carless, 2009b).

CONSEQUENCES OF THE PERFORMANCE NARRATIVE

We have suggested that those who tell discovery and relational narratives experience few tensions between their experiences and their story—that is, there is narrative alignment between how they experience life and how they story life. There is, however, significant narrative tension and a lack of fit between these alternative narrative types and the expectations of the dominant (i.e., performance) narrative. During the time these women played on the tour, they generally perceived that others—expecting performance stories—failed to accept, validate, or understand their lives. Thus, these women were more likely to experience psychological difficulty and trauma *within* sport culture than outside it (for example, after retirement). In their lives outside of sport, narrative, continuity, coherence, and fit are possible across the life span—before, during, and after their sport careers.

In contrast, for those who articulated a performance story, narrative alignment was possible only within the competitive high-performance environment and even then only if their experiences continued to match the performance narrative's specific and narrow contours. In line with narrative theory, when the concrete experiences of their lives no longer aligned with the performance stories they told, psychological problems resulted (Carless & Douglas, 2009; Douglas & Carless, 2009a). For example, all women who told performance-type narratives experienced psychological trauma when they played poorly to the extent that life was described as a "yo-yo" and a "roller-coaster."

Perhaps the most troubling story was told by a young woman who storied the early part of her life as "a fairy tale" in which she won everything possible (Douglas & Carless, 2009a). This individual told numerous stories about her triumphs, including how she would continue to win after becoming pregnant and having a baby. When she did not keep winning after the child was born, her concrete experience began to drift apart from the fairy-tale performance stories that she continued to tell. At this point in her life, she was unable to create an alternative story that would link, in a coherent way, her past self with a future self that she found acceptable. The performance narrative offered no narrative resources to help her create an alternative story in keeping with her changing experiences. Her story of the future had been entirely centered on winning, and the only possible self that was constructed in that telling was "champion golfer."

While it is true to say that the storyteller's identity and role had changed through becoming a mother, and that this role offered the possibility to story herself in multiple ways that could have staved off the problems associated with an exclusive athletic identity, she did not value these identities. Her story followed the performance narrative script that values only winners and winning. Although motherhood is valued in wider society, this individual was primarily immersed in a sport culture dominated by a performance narrative that places tournament success above familial responsibility. Therefore, rather than engaging with the additional identity of mother and the role of caregiver and nurturer providing some balance, these seemingly alternative roles merely increased the tensions in her life. As McLeod (1997) has observed, when an individual fears a negative reaction to her story, it is likely that she will remain silent. This storyteller was silenced because she felt unable, as a mother, to say, "I didn't want my baby" or "I blamed him." After some months of trauma, this young mother—unable to story her life in a way that aligned with her experiences and unable to construct a future story from her current position—attempted suicide.

While this case is particularly serious, stories of depression, despair, chaos, and silence were told by *all* the women with performance narratives when their objective experiences (i.e., results) curtailed their opportunities to sustain a story of winning. Our findings are in line with previous narrative research that shows that reliance on a single dominant narrative can be problematic when a person's life experiences, for whatever reason, no longer align with the profile of the chosen narrative (Frank, 1995; Smith & Sparkes, 2005; Sparkes, 1998). Poor performance, retirement or withdrawal, and serious injury are potentially problematic episodes when an athlete may struggle to reconcile or make sense of the dramatic changes occurring within her life (see, for example, Sparkes, 1996, 1998; Kerr & Dacyshyn, 2000). At these times, the performance narrative fails to fit the individual's experiences, and alternative narrative resources are required.

CONCLUSION

Returning to questions posed in the introduction, we would like to conclude by emphasizing three key points that we see as directly relevant to sport psychologists and to the ethical obligations associated with this role. First, the existence of alternatives to the performance narrative shows that there is more than one way to *be* a successful elite athlete. Alternative ways of being offer hope because they show that, contrary to widely held assumptions in sport, athletes are *not* fixed and finalized—we can and do have potential to change our stories and lives, we don't have to be *just* athletes, and the main goal does not *have* to be winning. Instead, we can prioritize our relationships above our sport performance and don't have to face withdrawal from sport as a time of loss or trauma.

These insights provide an opportunity for sport psychologists to become open to alternative narratives that inevitably bring their own particular possibilities and difficulties. As Etherington (2007) has shown, "we can invite stories that help people make sense of their lives in ways that do not reinforce internalized negative and stigmatizing stereotypes based on concepts of identity as fixed" (p. 467). Thus if sport psychologists want to provide opportunities for athletes to story their lives differently, it is first necessary to share the kinds of stories that show alternatives to be possible. In our work with students, elite athletes, and coaches, sharing the three different types in the form of stories has provided an opportunity to show that alternatives are possible and to open up discussions about different ways of being. These alternatives provide a bridge to silenced stories and have been particularly helpful for athletes who have felt alone or silenced. Awareness of these alternatives provides the individual with options in terms of both identity development and life horizons.

A second point we want to make relates to the ways particular narratives are privileged in sport environments. Currently, performance-type stories dominate elite sport culture and permeate the language and discourse of coaches, managers, performance directors, selectors, governing bodies, sport strategy documents, and the sport media. Similarly, many of the theories and practices of contemporary sport psychology (e.g., mental toughness, self-confidence) are predicated on an unconditional acceptance of performance values as the best or only way (Van Raalte & Andersen, 2007). Alternative stories and, therefore, the values and perspectives associated with them are routinely silenced

(Douglas, 2009). From this perspective, the problem lies not so much in the psychological processes of individual athletes but in ingrained sociocultural values and assumptions among those who participate in sport. While, in the long term, cultural changes *are* necessary, a practical first step involves individual action. It follows that there are two ways in which sport psychologists might help.

First, through becoming aware of and reflecting on the ways in which their current practices and dialogue may serve to silence or impede alternative stories, psychologists can invite and support different stories that are closer to some individuals' experiences. Sharing these stories is likely to enhance an athlete's psychological well-being and build a more open and trusting relationship between the psychologist and the athlete. Second, armed with knowledge of the dangers of wholehearted subscription to the performance narrative, we believe that sport psychologists have an ethical duty to begin to question and challenge those exchanges and practices that perpetuate totalitarian performance-focused values and beliefs. We recognize that taking such a stance is difficult (many practitioners are employed not by individual athletes but by governing bodies or sport teams), yet it is not impossible. These two approaches will begin to open up space for alternative narratives to coexist within sport culture.

Finally, we believe that sport psychology research has the potential to make a greater contribution to athletes' careers and lives in two key ways. The first relates to beliefs concerning the presentation of sport psychology knowledge to athletes. When Kitrina reflected on the diet of watered-down and paraphrased findings she was fed as an elite athlete, it seemed that she was considered to be part of a population that was unable or unwilling to digest a more substantial diet. In our experience, however, when given the right environment, format, and topics, most athletes appear able and interested to consider philosophical, ethical, and psychological issues—and are capable of modifying their behavior or perspective accordingly. It is not helpful to athletes when psychologists assume that research must be diluted or "dumbed down." The second potential contribution relates to the need for psychologists themselves to become open to, and informed about, nonpositivistic research approaches such as narrative inquiry. In our experience and that of others (e.g., Smith & Sparkes, 2009), these approaches have shown the potential to expand, enrich, and problematize existing sport psychology knowledge and practice by providing and communicating a perspective that gets close to the ways in which athletes communicate and understand themselves within the unique sociocultural environment of elite sport.

IDEAS FOR REFLECTION AND DEBATE

1. Reflect on the notion that approaching applied practice through the lens of narrative inquiry allows applied practitioners to develop and extend their understanding of their own life histories.

2. Consider the career challenges that you might face if you opt to build a research or applied practice career based on themes of story analysis and storytelling rather than hypothesis testing.

3. This essay by Kitrina and David challenges a dominant sporting narrative and suggests that other narratives might also exist and be powerful. Reflect on this theme and consider how many different sporting narratives you have encountered.

4. Finally, reflect on how different narratives might have implications for different approaches to the support of athletes and consider how these different approaches might require adjustments to applied training or applied curricula more generally.

Acknowledgments: We offer our sincere thanks to the participants who generously shared stories of their lives. Without them this research and essay would not have been possible.

REFERENCES

Alder, P.A., & Alder, P. (1989). The gloried self: The aggrandizement and the constriction of self. *Social Psychology Quarterly, 52*(4), 299–310.

Bruner J.S. (1986). *Actual minds, possible worlds.* Cambridge, MA: Harvard University Press.

Carless, D., & Douglas, K. (2009). "We haven't got a seat on the bus for you" or "All the seats are mine": Narratives and career transition in professional golf. *Qualitative Research in Sport and Exercise, 1*(1), 51–66.

Chase, S. (2005). Narrative inquiry: Multiple lenses, approaches, voices. In N. Denzin & Y. Lincoln (Eds.), *The handbook of qualitative research* (pp. 651–679). Thousand Oaks, CA: Sage.

Crosset, T.W. (1995). *Outsiders in the clubhouse: The world of women's professional golf.* New York: State University of New York Press.

Crossley, M. (2000). *Introducing narrative psychology: Self, trauma and the construction of meaning.* Buckingham: Open University Press.

Denzin, N.K. (2003). *Performance ethnography.* Thousand Oaks, CA: Sage.

Douglas, K. (2004). *What's the drive in golf? Motivation and persistence in women professional tournament golfers.* Doctoral dissertation, University of Bristol.

Douglas, K. (2009). Storying my self: Negotiating a relational identity in professional sport. *Journal of Qualitative Research in Sport and Exercise, 1*(2), 176–190.

Douglas, K., & Carless, D. (2006). Performance, discovery, and relational narratives among women professional tournament golfers. *Women in Sport and Physical Activity Journal, 15*(2), 14–27.

Douglas, K., & Carless, D. (2008a). Using stories in coach education. *International Journal of Sports Science and Coaching, 3*(1), 33–49.

Douglas, K., & Carless, D. (2008b). Training or education? Negotiating a fuzzy line between what "we" want and "they" might need. *Annual Review of Golf Coaching,* 1–13.

Douglas, K., & Carless, D. (2008c). The teams are off: Getting inside women's experiences in professional sport. *Aethlon: The Journal of Sport Literature, XXV*(I), 241–251.

Douglas, K., & Carless, D. (2009a). Abandoning the performance narrative: Two women's stories of transition from professional golf. *Journal of Applied Sport Psychology, 21*(2), 213-230.

Douglas, K., & Carless, D. (2009b). Exploring taboo issues in professional sport through a fictional approach. *Reflective Practice, 10*(3), 311–323.

Etherington, K. (2007). The impact of trauma on drug users' identities. *British Journal of Guidance & Counselling, 35*(4), 455–469.

Frank, A.W. (1995). *The wounded storyteller.* Chicago: University of Chicago Press.

Frank, A.W. (2000). The standpoint of the storyteller. *Qualitative Health Research, 10*(3), 354–365.

Gilligan, C. (1993). *In a different voice: Psychological theory and women's development.* Cambridge, MA: Harvard University Press.

Kerr, G., & Dacyshyn, A. (2000). The retirement experiences of elite, female gymnasts. *Journal of Applied Sport Psychology, 12,* 115–133.

Lieblich, A., Tuval-Mashiach, R., & Zilber, T. (1998). *Narrative research: Reading, analysis and interpretation.* London: Sage.

McAdams, D. (1993). *The stories we live by.* New York: Guilford Press.

McLeod, J. (1997). *Narrative and psychotherapy.* London: Sage.

Miller, J.B. (1976). *Toward a new psychology of women.* Boston: Beacon Press.

Neimeyer, R., Herrero, O., & Botella, L. (2006). Chaos to coherence: Psychotherapeutic integration of traumatic loss. *Journal of Constructivist Psychology, 19,* 127–145.

Richardson, L. (1995). Narrative and sociology. In J. Van Mannen (Ed.), *Representation in Ethnography* (pp. 198–222). Thousand Oaks, CA: Sage.

Somers, M. (1994). The narrative construction of identity: A relational and network approach. *Theory and Society, 23,* 605–649.

Smith, B., & Sparkes, A.C. (2005). Men, sport, spinal cord injury, and narratives of hope. *Social Science and Medicine, 61,* 1095–1105.

Smith, B., & Sparkes, A.C. (2009). Narrative inquiry in sport and exercise psychology: What can it mean, and why might we do it? *Psychology of Sport and Exercise, 10*(1), 1–11.

Sparkes, A.C. (1996). The fatal flaw: A narrative of the fragile body-self. *Qualitative Inquiry, 2(4),* 463–494.

Sparkes, A.C. (1998). Athletic identity: An Achilles' heel to the survival of self. *Qualitative Health Research, 8*(5), 644–664.

Sparkes, A.C. (2003). Bodies, identities, selves: Autoethnographic fragments and reflections. In J. Denison & P. Markula (Eds.), *Moving writing* (pp. 51-76). New York: Peter Lang.

Sparkes, A.C. (2004). Bodies, narratives, selves, and autobiography: The example of Lance Armstrong. *Journal of Sport and Social Issues, 28,* 397–428.

Sparkes, A.C., & Douglas, K. (2007). Making the case for poetic representations: An example in action. *The Sport Psychologist, 21(2),* 170-189.

Sparkes, A.C., & Smith, B. (2002). Sport, spinal cord injury, embodied masculinities, and the dilemmas of narrative identity. *Men and Masculinities, 4*(3), 258–285.

Van Raalte, J., & Andersen, M. (2007). When sport psychology consulting is a means to an end(ing): Roles and agendas when helping athletes leave their sports. *Sport Psychologist, 21,* 227-242.

Werthner, P., & Orlick, T. (1986). Retirement experiences of successful Olympic athletes. *International Journal of Sport Psychology, 17,* 337–363.

REPRESENTING APPLIED RESEARCH EXPERIENCES THROUGH PERFORMANCE:

Extending Beyond Text

David Llewellyn
Liverpool John Moores University, United Kingdom

David Gilbourne
University of Wales Institute, Cardiff, United Kingdom

Carmel Triggs
University of Chester, United Kingdom

In this essay, the two Davids and Carmel present a representational challenge to applied qualitative researchers and suggest that the insight and authenticity offered by in-depth data sources such as life histories, autoethnographies, and ethnographies can be disseminated through the performing arts. This essay posits drama as a mechanism that allows narratives to be brought to life and holds that the physicality and interpretation offered though performance can serve to embody the emotionality of the lived experience. We also discuss how drama might engage and encourage reflection in audience members, be they sport psychologists or the general public. By way of illustration, the journey from research text to performance is briefly considered through examples of recently presented material. In summary, this chapter outlines a case for using performance as part of applied practice in sport psychology.

INTRODUCTION

Following a performance of the ethnodrama *Fates, Mates and Moments* (Gilbourne, 2007), presented at a conference workshop (Gilbourne & Llewellyn, 2008) on storytellers and story analysts in Cardiff, one delegate asked a fundamental question: "Isn't this just entertainment?" That query challenged the providence, validity, and efficacy of ethnodrama as a process of communication within sport social sciences. The question not only points toward the problem of defining and locating the dramatic territory of ethnodrama in the already crowded lexical landscape of, as Saldana has termed it, reality theater; it also challenges the validity of dramatizing the data for dissemination within the academic community and beyond (Saldana, 2005). Our intention is to address this question both from the ethnodramatist's (Gilbourne & Triggs) and from a theater director's (David Llewellyn's) stance. In this essay, we initially seek to identify the recently established territory that ethnodrama has claimed in the field of reality theater and applied theater practice, then consider the function and potential of ethnodrama in the landscape of qualitative research in sport social sciences. We undertake this task with reference both to the dramatic canon of documentary-based plays and to a range of recently written and produced ethnodramas representing sport narratives (Gilbourne, Triggs, & Merkin, 2006; Gilbourne & Llewellyn, 2008).

ETHNODRAMA AND THEATER

Ethnodrama has been described as "a new form of theatre" (Mienczakowski & Morgan, 2001) that seeks "to translate action research into reflexive, reflective performances." However, as Saldana (2005) points out, for more than 2,500 years theater has been "telling stories" and "representing social life on stage interpreted artistically by playwrights and actors with perceptive insight into the human condition" (p. 4). Although the claim that playwrights and actors have the privilege of "perceptive insight" can be challenged, the aspiration that Shakespeare articulated through the character of Hamlet indicates a more profound purpose than just entertainment:

> *The purpose of playing, whose end, both at the first and now, was and is, to hold as 'twere the mirror up to nature; to show virtue her own feature, scorn her own*

image, and the very age and body of the time his form and pressure.

(Hamlet, act 3, scene 2)

Despite the widely held view of drama as primarily a vehicle of fiction, dramatists from classical antiquity to contemporary times have used a range of factual materials to inform their scripts. Aristotle's classical theory of art, for example, established various paradigms relating to dramatic practice, and in the *Poetics* (335 BCE/1997) he asserted that dramatic characters should be based on historical figures. The impulse to incorporate factual material into plays has been a sustained feature of dramatic literature in the West since its earliest days. For example, the reality of the wars of Ancient Greece provided the documentary backdrop for the classical tragedies of Aeschylus' *Agamemnon* (458 BCE), and even fanciful comedies such as Aristophanes' political satire *Lysistrata* (411 BCE) were informed by historical events, in this case the Peloponnesian War. Indeed, connections with historical realities and documents of the time are evident even in plays featuring characters, locations, and narrative action that are essentially fictional and set in fantasy worlds (e.g., Shakespeare's *A Midsummer Night's Dream* and *The Tempest*) in which the relationship to the real is essentially metaphorical. Contemporary events and the documented history of the time are evident in *A Midsummer Night's Dream,* the blessing of the marriage of the Earl of Leicester by the fairy queen is regarded as a direct reference to Queen Elizabeth, and the report of a shipwreck off Bermuda informed the writing of *The Tempest.* Although in both cases the material has been crafted by the dramatist and hopefully produced by the director to entertain the imagination of an audience, the aspiration to illuminate the human condition remains the primary purpose. Entertainment is the means, not the end.

It is in the latter part of the 20th century and, in particular, in the 21st century, however, that playwrights and ethnographers have extensively exploited the potential of ethnographic and documentary-based material to inform their work. For example, Gregory Burke's (2005) interviews with soldiers who had resigned their commissions from a Scottish regiment provide the verbatim for the National Theatre of Scotland's critically and commercially acclaimed *Black Watch* (2006). Liverpool sex workers provided the verbatim for *Unprotected* (Wilson, 2006), and thousands of interviews provided the material for Eve Ensler's (2000) internationally successful *The Vagina Monologues.*

This verbatim approach to playwriting foregrounds and embodies empirical data in production, as we have indicated playwrights have always engaged with and embedded fact into their fictions. However, if the database extends legitimately to the playwright's lived and learned experience, as well as factual material gleaned from a rigorous observer's point of view, then, as Saldana (2005) asserts, "all playwrights are ethno-dramatists" (p. 4).

The documentary drama is a well-established and distinct genre of dramatic literature. The potential of plays that feature and foreground factual material and qualitative data to effect social change has attracted many radically minded dramatists and directors to adopt and exploit the form for both didactic and political purpose. Taking inspiration from the development of a newsreel aesthetic in films, documentary drama was adopted enthusiastically by theater, radio, and television dramatists in the latter part of the 20th century. The responses of critics and scholars have produced an expanding nomenclature for this work, and the terms *docudrama, documentary drama, drama documentary, faction, creative nonfiction,* and the aforementioned *verbatim drama* have all been coined to describe variants of the genre. To this list we must now add *ethnodrama* and, in a more recent development, Gilbourne's conception of *informed fiction* (presented by Gilbourne & Llewellyn, 2008) as an eclectic mode of writing founded on ethnographic and autoethnographic sources, as well as ideas and material from blogs, newspapers, television, radio, and other media.

The effect that reality theater has had on society lends weight to the notion of ethnodrama as a potential means of education and social change. Peter Watkins' *The War Game* (1965), a documentary drama based on the impact of a nuclear attack on Britain, was banned by government in fear of its power to stir up antinuclear sentiment and public panic. Educators, however, regarded the drama as a vital source of information and showed it "privately" in the majority of secondary schools in England in the 1960s. Jeremy Sandford's *Cathy Come Home* (1966) created a national outcry about the plight of homeless persons in mid-1960s Britain and gave rise to the charity known as Shelter. Sandford's *Edna the Inebriate Woman* (1971) provoked parliament to change the law with regard to vagrancy. Indeed, Mienczakowski and Morgan (2001) recognized that ethnodrama has the power to influence participants and audiences.

Ethnodramas (i.e., written plays) and ethnotheater (i.e., performed plays) constitute a notable 21st-century development in the field of qualitative inquiry in the social sciences. This experimentation with arts-based modes of research representation is exemplified by a range of publications and practices in the field that have been conducted by, among others, Bagley and Cancienne (2002), Barone (2002), Mienczakowski and Morgan (2001), and Saldana (2005). It can also be seen in efforts to articulate sport ethnographies through drama in a range of ethnodramatic forms in the work of Gilbourne, Llewellyn, Triggs, and Merkin from 2005 through 2010.

Kruger's (2008) somewhat reductive view in *Ethnography in the Performing Arts: A Student Guide* asserts that ethnodrama is not a means for research but instead "resembles performed research" (p. 67) and serves the aim of promoting "wider understandings for participants"; the author seeks to achieve social impact and change by using an ethnodrama to deliver narratives that inform, disturb, confront, and hold the attention of an audience. Thus an ethnodrama in Kruger's view can be described not only as a means of disseminating data as "just entertainment" but also as a form of applied drama designed to elicit change. Although the term *applied* refers to the educational content and purpose of ethnodramas like those developed by Mienczakowski and Morgan (2001) toward the professional education of health workers, Kruger's perspective does not fully recognize the value that an ethnodrama and ethnotheater can bring to an ethnographic report.

There is an enormous difference between drama and any other form of literature. A play script is a blueprint for performance. It is a literature that is intended to walk, to sound, to see, to be inflected with gesture and with the breath and the rhythms and the emotional dimensions of life. It is a literature intended to be embodied by three-dimensional human performers working in real time in front of a real audience. It is an artifact that is at one and the same time essentially false and essentially true—false in the sense that acting is fundamentally pretending, though this pretense is performed before audience members who contract to adopt a state of mind that suspends disbelief (Coleridge, 1817/1983) in order to allow what is clearly false to be experienced as true.

In rehearsal and production, actors, designers, and directors work together, primarily through the dialogue and action of the text, to tell the story of the drama. However, for the realization of the story to be both convincing and expressively effective, the artistic direction must take account of a range of nonverbal details in order to re-create the detailed and layered nature of human consciousness and behavior. These details include characters' unspoken thoughts, sometimes referred to as the subtext, which both precede and accompany the text in performance and inform the character's emotional journeys attendant to the action. These nonverbal signs are embodied in the live presence of the actor in performance, and their effectiveness is determined in part by the actor's imaginative engagement in the role and his or her intellectual purchase on the world of the script. These elements that are beyond the text are vital to the effective re-creation of life onstage and they affect the actor's treatment of the words and the physical expression of character and feeling through the presence of the body languages of movement, gesture, and facial expression. It is the presence of these in performance, if convincingly portrayed and produced, that helps an audience further engage and empathize with the situation portrayed and with the attendant emotional landscape of the narrative. The distinctive impact of a story told through a dramatic text in performance results in part from the facility of the actor to incorporate this broader representation (i.e., broader than the written text alone affords) of the multifaceted nature of the human condition. Moreover, because a theater text is embodied by a human being working in real time before a real audience, the impression derived is the closest of all the media of expression to the direct experience of life.

As Grotowski (1968) pointed out, all that is required to make theater is an actor, a space, and an audience. More often than not, however, theater makers employ a more expansive range of expressive means to augment the script and its vocal and physical interpretation by the actors before an audience. These means include elements of scenery and stage design, stage properties, costumes, and lighting and sound effects that function together with the script and the performance to create, as Gestalt theory suggests, an overall effect that is greater than the sum of its constituent elements. The documentary foundations of ethnotheater often predicate the inclusion in the scenography of technical elements such as photography, film, and sound archive material in order both to convey information and to provide the feel of reality. This layering of languages and signs cogently engages our experience of the real world and posits an ethnodrama not only as a vehicle of disseminating data in an entertaining way but also as a means by which aspects of human experience, authenticated by data produced by social scientists in narrative form, can be realized in order to reveal new insight through the communication of meaning and emotional moment in live theater.

SPORT-BASED ETHNODRAMA EXAMPLES

The following examples, derived from our own endeavors to produce ethnographic drama based in sport cultures, illustrate how nonverbal elements play their part. *Your Breath in the Air* (Gilbourne, Triggs, & Merkin, 2006) is an ethnodrama rooted in the autoethnographic writings of Gilbourne and Triggs. The premier ran for a short season at Unity Theatre Liverpool and was open to both academic delegates attending the Liverpool John Moores Qualitative Research Conference and public audiences. The play documents experiences of football (called *soccer* in the United States) fans and highlights contrasting experiences within fandom.

The play is set in an invented location of a railway station platform. This place provided a plausible, literal, and metaphorical junction for the contrasting autoethnographic narratives of the Nottingham Forest fan (Gilbourne) and the Liverpool fan (Triggs) embodied in the drama, respectively, as the characters Steve and Laura. The narratives were fused into a script and performed through the medium of ethnodrama. The play locates the autoethnographic narratives in a fictional context that includes the additional fictional characters of Rob and Shaun, whose dramatic function provoked the inciting incidents that realized the telling of the autoethnographic narratives. This blurring of fact and fiction, necessitated by the desire to provide a realistic world within which the narratives could credibly emerge and thus engage an audience both intellectually and emotionally, caused some delegates to question the legitimacy of the work. However, as Saldana (2005) points out, the theater is a medium that accommodates the simultaneous use of fictionalized and nonfictionalized social life in order to portray the human condition. Moreover, such combinations and emphases can be employed to stimulate and facilitate reflection. Although there is a tension between the need to root work of this kind in the products of rigorous research and the need to create an engaging and effective piece of theater, there is also value in dramatizing and producing this kind of research data as theater. That value can be best illustrated by a close analysis of the text and the attendant production rhetoric employed by Merkin in two exemplary sections and scenes from *Your Breath in the Air*.

Narratives as Script

The first example features Gilbourne's autoethnographic narrative, told in the play by the character Steve; the second features Triggs' narrative, told through Laura. The two narratives illustrate and contrast the experience of soccer fandom in the lives of Gilbourne and Triggs, and they were integrated in the play to show the divergent fortunes of the two soccer clubs in a story line that paralleled different time frames in the authors' own lives. In keeping with this focus, the scenography featured archive film of significant cup and league matches between the two clubs and reflected on how their fandoms informed the ways in which the respective authors grew up and developed relationships with their fathers.

In the following section, we seek to illustrate the nonverbal language and signs produced by the actor's work in a short extract from the play. The original written script appears in boldface font, the subtexts are rendered in italics, and the scenography appears in standard font. In this example, the analysis foregrounds the expressive values of the languages of facial expression, body language, stage movement and imagery, vocal inflection, and gesture, all of which contribute to and indicate elements of the seminal and emotional journeys of the characters.

> The stage is set and indicates a railway station platform somewhere between Liverpool, Nottingham, and Hartlepool. A railway timetable is seen at stage right and a rubbish bin at stage left, and two typical railway platform bench seats face the audience. On one bench, Steve and Rob, both Nottingham Forest fans, are talking about Brian Clough, a past and iconic manager of Nottingham Forest Football Club in the UK. Steve and Rob are positioned physically close to each other to underscore their mutual allegiance. Shaun, a Liverpool Football Club fan, is at a distance but listening in to their conversation.

> **Steve:** Brian hated that ya know . . . the fact he ended his time at Forest with relegation. . . . That relegation haunted him.

> *[Subtext: And I am still haunted by it.]*

> As part of his attempt to put his lifelong association with Nottingham Forest Football Club as a fan behind him, Steve, unlike Rob, no longer wears the scarf or follows the matches. He remains locked not only in the memories of both the glory and the ignominy of the past but also in a powerful identification with the past manager. The subtext—negotiated in this case by the actor, the author, and the director—was shown not only by the vocal intonation employed on the final phrase of the line but also by the reaction of the performer playing Rob to Steve's introspec-

tive reflection and the evident change in his facial expression. When Rob does not respond immediately, thus leaving an awkward pause, Steve turns away from direct eye contact with Rob in order to reflect on his own "haunting," thus indicating, in a gesture that goes beyond the text, the bitter gall of his feelings.

Shaun: Yeah he were [*sic*] great Cloughy!

[Subtext: I want to lighten things up—cheer him up and join in.]

Shaun's intention to get in on the conversation and lighten the mood by showing respect to Steve's hero and a degree of camaraderie with him was physically indicated in the performance by the bright and buoyant tone of his delivery and also by a move toward Steve. Steve's consequent rebuttal of Shaun's overture was shown by means of three nonverbal signifiers: an audible sigh accompanied the blocking body language of folding his arms across his chest and moving away from the bench, thus essentially blanking Shaun. Shaun's incomprehension was shown by a glance toward Rob with a facial expression suggesting the thought, *Is he mad?*

Rob: In Nottingham everyone called him "Brian" only them pundits ever called him Clough or Cloughy.

[Subtext: He doesn't know. Why should he? No need for a conflict—I'd better explain.]

With this line, Rob moves toward Shaun, literally and metaphorically closing the gap between him and the Liverpool supporter, who up until this moment had been mocking him aggressively for his support of a team of losers. Steve, who had moved upstage, turning his back on Shaun and the audience, hears Rob's conciliatory remark to Shaun and, realizing that his emotional reaction was unnecessarily extreme, turns and moves to rejoin them and continue the reminiscence.

Steve: Rob's right; it was always "Brian" . . . like he'd just popped in for a cup a tea.

Shaun: Didn't he hit some fans once . . . when they'd ran onto the pitch!

Steve: Yeah . . . and then . . . the next day . . . they apologized . . . to him!

All three laugh.

The image of the three characters laughing together in close quarters communicates, essentially through nonverbal means, the temporary resolution of the conflict.

Techniques That Capture the Moment

The following illustration, taken from a later scene, foregrounds the exploitation of technical aspects of the scenography. Here, Merkin's scenography features archive film footage of key football matches, including shots of the actual crowd with an accompanying sound track and the use of nonrealist lighting effects such as single spotlight in contrast with the realist effect of general cover illumination. These design elements work to locate the football matches in their respective times and add color and depth to the texture of the contrasting emotional landscapes and journeys explored in the drama.

In this scene, Laura is telling her story of watching the European Cup Final, played by Liverpool and Milan in Istanbul, with her dad when she was younger. Her first line responds to an observation made by another character that many of the Liverpool fans left at halftime when they were losing. As before, the script of the original play appears in boldface font, the commentary is rendered in italics, and technical indication appears in standard font.

> **Laura:** I could never do that. . . . They don't lose on purpose. . . . I don't understand it. . . . The real fans stayed behind 'em and then . . . we started singin' . . . "You'll Never Walk Alone.". . . It got louder and louder. . . . Blokes were shoutin' . . . make 'em hear us in the changing rooms . . . and we did, we sang and sang [music*]. I wanted the boys ta hear us . . . to hear me. . . . I wanted them ta know we were still there for 'em. . . . And they heard us . . . they heard us in the changing rooms . . . they said after.

> *The sound of the Liverpool anthem sung by the fans was played at a very low volume to underscore the final three lines at an almost subliminal level as if it were being heard in the changing rooms by the players.

> **Shaun:** Did ya really believe we'd turn it 'round, though?

> **Laura:** If I'm honest . . . no . . . but when they came out [cheers and chanting: "Liverpool . . . Liverpool*], it was 'right. . . . They've got a job ta do and so have we . . . so I got stuck in. . . .

> *Chants and a huge crowd roaring as a goal is scored.

At this moment the recording of the cheers and chant was played at a high volume to suggest both the start of the second half and the shared recollection of the event by Shaun and Laura.

Shaun: Alonso was awesome. . . .

*Archive footage shows Xabi Alonso preparing to take his penalty.

Laura: Another game another day you'd say. . . . No way he should take a penalty. . . . Fair dos [to be fair] though he had the guts ta take it. . . . [*Film] When it went in . . . off the rebound . . . it was wild . . . just mayhem. . . . Dad lifted me off the floor . . . just pure jubilance. . . . Afterwards I thought, *Everyone should experience this.* I really believe that. . . .

*Film: The strike, the goal, the cheering. Film off and sound to silence.

Shaun: We were level! Then the penalties. . . . The players must have been . . .

The film played on the upstage cyclorama not only added color but was also used to take the audience (the Liverpool fans, at least) back into the moment when they saw the game played on television. Cutting away from the film and the sound brings us back to the theatrical reality of Laura telling her tale.

Laura: Don't ask me about the players. . . . I tell ya . . . I was wrecked. . . . I was so frightened that after all that . . . we might still lose. . . . I hate watchin' pens [penalties] anyway. . . .

Shaun: Ya must have watched. . . . Tell me ya watched 'em!

Laura: I did. . . . Me dad made me . . .

Stage light: Change from general cover narrow to a spotlight focusing on Laura.

Laura: . . . I just felt sick, so nervous. . . . Me and me dad, we came to a compromise. . . . I crouch down . . . knees bent a bit. . . . I've not got a clear view—it's like a view through the crowd . . . then . . . I remember. . . he misses. . . . Their player misses. . . . Still early days though. . . . Back into me crouch position again. THEN . . . it's "if they miss we win." . . . Everyone's checkin'. . . . "That's right . . . if they miss we win.". . . Oh God . . . I know that's right but still asked me dad. . . . Then I'm off again crouchin'. . . . It's me favorite place ever. THEN . . . I'm huggin' me dad . . . people are in tears . . . I've never seen so many grown men cryin' in one place. . . . It was surreal. Me dad, he turns to me and says to me . . .

Stage light: Another circle of light appears directly alongside her. Laura moves into it to play her dad. Her spotlight fades to black.

Laura: . . . Remember this night . . . remember it when I'm dead and gone, promise me you'll always remember this.

Stage light: Spotlight fades to black; Laura returns to her original place; her spotlight illuminates her.

Laura: . . . I will, I will. We've done it. . . . I've seen us do it, Dad!

Stage light switches to general cover.

The lighting effects focus the audience's attention on the storyteller and suggest the intensely personal experience of the moment while also indicating the father's presence without the need to characterize the father's voice through the work of the actress playing Laura. The return to the general cover brings the audience back into the play's present time.

When ethnographies are played out as ethnotheater, the communication of meaning is contingent not only on the words written and spoken but also on what is put in the scene by the actors and the director. The value and the validity of the artifact as means of representation are enhanced by the way in which the nonverbal elements of subtext, stage imagery, and design inform the complex detail of human experience, consciousness, and emotional journey.

Storytelling as Theatrical Monologue

In 2008, at the 12th European Congress of Sport Psychology in Halkidiki, Greece, Gilbourne and Llewellyn worked with actors to present and perform ethnodramatic work. They reprised a scene from *Your Breath in the Air* and introduced an autoethnographic prose narrative written by Jim McGuiness (2006). This narrative monologue piece was an autoethnographic case study that focused on dysfunctional sport performance in the context of family bereavement and on the impact of feelings of loss and guilt on elite sport performance.

Autoethnographic prose narrative lends itself, with its central protagonist's perspective, to the form of the theatrical monologue. In theater parlance, this form goes by the name of the one-man or one-woman show and is an established style of dramatic writing that relies heavily on storytelling technique in performance. This approach contrasts with the realist conventions employed in *Your Breath in the Air.* In the realist form of dramatic writing and performance, social interaction is staged through dialogue and action, and audience members participate as voyeurs. The monologue form, however, predicates that the performer acknowledge the presence of an audience by speaking directly to them and thus lends itself to the verbatim account of an ethnographic case study. In the case of McGuiness' piece, there was no recourse to a playwright's invention. The script used in the performance was taken verbatim from an account, which originally formed an element of his unpublished master's thesis, that was written from the perspective of his experience as a professional Gaelic football player.

It was clear that the representation of the author by an actor in performance entertained in the sense that the playing commanded the audience's attention and communicated the story content. The reception, both in the playing and in the questions and comments following the performance (and beyond in the conference fringe), demonstrated the value of telling the story through the psychology of an actor embodying the role in a live performance because it manifested and heightened the experience of the emotional and mental turmoil that lay at the root of the player's dysfunction. The fact that an audience, many of whom were sport psychologists, had collectively shared the autoethnography provided common ground for critiquing the application of conventional instrumental theoretical approaches.

As with *Your Breath in the Air,* which exploits a realist approach, the audience here engaged not only with the content of the narrative but also with the protagonist's emotional journey. In the McGuiness piece, despite the use of direct address and the absence of any location or dramatic motivation to cause the speech, the performer's vocal and physical embodiment of character—coupled with the subtextual triggers of the nonverbal aspects of performance as manifested in the pauses and phrasing of the speech and the use of significant gestures and body language—enhanced and illuminated the significance and effect of the raw text. In this instance, the actor and director were privileged to work with McGuiness to achieve maximum authenticity.

CONCLUSION

Material that is presented in this form holds the attention and can serve as a source of pleasure for an audience; as a result, ethnography presented in this way has greater potential to be disseminated beyond the confines of the academic qualitative research community. Thus reality theater, specifically ethnodrama, provides a way to achieve educational objectives of communicating information and eliciting change, and its efficacy is evident both in the history of documentary theater and in the contemporary use of ethnodrama in training. This essay, however, has sought to illustrate the potential of this relatively recent application of drama to ethnography. If the purpose of qualitative research is to gain insight into the issues that underlie a research problem by gathering (often from small samples) nonstatistical feedback and opinions rooted in people's feelings, attitudes, motivations, values, and perceptions—and if one of its central aims is to "learn about how and why people behave, think and make meaning" (Ambert, Adler, Adler, & Detzner, 1995)—then the dramatization of data offers more than just an entertaining diversion.

As Oscar Wilde (1895) pointed out in *The Importance of Being Earnest,* "the truth is rarely pure and never simple," and it would be fallacious to suggest that authenticity and truth can be fully realized by dramatizing the ethnographic report. Furthermore, the processes of selection and editing during the making of a performance, along with the inevitable vagaries of the performance's reception, determine a subjective and partial purchase on the material. As Saldana (2005) points out, the staging of reality-based work is a "risky business," and in our own experience it has been evident that ethnodrama has the capacity to disturb the sensibilities of conservative-minded researchers who value the enduring quality and relatively emotion-free zone of the journal article. Indeed, it has not been our intention in writing this article to deny or denigrate the validity and value of well-established forms of ethnography; we have intended, rather, to argue that ethnodrama constitutes a valuable addition to the research landscape of qualitative inquiry. With its value as a vehicle of dissemination, education, and training established, it is our contention that dramatizing and theatricalizing the data add more to the ethnographic report than just entertainment.

IDEAS FOR REFLECTION AND DEBATE

1. Research presented through the medium of theater (i.e., ethnodrama) offers a different approach to the process of dissemination. Who might the potential beneficiaries be?

2. The scripted examples presented in the chapter emphasize direction, subtext, and the re-creation of contextual markers to suggest that applied research needs to be of a particular type in order to provide such depth and clarity. What might this research be? How might it be conducted? What are the ethical dilemmas associated with transferal to performance?

3. Comment on the following statement: "Qualitative research in sport and exercise is only just showing signs of being insightful enough to warrant sharing with dramatists and the public more widely."

4. How might ethnodrama be used within the applied sport psychology curriculum?

REFERENCES

Ambert, A., Adler P., Adler, P., & Detzner, D. (1995). Understanding and evaluating qualitative research. *Journal of Marriage and the Family, 57*(4), 879–893.

Aristotle. (1997). *Poetics* (S.H. Butcher, Trans.). New York: Courier Dover. (Original work published 350 BCE)

Bagley, C., & Cancienne, M.B. (2002). *Dancing the data.* New York: Peer Lang.

Barone, T. (2002). From gene blurring to audience blending: Reflections on the field emanating from an ethnodrama. *Anthropology and Education Quarterly, 33,* 255–267.

Burke, G. (2006). *Black watch.* Performance at Edinburgh Festival, Edinburgh Training Corps Drill Hall, Edinburgh, Scotland.

Coleridge, S.T. (1983). *The collected works of Samuel Taylor Coleridge: Biographia literaria.* Princeton University Press: New Jersey. (Original work published 1817).

Ensler, E. (2000). *The vagina monologues.* New York: Dramatists Play Service.

Gilbourne, D. (2007, July). Self-narrative: Illustrations of different genres and explorations of the underlying rationale for writing. In B. Smith (Chair), *Symposium: Narrative and its potential contribution to sport and health psychology.* Symposium conducted at the 12th European Congress of Sport Psychology, Halkidiki, Greece.

Gilbourne, D., & Llewellyn, D. (2008). Fate, mates and moments: Performance of informed fiction. Presentation at Story Analysts and Storytellers, Cardiff: UK.

Gilbourne, D., Triggs, C., & Merkin, R. (Director). (2006). *Your breath in the air.* Unity Theatre Liverpool presentation at the 2nd International Qualitative Research Conference, Liverpool, England.

Grotowski, J. (1968). *Towards a poor theatre.* London: Eyre Methuen.

Kruger S. (2008). *Ethnography in the performing arts: A student guide.* Lancaster: Palatine (the HEA Subject Centre for Dance, Drama and Music).

McGuinness, J. (2006). *Making it and faking it.* Unpublished master's thesis, Liverpool John Moores University, Liverpool, England.

Mienczakowski, J., & Morgan, S. (2001). Constructing participatory experiential and compelling action research: Participative inquiry and practice. In P. Reason & H. Bradbury (Eds.), *Handbook of action research: Participatory inquiry and practice* (pp. 219–227). London: Sage.

Saldana J. (2005). *Ethnodrama: An anthology of reality theatre.* Walnut Creek, CA: Altamira.

Sandford, J. (1966). *Cathy come home* [Television broadcast]. The Wednesday Play. London: BBC Television.

Sandford, J. (1971). *Edna the inebriate woman* [Television broadcast]. Play for Today. London: BBC Television.

Watkins, P. (1985). *The War Game.* The Wednesday Play [Television broadcast]. London: BBC Television. (Original work published 1965).

Wilde, O. (1895). *The importance of being earnest.* London: St. James Theatre.

IN PRAISE OF QUANTITATIVE METHODS:

How Numbers Can Change Culture

Harriet D. Speed
Victoria University, Australia

Mark B. Andersen
Victoria University, Australia

Many qualitative researchers make impassioned pleas for sport cultures to change. They tell tales of sexism, racism, homophobia, abuse, and exploitation. Harriet and Mark argue that these calls to arms are important and worthy of attention, yet the degree to which such studies actually change culture is unknown. They discuss the issue of research effecting change and tell the story of a quantitative study on the health and welfare of jockeys in the Australian racing industry. The tale explores how predominantly numbers-oriented research led to cultural changes in an exploited population and challenges applied qualitative researchers to ask themselves how their own research might be developed in order to make a real difference in the lives of athletes through cultural change.

I often say that when you can measure what you are speaking about, and express it in numbers, you know something about it; but when you cannot measure it, when you cannot express it in numbers, your knowledge is of a meager and

unsatisfactory kind; it may be the beginning of knowledge, but you have scarcely, in your thoughts, advanced to the state of Science, whatever the matter may be.
      William Thomson (Lord Kelvin), 1883

INTRODUCTION

Lord Kelvin's quote reflects the pervasive late-19th-century faith in science and numbers to provide us with certainty about the world. About 20 years after the time of this quote, Lord Kelvin's snug, secure, and certain world would begin to crumble with Einstein's special theory of relativity, and faith in numbers and measurement would take another huge body blow in the 1920s from Heisenberg's uncertainty principle. Today, Lord Kelvin sounds naïve, and we have used him to introduce this chapter with a sense of irony, because, in general, we don't have a lot of faith in numbers, either, especially how they are used in applied sport psychology research. But we don't want to defenestrate the numbers baby with the bath water. We do think numbers can be useful even if they contain mild to moderate levels of uncertainty. It is a matter of degree.

Much qualitative research contains high levels of uncertainty, but we live in an uncertain universe, and that's just fine. Qualitative research can also contain high levels of certainty. For example, in case study research, if we have established rapport, developed trust, critically examined our biases, reduced power differentials, acted collaboratively with the participant, imparted empathy and care, expressed deep appreciation for the participant's story, and sought out some devil's advocates for our interpretations, then we can be reasonably certain that we have gotten most of the participant's tale right. At this idiographic level, qualitative research can have as much (or more) certainty as quantitative approaches do.

A great deal of quantitative research in applied sport psychology is highly uncertain (especially with small samples). It is when we want to say things about populations and project research findings from samples onto those populations that we want to be reasonably sure we have got it right. Statistics are all about probabilities (levels of uncertainty), and they offer us ways to think about how confident we can be in our projections onto populations. If sample sizes are small, or standard deviations and confidence intervals are large, then our uncertainty is substantial. For example, if we survey 10 primary school teachers and half of them say they experience frequent depressed mood, we don't have much confidence or certainty about the prevalence of depressed mood in the population of these educators. If, however, we survey 1,000 teachers and 500 say they often experience depressed mood, then, assuming that the measure we are using is valid, we can be fairly confident or certain that we are on to something. For many questions regarding populations, we just have to use numbers, and lots of them.

Qualitative and quantitative sport studies are published in journals that powerful administrators are unlikely to read, and many messages that researchers and academics consume may not necessarily reach those with the power to bring about change. Furthermore, power brokers in sport governing bodies are well known for preferring numbers to narratives and, when faced with qualitative data, may ask questions such as "How widespread is the problem?" and "How many people are affected?" In the past 10 to 15 years, quantitative research in applied sport psychology has come under fire from postmodernist and poststructuralist researchers. Some of the criticisms have merit; some do not. A considerable amount of quantitative research in our field has involved the extensive use of self-report measures, and many of the instruments used are arbitrary metrics. They provide little or no information about where a given score on the instrument "locates an individual on the underlying psychological dimension or how a one-unit change on the observed score reflects the magnitude of change on the underlying dimension" (Blanton & Jaccard, 2006, p. 28). Arbitrary metrics, unless they are connected to or calibrated against real-world behaviors (e.g., running time, distance objects are thrown), are usually not easily interpretable. Andersen, McCullagh, and Wilson (2007) reported that 44% of quantitative articles in three of the top sport psychology journals used only arbitrary metrics without real-world referents. They suggested that, in real-world practical terms, such research is relatively meaningless, and they called into question much of the past applied sport psychology research using arbitrary metrics. They gave the following example:

> *In an example of anxiety measurement, one may be able to say that Johnny has a score of 42 on a cognitive competitive state-anxiety scale, and Mary has a score of 21, but one certainly cannot say that Johnny has double the anxiety of Mary. One also cannot say anything about Johnny's competitive behavior versus Mary's unless the state anxiety scores are calibrated in some way against real-world behavioral*

variables. One can say that Johnny appears to have more anxiety than Mary, but how much more? We don't know, and the question becomes "So what?" unless we observe some differences in behavior or performance. We need to have measures of attitudes, personality, motivation, and so forth, but we need to be sure these measures are related to behaviors such as performance and exercise.

(Andersen et al., p. 665)

The researchers did not, however, call for a replacement of quantitative methods by qualitative ones; rather, they suggested that journal editors more carefully screen quantitative studies to ensure that published research on professional practice and sport psychology interventions for behavioral change connects closely to real-world variables. The question is about how certain we can be that our arbitrary metrics have some real meaning.

Qualitative research in applied sport psychology is also deserving of criticism. Much of the early qualitative research (see, for example, Scanlan, Ravizza, & Stein, 1989) amounted to little more than verbal factor analyses and the grouping of raw data themes into secondary and higher-order themes that often appeared as though researchers were finding their own prejudices and biases. Later, around the year 2000, case studies began to emerge. One positive aspect of these case studies was that they illustrated real-world language and dialogue that occurs when sport psychology practitioners sit down and work with athletes and coaches.

A different branch of qualitative research seems to have become not more but less connected to real-world experience in that the arcane language of the postmodernist and poststructuralist researcher may be comprehensible to those in academia but comes across as largely divorced from meaningfulness and the experiences of coaches, athletes, and practitioners. In terms of language, for example, one often is left to ponder the depth of such redundant terms as "lived experience" (we'd like to know what type of experience is not lived) and "the embodied self" (we don't know any selves that are not housed in bodies). Qualitative researchers often speak of "voices," which sounds symptomatic of psychosis. In addition, voices, such as one hears on the radio, can be "disembodied"; for proponents of embodiment, then, calling people "voices" seems antithetical. We believe we know what qualitative researchers mean by "voices" (expressions of selfhood), but it is the usage that is irksome. Other terms adopted into the qualitative research lexicon are used erroneously. Take, for example, the terms "reflexivity" and "reflexive practice." The misuse of these terms constitutes a misunderstanding of the English language. The root word for both these terms is "reflex," which is an unthinking process (e.g., a knee jerk). So, to be reflexive is to be unthinking, which completely contradicts what the researchers really want to say. These minor abuses of language are off-putting enough, but when phrases such as "deconstructing the gendered-embodied self" appear, we want to run away. How would coaches and administrators respond to such language? For the power brokers in sport, a lot of the language of qualitative research may be alienating or even incomprehensible.

Many proponents of qualitative methods call for cultural change, but one wonders whether qualitative representations of data and research can substantially influence sporting cultures. The powers that be in sport, who may have influence on potential cultural change, are not academics but administrators, managers, coaches, officials, and members of governing bodies. These people, the potential real agents of change, are much more interested in quantification (How much? How long? How prevalent? How expensive?) than they are in a poststructural analysis of the narratives or stories from athletes and coaches.

The story we would like to tell now is a quantitative one. It is about how numbers and people in power helped initiate profound cultural changes that affected an exploited, underserved, and vulnerable group of athletes. It is about thoroughbred horse racing, jockeys, and the lives of athletes after retirement (Speed, 2007). Much credit must be given to the power brokers; they wanted change, and they wanted the numbers to quantify the problems within the culture (e.g., percentage of jockeys experiencing postcareer health problems). Those numbers told the power brokers stories, many of which were disturbing, in a language they understood.

BACKGROUND: THE SPORT

The sport of thoroughbred (flat race) horse racing has had a long association with the Australian people, nowhere more so than in the state of Victoria. Throughout Australia, horse racing is conducted year round; there is no off-season respite period. During the 1999–2000 season (the period during which the research was conducted), Victoria's racing industry hosted 578 metropolitan and provisional (rural) race meetings covering 360 days of the year. Horse racing is also one of Victoria's largest financial industries, and the Victorian Racing Club contributes an annual provision to the government of more than $140 million in taxes from wagering and generates many hundreds of million dollars for the state's economy (Racing Victoria Ltd., 2001).

Jockeys come from a variety of backgrounds. A jockey is characteristically small in stature and typically leaves school at around 14 or 15 years of age after completing only basic secondary education requirements. Traditionally, jockeys have family connections to the racing industry (e.g., a horse-owning family) or are the sons and daughters of jockeys. Most are motivated by their love of horses and riding, though there is a growing trend of new recruits from outside the racing community being drawn to riding careers by the perceived glamour of the jockey's life, the media exposure afforded to the sport, and the (perceived) opportunity of substantial financial rewards for success.

In reality, the careers of the professional jockeys are usually far from glamorous, and for the majority the financial rewards are modest at best. It is a career of long hours, strict discipline, and constant high risk to personal health. Every day, jockeys face the demands to maintain low weight and high fitness, and every ride (training horses in practice on the track and racing) entails the risk of career-ending injury, severe disability, and even death. Retirement may come at any time and without warning. Jockeys who are fortunate enough to have long careers are likely to contend with deteriorated physical condition upon retirement due to the stringent demands they must meet to sustain their sport involvement.

Racing is life for many jockeys and has been since their early teenage years. The aim of the research we describe in this chapter was to determine how jockeys cope with retirement from the sport and what can be done to make life after riding more meaningful and manageable. Anecdotal reports have suggested that although some top jockeys have access to professional services and support networks and retire from riding to secure home and employment bases, there are also many who do not, sometimes with tragic consequences. In the 18 months preceding the research, three retired jockeys had taken their own lives. All three were young men: two in their 30s, the other in his 50s. Although the full range of their reasons for choosing to end their lives will probably never be known, considerable speculation in the industry and among friends pointed to an inability to cope with the challenges they faced after retiring from riding, coupled with a lack of support networks.

These tragic events shocked the power brokers in the industry and were part of the reason for conducting the research.

THE RESEARCH

The research was developed in response to a call by the state minister for racing for an investigation into the welfare of retired jockeys so as to identify strategies for the government and the racing industry to provide better options for jockeys when they leave their riding careers. The investigation was part of a comprehensive series of four studies, but for this chapter we will focus on (a) quantification of the range of situational and personal experiences of retired jockeys as they relate to retirement from racing, (b) examination of the perceptions and attitudes of jockeys currently engaged in the sport toward retirement and available support services, (c) current trends and issues in the retirement of jockeys in Victoria, Australia, from the perspectives of both retired and current jockeys, and (d) retirement support services and strategies made available to jockeys by racing bodies in Victoria.

Participants were former jockeys ($n = 72$) who had retired from racing careers during the past 10 years and current jockeys who were racing in Victoria at the time of the research, under either full license ($n = 82$) or apprenticeship ($n = 22$). All participants were mailed a questionnaire designed specifically for the study. In addition, five of the former jockeys and five of the full-time licensed jockeys who returned completed questionnaires also participated in face-to-face interviews with a member of the research team.

The questionnaires were tailored individually for the three participant groups (former jockeys, licensed jockeys, and apprentices). All questionnaires contained items relating to participants' demographic details and racing careers (e.g. commencement age, duration), recent financial and employment circumstances, and retirement planning. The questionnaires also provided an opportunity for participants to comment on what they considered to be the most important issues that needed to be addressed by the Victorian racing industry and on specific strategies and support services to assist jockeys in preparing for, and coping with, retirement. The retired jockeys' questionnaire contained additional items relating to retirement from racing, (e.g., reasons for retirement), problems experienced since retiring (e.g., financial, employment, educational, social, health-related), and awareness and use of resources provided by the racing industry and other parties to assist them in their adjustments to retirement. The licensed and apprentice jockeys' questionnaires included specific items that addressed problem areas experienced by jockeys during their racing careers and their perceptions of, and attitudes toward, retirement from racing. See figure 3.1 for an example of questionnaire items that address psychological and physical health concerns.

The interviews with 10 former and current jockeys who completed the survey followed the same lines of inquiry. The themes that emerged from the interviews were quantified (e.g., 90 percent of interviewees expressed concern about future financial circumstances), and they corroborated the questionnaire data and provided quotes for media and industry promotions. These quantified qualitative data constituted only a small portion of the overall research results.

THE RESEARCH OUTCOMES

Some jockeys saw retirement from riding as an opportunity for personal growth and development and a time to engage in family commitments or extend social networks. For a significant number of other jockeys, however, retirement had at times been stressful periods in their lives, characterized by limited employment opportunities, financial hardship, poor physical health, and psychological and emotional distress. Although these difficulties were eventually overcome by some jockeys, others continued to struggle long into their retirement.

This main result is perhaps not surprising, given that retirement for most jockeys (>70 percent) who participated in the study was sudden and unplanned due to injuries, weight problems, or lack of rides. Few jockeys had retirement plans in place at the time of their retirement, and it was clear that most retired jockeys hadn't even contemplated life beyond riding before their careers ended. Although many current jockeys (50 percent) often thought about their future after racing, only a few (<10 percent) were taking any action, or intending to take action, to prepare for their retirement.

Financial Security

Jockeys have the potential to earn significant sums of money, but only a small number of jockeys take a substantial share of the available monies, and many jockeys earn what would be an average income (or less) in the general work force. One result indicated that 60 percent of jockeys had experienced financial difficulties at some time during

Please indicate the extent to which you have suffered from or have been susceptible to each of the health issues listed below during your racing career so far. Please comment on any issues if you wish.

Response codes:

1	2	3	4	5
not at all	rarely	sometimes	often	very frequently

Circle one

Health Issues	Response	Any comments?
Functional health:		
• Liver problems	1 2 3 4 5	
• Kidney problems	1 2 3 4 5	
• Immune system problems	1 2 3 4 5	
• Arthritis	1 2 3 4 5	
Structural health:		
• Back problems	1 2 3 4 5	
• Hip problems	1 2 3 4 5	
• Other joint problems	1 2 3 4 5	
• Osteoporosis	1 2 3 4 5	
• Dental problems	1 2 3 4 5	
Weight management:		
Excessive weight gain	1 2 3 4 5	
Use of laxatives, diuretics, or medication/ drugs for weight control	1 2 3 4 5	
	1 2 3 4 5	
Use of vomiting for weight control	1 2 3 4 5	
Other _____ *(optional)*		
Psychological health:		
• Inability to cope	1 2 3 4 5	
• Strong emotional feelings (e.g. anger, despair)	1 2 3 4 5	
	1 2 3 4 5	
• Low general self-confidence	1 2 3 4 5	
• Gambling issues		
Other _____ *(optional)*		
Other health problems (please specify):		
•	1 2 3 4 5	
•	1 2 3 4 5	
•	1 2 3 4 5	
•	1 2 3 4 5	

© Harriet D. Speed. From the "Welfare of Retired Jockeys Questionnaire" in H.D. Speed, 2007, *The welfare of retired jockeys* [Melbourne, VIC, Australia: Centre for Ageing, Rehabilitation, Exercise and Sport (CARES)].

Figure 3.1 Examples from the questionnaire on the welfare of retired and current jockeys.

their retirement periods, and many continued to have serious concerns about their future financial circumstances and employment potential. Despite these difficulties and concerns, few jockeys (<15 percent) had sought professional financial advice or developed financial plans during their racing careers, and only one-third of those who participated in the research had done so since retiring.

Many jockeys were either dissatisfied with their current financial situation (43 percent) or very concerned about their future financial circumstances (50 percent). Underlying the financial problems experienced by some retired jockeys was the sudden and unexpected termination of their riding careers due to injury and the abrupt transition into retirement that inevitably ensued. Both retired jockeys (96 percent) and current licensed jockeys (94 percent) agreed that a compulsory superannuation scheme (retirement benefits plan) should be introduced. In Australia, superannuation is compulsory across almost all government and industry employment sectors, including professional sport, and both employees and employers contribute funds. Jockeys are one of the few remaining employee populations without compulsory superannuation. Most retired jockeys (93 percent) and current jockeys (86 percent licensed jockeys, 71 percent apprentices) also agreed that a professional financial counseling service would be beneficial for both retired and current jockeys. Despite retirement being in the distant future, nearly 60 percent of apprentice jockeys had major concerns about their financial circumstances once they retired from riding, but none of the apprentices surveyed had developed any financial plans.

Training and Education

Although most retired jockeys (70 percent) had secured employment after retirement from riding, many (40 to 50 percent) found their employment options severely restricted by limitations in their education, knowledge of job processes, and employment histories. Few retirees had engaged in further education or job skills training either during their riding careers or upon retirement. Aside from the issues of financial security and job satisfaction, some jockeys (25 percent) found that their lack of prior education and their limited job skills undermined their self-esteem and self-confidence, creating additional issues for them to cope with once they left the racing industry. Of particular concern was the limited, or complete lack of, computer skills in 78 percent of retired jockeys, leaving many of them at a competitive disadvantage when applying for and undertaking employment outside of the racing industry. Some 68 percent of current jockeys also had little or no computer skills.

Few current jockeys (8 to 11 percent) had taken, or were taking, action to prepare themselves for retirement with respect to employment opportunities, education, or job skills training. Most retired jockeys believed that job skills training (86 percent) and career counseling (89 percent) should be provided to jockeys during their riding careers or once they retired from riding (93 percent and 87 percent, respectively). The majority of retired jockeys (82 percent) also believed that nonracing jobs and career opportunities within the industry would assist in the adjustment to retirement. With limited prior work experience and education, leaving the racing industry to pursue employment elsewhere may not be perceived as a realistic option for some jockeys, whose self-confidence and sense of identity are deeply entrenched in racing.

Health

There is unequivocal evidence that many jockeys struggle with weight problems and health issues during their riding careers. More than 50 percent of the retired jockeys surveyed identified weight problems or injury as the main reason for their retirement from riding. For some jockeys, this struggle continued well into their retirement years. Since retiring, more than 40 percent of jockeys had frequently experienced back problems, arthritis, and other joint problems, and a small number had experienced excessive weight gain. Given the physical demands of riding and the absence of an off-season, it is perhaps not surprising that structural problems (e.g., in the back and joints) continue to pose problems for jockeys once their riding careers end.

Although many jockeys were satisfied overall with their lives since retiring from riding, some jockeys found retirement to be a stressful period associated with lowered self-esteem, lack of direction or purpose, loss of personal identity and social networks, and a sense of being disconnected from or forgotten by the racing industry.

A significant number of recently (<6 years) retired jockeys (28 percent) reported that emotional distress (e.g., inability to cope) had been a major problem since retiring from racing. In contrast, few (5 percent) long-term retired jockeys had experienced (or remembered experiencing) high levels of emotional distress during their retirement. Emotional distress in jockeys who have recently retired may reflect the difficulties that jockeys have in the transition from a riding career to retirement, reinforcing the need for early preparation for retirement and, for some jockeys, access to personal counseling.

A low but significant number of current jockeys (13 percent) indicated that emotional distress had also been a major problem during their riding careers. In addition, most of the interviewed jockeys provided examples of psychological problems that they, or a jockey they knew, had experienced, including severe mood disturbance (e.g., symptoms of depression), despair, loss of confidence, and anxiety. Frequently, these problems were related to injury, prolonged weight issues, or difficulties in the transition from apprentice to licensed jockey.

Dental problems were also problematic for some jockeys (17 percent), and in some cases these problems may have been related to the continued and excessive weight cutting that many jockeys engage in (stomach acids from vomiting erodes teeth; see Bishop & Deans, 1996) or to mouth injuries incurred from direct contact with horses' heads when riding.

Recognition and Social Opportunities

The life of a jockey is one of long hours, strict discipline, and high risk to personal health. There was a strong feeling among retired jockeys in the study that they received little or no recognition from the racing industry for their years of service. Formal recognition would be one way in which the industry can demonstrate its appreciation of the services provided by jockeys and formally acknowledge them as valued members of the racing community. Currently, however, the industry gives little if any formal recognition of retiring jockeys. Many jockeys (current and retired) believed that life membership or free entry on race days would be appropriate forms of recognition that would also provide opportunities for social engagement.

Although some retired jockeys leave the social networks developed during their riding careers and move successfully into new social groups, a significant number of jockeys experience difficulty in maintaining a social life within the racing industry or establishing new social contacts outside of the industry once they retire. Social contact with current jockeys and other racing personnel may help some retired jockeys, particularly those struggling in retirement, maintain some sense of security and stability in their lives thanks to the feelings of worth, competence, and belonging derived from continued social interaction with others who appreciate or understand their lives as jockeys.

Retirement Support Services

The jockeys indicated some confusion about the availability of retirement support services and retirement preparation opportunities for retired and current jockeys. According to industry personnel, the Victorian racing industry provides retired and current (apprentice and fully registered) jockeys with access to a range of education and job skill training programs through Racing Victoria's Education and Training Centre. The Centre's staff includes a dietitian, a sport psychologist, a physical fitness instructor, counselors, and social workers. Although the programs and services offered at the Education and Training Centre are aimed primarily at apprentice jockeys, access is also provided, where suitable, to current and retired jockeys.

Unfortunately, few jockeys (current or retired) appeared to be aware of the availability of these training programs and support services or how to access them. The majority of both retired jockeys (89 percent) and licensed jockeys (96 percent) indicated that they were not aware of any retirement support or planning services provided by the racing industry. Moreover, a significant number of retired jockeys felt that they had received little or no support from the racing industry once they had retired. Most apprentices (91 percent) were also not aware of any retirement or career planning services offered to current or retired jockeys, outside of those provided in the apprentice training program.

Jockey Representation

Jockeys are essentially self-employed contractors who operate independently of racing organizations. According to the Australian Workers' Union, this situation involves legal fiction because, on the one hand, the racing industry considers jockeys as independent contractors, but on the other hand, it regulates many of their working conditions, including their attire, licensing to race, competition insurance, health issues, and other areas of the jockeys' working environment. As a consequence, jockeys are denied rights that many employees enjoy, such as annual leave and superannuation—rights that professional athletes in other sports have won in the past.

A number of recommendations based on this quantitative research pointed directly to the Victorian Jockeys Association as one option through which the racing industry could address and implement a range of innovative strategies for supporting retired jockeys and better preparing current jockeys for retirement. One of the main findings of the research, however, was that within its current operations, the association is underresourced in terms of infrastructure provision, equipment, marketing, and availability of support personnel. Having no salaried positions and few of the essential equipment resources for fulfilling its duties, the association functions only by the support and energies of a few committed and dedicated staff.

INTERPRETING THE NUMBERS

We have probably overwhelmed some readers with all the numbers and percentages we reported. And in some ways, that was our intention, as it was in the original research (Speed, 2007) and in the resulting report to the racing industry. That report contained many more numbers than we have presented here. We believe the sheer volume of numerical data documenting issues that needed addressing in the racing industry made it quite clear to the power brokers that the problems were multifarious, extensive, and systemic. They knew problems existed, and the numbers Speed presented increased their conviction that changes needed to be made and helped them identify where to make them.

One of the main functions of quantitative research is to generalize data from a sample to the population in question (in this case, retired, current, and apprentice jockeys). These generalizations are the heart of the research and supply a picture of the state of affairs across the groups of interest. With a sample size of $N = 176$, we are reasonably certain that the numbers and percentages are close to what is happening in the population. What initially appear to be small numbers or percentages take on added significance and real-world meaning when projected onto the population. For example, only 13 percent of current jockeys reported experiencing emotional distress during their careers, but when that 13 percent is projected onto the Victorian population (currently about 300 jockeys) or the Australian population (about 1,000 jockeys), the problem is revealed as a large one in terms of prevention and the provision of services and resources.

Disseminating this quantitative research to the racing industry entailed helping the leaders understand and appreciate that even if some of the percentages seemed relatively low, the real-world problems for the industry and the jockeys were in many cases quite large. Big numbers (e.g., 94 percent of current jockeys want a compulsory superannuation scheme) ring loud and clear for industry stakeholders. It's the smaller numbers that require us to engage in a bit more examination and construction of meaning to realize their human significance.

RECOMMENDATIONS

This applied sport psychology research was directed toward improving the health and welfare of retired jockeys through recommendations for industry initiatives. Based on the quantitative results of the research, the report to the racing industry contained recommendations in the following areas:

1. Establishing a fully professional and independently funded jockeys' body to represent and pursue the interests of current and retired jockeys

2. Introducing an effective financial investment scheme (superannuation or pension fund) for jockeys

3. Providing current and retired jockeys with access to professional financial counseling services and actively encouraging jockeys to plan financially for their future

4. Reviewing the need for welfare funding assistance for retired and current jockeys and identifying the most effective mechanisms for meeting this need

5. Using innovative approaches and educational networks to provide retired and current jockeys with opportunities to develop career options outside of the racing industry through suitable training and education programs and career counseling services

6. Providing retired and current jockeys with access to retraining programs in job skills for nonriding positions in the racing industry

7. Introducing a mentoring scheme in which retired jockeys can support current jockeys, particularly those in the early or late stages of their riding careers

8. Providing retired and current jockeys with access to personal and confidential counseling and health services delivered by an agency outside of the Victorian racing industry

9. Providing retiring jockeys with formal recognition of their contributions to racing

RESPONSE TO THE RESEARCH OUTCOMES AND RECOMMENDATIONS

In November 2001, the findings of this research were presented in a report, titled *The Welfare of Retired Jockeys* (for the full report see Speed, 2007), to the Victorian minister for racing. The response of the Victorian horse racing industry to the recommendations made in the report amounted to a major cultural shift in the way the industry considered and treated its professional athlete population. The industry was ready for a change, the power brokers supported change, and the research provided the evidence (the numbers) of the need for radical reform and gave direction to move the industry forward. The industry is now considered, nationally and internationally, a leader in best practice in terms of the health and welfare of its personnel. Not only did the industry set out to eliminate exploitative and harmful practices; it also established a comprehensive suite of programs and services to promote the health and welfare of jockeys from their beginnings as apprentices through their careers and into their retirement. The following list highlights some of the key initiatives undertaken by the industry. It is by no means exhaustive, and numerous ongoing developments continue today.

- Allocating $1.1 million (AUD) over 3 years and $300,000 (AUD) per annum thereafter for jockey welfare assistance, training, and employment
- Establishing a dual financial investment scheme (the Racing Victoria Jockey Retirement Package); one part provides traditional superannuation benefits upon retirement from the work force, and the other part delivers benefits at the end of a jockey's riding career
- Introducing mandatory death and disability insurance
- Creating a jockey financial planning and management advisory service
- Employing an occupational welfare and safety coordinator
- Establishing a jockey development program focused on education and training, career transition and planning, tertiary scholarships, and job placement and retraining
- Developing a jockey assistance program—a free, confidential counseling service for apprentice, current, and retired jockeys and their immediate family members

- Launching a young jockey mentoring program to connect retired jockeys with apprentices, particularly final-year apprentices, to help them with the transition to the senior ranks
- Upgrading the resources of the Victorian Jockeys Association by creating a full-time, independently operated office
- Acknowledging the achievements and contributions of retired jockeys through initiatives such as family race days and race meeting admission rights (initiatives that led to National Jockey Celebration Day, held annually at race meetings across Australia)
- Funding further research and initiatives to address jockeys' welfare, including research into psychological and physical health issues resulting from career-long pathogenic weight management, review of the apprenticeship and employer deeds of agreement, enhancement of injury prevention programs, and introduction of licensing requirements to ensure participation in essential training seminars and activities

We need to applaud Racing Victoria Ltd., the peak industry body for horse racing in Victoria, for following through and addressing all of the recommendations based on the research, which included sensitive areas that they may not have anticipated when the research was initially funded. We are convinced that the racing industry's actions on this research were driven by numbers. Those numbers reflected the magnitude of the various problems within the industry and, in turn, drove the magnitude of the response. The one large uncertainty in our data lies in all our estimates of the extent of problems (e.g., depression, suicidal ideation, health issues, alcohol consumption). The population and the sample were mostly males, and males generally underreport symptoms of psychological, medical, and behavioral distress. We can be fairly certain that the numbers Speed (2007) presented to the industry are mostly underestimates of the prevalence and incidence of issues related to the health and welfare of jockeys. Speed strongly made that point to the industry.

The jockey study was only the beginning. Over the past 9 years, the racing industry has been proactive in funding quantitative studies across a diverse range of health and welfare issues, including research into the detrimental effects of occupational practices on the psychological and physical health of jockeys (McGregor & Speed, 2005; Speed, Carlson, & Iuliano-Burns, 2006). Most recently, they extended the research beyond jockeys to address the health and welfare of other contributors to the racing industry, including stable employees and horse trainers (Speed & Andersen, 2008). The recommendations from this latest research are being addressed by the racing industry and implemented today (Racing Victoria Ltd., 2008). The initial cultural changes in jockey care and management in the Victorian jockey population are now spreading across the other sectors of the industry both nationally and internationally.

CONCLUSION

We have both undertaken a significant amount of quantitative and qualitative research, but we consider the quantitative studies—especially the research about jockeys, stable employees, and horse trainers—to have been far more influential in effecting cultural change than any of our other research. What has become clear is that numbers can tell equally rich and maybe even more effective stories in terms of potential cultural change than many qualitative approaches. Perhaps, in this case of the health and welfare of jockeys, we have to give Lord Kelvin a bit of a nod when he said, "When you cannot express it in numbers, your knowledge is of a meager and unsatisfactory kind." For the racing industry, the knowledge gained through numbers was the opposite of "meager and unsatisfactory." We think Lord Kelvin would have approved.

IDEAS FOR REFLECTION AND DEBATE

1. What arguments (other than the ones presented in this essay) could you mount for the use of quantitative methods in applied sport psychology research and practice?

2. One of the major goals of applied sport psychology research and practice is behavioral change. What qualitative methods and research designs convincingly demonstrate positive behavior change without resorting to numbers?

3. Both quantitative and qualitative research are forms of exploitation. We exploit athletes' and coaches' time and energy for purposes of finishing our research degrees, succeeding in a "publish or perish" profession, getting promoted in academia, and even satisfying voyeuristic tendencies. Discuss the problems with and justifications for such exploitation beyond the rather tired defense of advancing knowledge.

4. Discuss the personal biases—the intrapersonal ones that stem from possibly questionable roots—that have led you to choose your research stance (qualitative, quantitative, mixed methods).

REFERENCES

Andersen, M.B., McCullagh, P., & Wilson, G.J. (2007). But what do the numbers really tell us? Arbitrary metrics and effect size reporting in sport psychology research. *Journal of Sport & Exercise Psychology, 29,* 664–672.

Bishop, K., & Deans, R.F. (1996). Dental erosion as a consequence of voluntary regurgitation in a jockey: A case report. *British Dental Journal, 181,* 343–345.

Blanton. H., & Jaccard, J. (2006). Arbitrary metrics in psychology. *American Psychologist, 61,* 27–41.

McGregor, M., & Speed, H.D. (2005, October). *The cognitive effects of wasting in jockeys: Was it worth the weight?* Paper presented at the annual conference of the Association for the Advancement of Applied Sport Psychology, Vancouver, BC, Canada.

Racing Victoria Ltd. (2001). *Annual report 2001.* Melbourne, VIC, Australia: Harding Media Services.

Racing Victoria Ltd. (2008). *Annual report 2008.* Melbourne, VIC, Australia: Harding Media Services.

Scanlan, T.K., Ravizza, K., & Stein, G.L. (1989). An in-depth study of former elite figure skaters: I. Introduction to the project. *Journal of Sport & Exercise Psychology, 11,* 54–64.

Speed, H.D. (2007). *The welfare of retired jockeys.* Melbourne, VIC, Australia: Victoria University Centre for Ageing, Rehabilitation, Exercise and Sport.

Speed, H.D., & Andersen, M.B. (2008). *The health and welfare of thoroughbred horse trainers and stable employees.* Melbourne, VIC, Australia: Victoria University Centre for Ageing, Rehabilitation, Exercise and Sport

Speed, H.D., Carlson, J., & Iuliano-Burns, S. (2006). *The influences of occupational practices on the skeletal health of Australian jockeys: A pilot study. Industry Research Report to Racing Victoria Ltd.* Melbourne, VIC, Australia: Victoria University Centre for Ageing, Rehabilitation, Exercise and Sport.

CRITICAL REFLECTIONS ON DOING REFLECTIVE PRACTICE AND WRITING REFLECTIVE TEXTS

Zoe Knowles
Liverpool John Moores University, United Kingdom

David Gilbourne
University of Wales Institute, Cardiff, United Kingdom

Ailsa Niven
Herriot-Watt University, United Kingdom

Being prepared to reflect on and develop would seem to be essential elements in any practitioner's skill base. In this essay, the emergence of reflective practice as a professional development tool for applied sport psychology practitioners is discussed through reference to diverse sources of literature support. These references are offered with a view to encouraging critical reflective practice and the writing of critical reflective texts. Critical social science is proposed as one thematic framework that might offer guidance and philosophical grounding for practitioners who seek to move beyond narrow and confining technical reflections on practice. With regard to writing, the authors promote narrative inquiry as an emerging genre that houses many examples of storytelling and reflective texts.

INTRODUCTION

We have opted to open this essay by talking a little about ourselves. Our thinking is that we really ought to start this way because our own experiences of reflective practice relate to different spheres of research activity. As a group, we have contributed to the reflective practice literature from the applied domains of sport coaching (Knowles, Gilbourne, Borrie, & Nevil, 2001) and applied sport psychology (Anderson, Knowles, & Gilbourne, 2004), and Zoe and Ailsa have been involved in developing reflective practice in professional training programs in the UK through the British Association of Sport and Exercise Sciences, the British Psychological Society, and the Open University. In contrast, David's interest in reflective practice is founded on engagement with the reflectively oriented methodology of action research (Gilbourne, 1999, 2000) and with the varieties of qualitative methods more generally. Though our academic and professional histories are different, we have all engendered a shared interest in reflective practice, one that houses a range of influences (in terms of literature) and interests (applied, pedagogic, and philosophic). In the present essay, we attempt to identify a number of critical issues that are somehow informed by elements of our own readings and professional activities.

According to Anderson, Knowles, and Gilbourne (2004), reflective practice is a process that helps applied practitioners explore decisions and experiences to aid understanding of their own practice. Reflective practice is well established across a number of applied professions, such as education (Osterman & Kottkamp, 1993), nursing (Morley, 2007), and sport coaching (Knowles et al., 2001; Knowles, Tyler, Gilbourne, & Eubank, 2006). Within the discipline of applied sport psychology, a number of articles have also reported on reflective practice processes and outcomes (e.g. Lindsay, Breckon, Thomas, & Maynard, 2007; Cropley, Miles, Hanton, & Niven, 2007; Jones, Evans, & Mullen, 2007; Tod, 2007; Woodcock, Richards, & Mugford, 2008). The sport psychology texts mostly present a positive evaluation of reflective practice, but points of challenge can be noted within elements of the literature. For example, Martindale and Collins (2005) acknowledged that reflective practice was a useful tool for the applied sport psychologist but argued that "there is still further need for clarification as to what we should actually be reflecting on (i.e., the content of reflection rather than the process) and crucially the criteria against which we are to reflect" (p. 311).

Such sentiments suggest that critical reflections on reflective practice are timely, particularly as reflective practice, the writing that stems from it, and the evaluation of both the practice and the writing all constitute relatively new experiences for those who practice in the field of applied sport psychology. In this essay, we consider challenges faced by reflective practitioners who are either required to document their reflections (say, for applied training accreditation purposes) or are personally motivated to share their reflective experiences in writing via journal articles or book chapters. In adopting this approach, we develop a critical position founded on our own view that contemporary examples of applied reflective practice within the domain of sport psychology illustrate a technical approach to both reflection and reflective writing.

In one example of a technical article based around reflective narrative from a trainee sport psychologist, Cropley et al. (2007) considered what constitutes effective practice. Previous research (Anderson, Miles, Mahoney, & Robinson, 2004) suggested six themes associated with the role of an effective sport psychologist (personable, able to provide good practical service, good at communicating, knowledgeable and experienced in sport psychology, and professionally skilled). These themes were used to headline a chronological collection of reflective extracts that were primarily technical in nature, as well as moments of reflecting on reflections. The latter material indicated staged reflection and, at times, critical reflection (see Knowles, Gilbourne, Tomlinson & Anderson, 2007, in press). For example:

> *I was able to talk to the client about some of the things he had been doing both in and outside of sport. In this sense I felt I was able to let the client know that I could be approached to discuss a range of issues, which seemed to improve the flow and quality of the conversation.* (p. 490)

This extract is an example of technical reflection based on the development of the interpersonal aspects of practice. Another technically based reflection considered the use of psychological skills training:

> *It [reflective practice] has increased my understanding of what professional skills actually are and their importance to the practice of applied sport psychology...and has allowed me to embrace the sometimes uncertain nature of the application of professional skills and provide the confidence and direction to seek answers to the problems that I have faced.* (p. 491)

The methodology used by Cropley et al. (2007) provides the reader with insight into a number of technical issues, and the writing provides evidence of practical, emotionally based reflection as well (though the technical information appeared to be dominant).

Our critique here might suggest that, to date, we are disappointed with the literature, but that is not the case. We accept that the existing articles, such as the one cited here, offer interesting insights into the process of reflective practice. Being supportive of contemporary texts does not, however, prevent us from asking critical questions such as what kind of texts we might expect in, say, 5 or 10 years. In response we would say that we hope for reflective practice to progress, both in terms of the scope of the process and the nature of the writing. Hoping for progress might appear laudable enough but we feel that progress needs to be nurtured and supported by individuals (of course) but also through reference to literature, both established and contemporary.

It is in this spirit that we aim to convince readers that progress in reflective practice as a process might be assisted by embracing underlying assumptions associated with critical social science as discussed by Habermas (1974), Carr and Kemmis (1986), and, more recently, authors such as Morly (2007). Therefore, the theme of engendering critical reflection is central to the first part of this essay. The second part of the essay considers the challenges in producing and structuring reflective writing and asks how such writing might be able to capture certain tenets of critical social science. That part of the essay considers how the narrative inquiry literature might provide a template for a more expansive phase of reflective practice writing.

In terms of structure, we first introduce a number of underlying assumptions that are associated with critical social science generally and critical reflective practice more specifically. This section of the essay positions critical social science as a perspective that might inform the process of reflection. Next, we consider how those who write reflectively might benefit from engagement with literature associated with the area of narrative inquiry.

CURRENT REFLECTIVE PRACTICE STUDIES

Anderson, Miles, et al. (2004) highlighted the notion that generating knowledge through engagement in reflective practice can serve different interests or purposes that can be described as technical (addressing standards, competencies, and development of the mechanical aspects of practice), practical (exploring personal meaning in a situation), or critical (examining how social, political, and economic factors constrain action). Knowles et al. (2001) had earlier described critical reflection as a process concerned more with how practice engages with issues of social justice and emancipation, and these themes recur across the critical social science literature. In one example from the field of education, Leitch and Day (2000) argued that reflection was a potentially empowering process (for both self and others, such as school pupils and colleagues).

The earlier thinking of Carr and Kemmis (1986) also considered the themes of emancipation and empowerment through an exploration of the even earlier writings of Habermas (1971, 1974). They argued the case for a critical social science that might help bring about a sense of challenge and thus aid reevaluation of the relationship between established theory and practice. By encouraging social science researchers to engage with the multilayered challenges that are to be found in any social situation, Carr and Kemmis developed a thesis for a critical social science approach to theory and practice and emphasized, like Habermas (1974), that they were keen to promote a form of social science that might uncover distortions and inequalities. Carr and Kemmis distinguish between critical theory and critical social science. In the field of applied sport psychology, critical theory can be understood through the demonstration of the development and progression of theoretical positions such as achievement goal theory. Within critical social science, however, the aim is to enlighten practice not by progressing theory but rather by challenging the efficacy of theory and to query the established processes that organize knowledge and so deliver applied action.

The previously mentioned aspirations are thought to be attained through personal and shared reflection (in the case of sport psychology that might be with groups, such as coaches or athletes). From such actions and from such points of challenge, theory can be deconstructed and reconstructed, but such engagement is described as being possible only when reflection and relationships are allowed to build without any sense of external coercion (see Carr & Kemmis, 1986). In Habermasian terms, a lack of coercion is fundamental to "the ideal speech situation," that is, one that allows reflection to be creative and open to the interests and well-being of others.

Morley (2007) provides a more recent example of reflective practice in nursing that is based on critical social science ideals. She cites Fook (2002) in explaining that her own aspirations for reflective practice, and for the nursing practice associated with it, are based on a sense of "furthering" society and doing so without any sense of domination or exploitation. Morley's ideas stress the importance of challenging both established theory and the establishment structures responsible for theory generation. Professional governing bodies are examples of institutions that might act as guardians to a range of contemporary critical theory and support the communication of such theory through journal and conference outlets.

In an earlier example of a reflective practice text that explores reflection in nurse teachers, O'Connor, Hyde, and Treacy (2003) cite Habermas (1971) directly as they argue, in encouraging terms, that reflection founded on the ideals of critical social science has the capacity to release practitioners from constraints and repression.

Sport psychology publications derived from critical interests are more difficult to find. In one rare example, Lindsay et al. (2007) highlighted the important role of reflective practice in pursuing congruence between the methods and the philosophy of applied sport psychology practice. This paper presented two accounts of consultancy sessions (conducted by the first author) with sport performers drawing on Gibbs' (1988) reflective cycle. The early accounts provide examples of what might be termed "technical reflection in action," which allow the reader to gain insight into the thoughts and self-questioning of a sport psychologist: "Each time a solution was rebuffed, either verbally or nonverbally, my internal dialogue spoke up: 'she's not buying that,' 'she's doubting your ability,' 'she doesn't think that would work'" (p. 341).

As Lindsay contemplates the tensions between attending to the client and also to himself, together with his own doubts about the efficacy of mental training, he displays a self-focused, technical, and uncertain approach to practice, one commonly seen in neophyte practitioners (Anderson, 1999; Holt & Strean, 2001; Knowles et al., 2007). Later, the text moves toward a more expansive phase suggesting critical reflection as it might be understood by Carr and Kemmis (1986) and other critical social science commentators cited earlier:

> *I felt betrayed by the tools I had learned in the formalised environment of the classroom. Was it just me who could not identify how to use them in this kind of situation?...What is most important in the work that we do? What is the fundamental core of this kind of work?*
>
> (Lindsay et al., 2007, p. 342)

This brief consideration of critical reflective practice from a range of practice domains emphasizes emancipation, suggests a sense of morality and justice in practice, and promotes the possibility of challenge and change. These aspirations have been presented here as a potential source of inspiration for those involved in reflective practice, and they offer another (more expansive) boundary point for reflection. The new boundary that is critical reflection, based on the philosophy of critical social science, offers the potential for reflective practice to move beyond technical matters and toward a greater appreciation of self as an agent of fairness, one who might contest elements of the status quo—and possibly one who might invoke change. Critical social science, therefore, is suggested here as one philosophical backdrop that might help guide practitioners toward engagement in critical reflective practice. In promoting this particular idea, we respond to the earlier question raised by Martindale and Collins (2005) about what we might (or should) be reflecting on. Having built this case, we find it also important to stress that, in promoting critical reflection via the assumptions of a critical social science, we do not intend to denigrate the value of technical reflection. Different circumstances are likely to require different types of reflection, and our case is not that critical reflection is good and technical reflection is bad but rather that all reflection has a place. We do, however, feel that critical reflection requires debate and development.

EXPANDING THE BOUNDARIES OF REFLECTIVE WRITING

Having made a case for reflective practice (as a process) to embrace a critical social science perspective, we now turn our attention to the challenges of writing reflectively. In particular, writing reflectively in a manner that captures elements of a critically engaged reflective process suggests to us a need to consider where authors might find support and inspiration for doing this kind of work. We have offered a critical perspective on the methodological status quo within applied sport psychology and by portraying it as an epistemological backdrop against which reflective writing presently takes place.

A number of commentators (e.g., Biddle, Markland, Gilbourne, Chatzisarantis, & Sparkes, 2001; Gilbourne & Richardson, 2006; Knowles et al., 2007) have identified that qualitative research in sport and exercise psychology leans heavily toward a postpositivist doctrine, in which prior theory, often established via quantitative means, drives and shapes the nature of any qualitative inquiry. Qualitative texts therefore tend to be theory led and reinforce an author-evacuated style of presentation (Brown, Gilbourne, & Claydon, 2009). Sparkes (2002) refers to such texts as *realist tales.*

This tendency to foreground established theory runs counter to elements of critical reflective practice that promote engagement with self both in a specific context and amidst the wider complexities of culture and society. Consequently, we would argue that the distal nature of the authorial voice, in both quantitative and qualitative texts, offers little literary encouragement or indeed illustration for the reflective practitioners of the future. Against the backdrop of these underlying methodological challenges, it is not so surprising that most contemporary reflective practice texts in sport psychology provide examples of technical and practical reflection (e.g., Clarke, 2004; McCann, 2000).

In making this case, we do not seek to reopen old disputes between qualitative and quantitative research or to pillory postpositivism and the realist tales that emanate from it; rather, we seek to make a straightforward critical observation that self-narratives (for that is what reflective writing often comes down to) remain rare. The corollary is that reflective practitioners who are required, or who seek, to write about their own practice find that self-narrative exemplars, illustrations, and inspiration are thin on the ground.

For would-be authors, one way forward is to consider the possibilities offered through the narrative inquiry literature. Smith and Sparkes (2009a) define narrative inquiry and narrative itself as "a complex genre that routinely contains a point and characters along with a plot connecting events that unfold sequentially over time and in space to provide an overarching explanation or consequence. It is a constructed form or template which people rely on to tell stories" (p. 2).

This comment enables several key observations. First, it depicts narrative as a time-based and interpersonally engaged story with a story line that might have qualities similar to those of any plot in any book (or film or play). Thus a reflective practice writer might begin to see himself or herself as a storyteller, which is described by Smith and Sparkes (2009b) as someone who "move[s] away from abstract theorizing, explaining, and thinking about stories towards the goal of evocation, intimate involvement, engagement and embodied participation with stories" (p. 281). An applied sport psychologist who reflects on the complexities of practice is likely to include characters (e.g., coaches, parents, athletes) as points of reflection, and in considering a longitudinal reflective practice process as something that builds a story line we suggest aligning reflective practice writing with storytelling and thus moving (however surreptitiously) toward engagement with literary (as opposed to scientific) devices and structures. The expectations and assumptions associated with the critical social sciences as sketched out here also relate to definitions of narratives that are expected to be personally derived, socially and culturally shared (indicative of relationships with others), contextually based, and involving processes of illuminating, inquiring, interpreting, making sense, and generating knowledge.

Given our depiction of reflective practice writing as a process with aspirations similar to those espoused in narrative inquiry, it is perfectly reasonable to promote narrative inquiry as a source of guidance and illustration for reflective writing. Indeed, we can readily identify several points of commonality between narrative definitional and reflective literature. For example, within the broad genre of narrative inquiry, narratives are expected to demonstrate a personally grounded depiction of context. Reflective practice as a process—and the writing that stems from it—is also contextually bound. Similarly, the narrative emphasis on illumination, sense making, and knowledge generation mirrors aspirations within the reflective practice literature. Consequently, it seems logical to depict narratives as textual structures or frameworks that house many qualities associated with reflective practice writing, and, as a result, narrative sources might offer reflective practice writers' points for comparison or illustration. An associated stylistic point relates to earlier observations made by Knowles et al. (2007), who noted that the written product of reflective practice is likely to be made in a narrative first-person format:

> *In the domain of sport and exercise, the act of writing about reflective practice is in its infancy. That being the case, it seems timely to suggest that in order for reflective practice to be shared with peers, it needs to develop a particular epistemology (or voice), and logic dictates that it should be based around the notion of self narrative. Reflective processes, of course, might embrace events, thoughts and emotions experienced by others, but such stories would inevitably be told through the reflective gaze of the author.* (p. 111)

This point relates back to the brief critical depiction of qualitative research in applied sport psychology as being dominated by a postpositivist mindset. Central to this critique is the notion that qualitative texts tend to be author evacuated in style and that as a result reflective practice writers in the present, and those of the future, risk being starved of first-person, author-involved texts. In contrast, the narrative inquiry literature, particularly the storytelling arm of the genre, is filled with examples of author-involved writing through conventions such as autoethnography (Douglas, 2009; Gilbourne, 2002, 2010; Sparkes, 1996; Stone, 2009). These texts place the authors centrally within the text (or story) and so offer reflective practice writers an ideal stylistic template from which to develop their own approach to reflective, self-referenced writing.

Smith and Sparkes (2009a) state that adopting a narrative perspective (or structure) has the potential to make a positive contribution through future scholarship on psychological research into sport and exercise. In this regard, narratives of self are viewed as research-based scholarly pieces in which authors are effectively researching (through reflection, deconstruction, and reconstruction) aspects of their own history. Narrative inquiry also offers specific ideas about issues such as the structure of the content of such stories. For example, temporality—the time period and means through which the data are collected or the story is derived—offers a structural template for reflective practitioners who are developing longitudinal accounts and may wish to paraphrase these for later publication purposes. It is possible that such a template might also provide a permission of sorts to write in this way, thus moving illustrations of texts beyond the restrictions of postpositivism as described earlier. The criteria for defining narrative put forth by Smith and Sparkes (2009a), as discussed earlier, might also offer some tangible markers against which reflective narrative might be evaluated.

CONCLUSION

We have sought to promote ways in which three broad areas of literature (critical social science commentary, critical reflective texts, and narrative inquiry texts) can act as points of inspiration and guidance for those engaged in reflective practice. Our case is that these different sources exhibit a symbiotic quality and that, together, they have the potential to assist the progression and development of reflective practice in the domain of applied sport psychology. More specifically, we associate writings on critical social science and critical reflection as a backdrop from which critical reflective practice might develop in applied sport psychology. Similarly, we have suggested that the emerging genre of narrative inquiry (particularly, storytelling) houses stylistic illustrations and structural references for those engaged in reflective practice writing.

IDEAS FOR REFLECTION AND DEBATE

1. Who are the gatekeepers for the development of reflective practice in the field of applied sport psychology? What have they contributed to the development of the genre to date? What are the strengths and weaknesses of present guidelines for undertaking reflective practice?

2. Access to differing forms of literature might be required to engender a greater understanding of critical social science. What might these forms of literature be?

3. Why might a critical social science agenda result in challenges to applied practice in sport psychology? What specific challenges might you expect to emerge from such developments?

4. How might engagement with the ideals of critical social science affect your own applied practice?

REFERENCES

Anderson, A.G. (1999). Reflections of a budding sport psychologist: First meetings. In H. Steinberg & I. Cockerill (Eds.), *Sport psychology in practice: The early stages* (pp. 30–37). Leicester: British Psychological Society.

Anderson, A.G., Knowles, Z., & Gilbourne, D. (2004). Reflective practice for sport psychologists: Concepts, models, practical implications and thoughts on dissemination. *The Sport Psychologist, 18,* 188–203.

Anderson, A.G., Miles, A., Mahoney, C., & Robinson, P. (2004). Evaluating the effectiveness of applied sport psychology practice: Making the case for a case study approach. *The Sport Psychologist, 16,* 433–454.

Biddle, S., Markland, D., Gilbourne, D., Chatzisarantis, N., & Sparkes, A.C. (2001). Quantitative and qualitative research issues in sport psychology. *Journal of Sport Sciences, 19,* 777–809.

Brown, G., Gilbourne, D., Claydon, J. (2009). When a rugby career ends: A short story. *Reflective Practice: International and Multidisciplinary Perspectives, 10*(4), 491-500.

Carr, W., & Kemmis, S. (1986). *Becoming critical: Education, knowledge and action research.* London: Falmer Press.

Clarke, P. (2004). Coping with the emotions of Olympic performance: A case study of winning the Olympic gold. In D. Lavallee, J. Thatcher, & M. Jones (Eds.), *Coping and emotion in sport* (pp. 239–253). New York: Nova Science.

Cropley, B., Miles, A., Hanton, S., & Niven, A. (2007). Improving the delivery of applied sport psychology support through reflective practice. *The Sport Psychologist, 21,* 475–494.

Douglas, K. (2009). Storying myself: Negotiating a relational identity in professional sport. *Qualitative Research in Sport and Exercise, 1,* 176–190.

Fook, J. (2002). *Critical social work.* London: Sage.

Gibbs, G. (1988). *Learning by doing: A guide to teaching and learning methods.* Oxford, England: Oxford Brookes University Further Education Unit.

Gilbourne, D. (1999). Collaboration and reflection: Adopting action research themes and processes to promote adherence to changing practice. In S. Bull (Ed.), *Adherence issues in sport and exercise.* Chichester, England: Wiley.

Gilbourne, D. (2000). Searching for the nature of action research: A response to Evans, Hardy and Fleming. *The Sport Psychologist, 14,* 207-214.

Gilbourne, D. (2002). Sports participation, sports injury and altered images of self: An autobiographical narrative of a lifelong legacy. *Reflective Practice, 3,* 71–88.

Gilbourne, D. (2010). "Edge of Darkness" and "Just in Time": Two cautionary tales, two styles, one story. *Qualitative Inquiry, 16*(5), 325-331.

Gilbourne, D., & Richardson, D. (2006). Tales from the field: Personal reflections on the provision of psychological support in professional soccer. *Psychology of Sport & Exercise, 7,* 325–337.

Habermas, J. (1971). *Knowledge and human interest.* London: Heinemann.

Habermas, J. (1974). *Theory and practice.* London: Heinemann.

Holt, N.L., & Strean, W.B. (2001). Reflecting on initiating sport psychology consultation: A self-narrative of neophyte practice. *The Sport Psychologist, 15,* 188–204.

Jones, L., Evans, L., & Mullen, R. (2007). Multiple roles in an applied setting: Trainee sport psychologist, coach, and researcher. *The Sport Psychologist, 21,* 210–226.

Knowles, Z., Gilbourne, D., Borrie, A., & Nevill, A. (2001). Developing the reflective sports coach: A study exploring the processes of reflective practice within a higher education coaching programme. *Reflective Practice, 2,* 186–201.

Knowles, Z., Tyler, G., Gilbourne, D., & Eubank, M. (2006). Reflecting on reflection: Exploring the practice of sports coaching graduates. *Reflective Practice, 7,* 163-179.

Knowles, Z., Tomlinson, V., Anderson, A., & Gilbourne, D. (2007). Reflections on the application of reflective practice for supervision in applied sport psychology. *The Sport Psychologist, 21,* 109–122.

Leitch, R., & Day, C. (2000). Action research and reflective practice: Towards a holistic view. *Educational Action Research, 8,* 179–193.

Lindsay, P., Breckon, J.D., Thomas, O., & Maynard, I.W. (2007). In pursuit of congruence: A personal reflection on methods and philosophy in applied practice. *The Sport Psychologist, 21,* 335–352.

Martindale, A., & Collins, D. (2005). Professional judgment and decision making: The role of intention for impact. *The Sport Psychologist, 19,* 303–317.

McCann, S.C. (2000). Doing sport psychology at the really big show. In M.B. Andersen (Ed.), *Doing sport psychology* (pp.209–222). Champaign, IL: Human Kinetics.

Morley, C. (2007). Engaging practitioners with critical reflection: Issues and dilemmas. *Reflective Practice, 8,* 61-74.

O'Connor, A., Hyde, A., & Treacy, M. (2003). Nurse teachers' constructions of reflection and reflective practice. *Reflective Practice, 4,* 107–119.

Osterman, K., & Kottkamp, R. (1993). *Reflective practice for educators.* Newbury, California: Corwin Press.

Smith, B., & Sparkes, A.C. (2009a). Narrative inquiry in sport and exercise psychology: What can it mean and why might we do it? *Psychology of Sport & Exercise, 10,* 1–11.

Smith, B., & Sparkes, A.C. (2009b). Narrative analysis and sport and exercise psychology: Understanding lives in diverse ways. *Psychology of Sport & Exercise, 10,* 279–288.

Sparkes, A.C. (1996). The fatal flaw: A narrative of the fragile body-self. *Qualitative Inquiry, 2,* 463–494.

Sparkes, A.C. (2002). *Telling tales in sport and physical activity: A qualitative journey.* Champaign, IL: Human Kinetics.

Stone, B. (2009). Running man. *Qualitative Research in Sport & Exercise, 1,* 67–71.

Tod, D. (2007). The long and winding road: Professional development in sport psychology. *The Sport Psychologist, 21,* 94-108.

Woodcock, C., Richards, H., & Mugford, A. (2008). Quality counts: Critical features for neophyte professional development. *The Sport Psychologist, 22,* 491–506.

REPRESENTING MULTILAYERED LIVES:
Embracing Context Through the Storied Self

David Gilbourne
University of Wales Institute, Cardiff, United Kingdom

David Llewellyn
Liverpool John Moores University, United Kingdom

This essay promotes the sustained progression of autoethnographic writing and builds on issues highlighted in essay 4. The discussion particularly emphasizes the way in which autoethnographic tales provide insights in the true depth of personal experience, as well as the context from which a life is recalled and storied for others to share. In a critical observation of dominant methodology, we propose that the entrenched nature of postpositivist doctrine in sport-based, qualitative inquiry is one possible reason for the painfully slow emergence of new writing forms. Examples and illustrations from recent autoethnographic texts highlight the strengths and reach of the storied self.

INTRODUCTION

As first author, I (David Gilbourne) have written this essay through my own eyes. The second author (David Llewellyn) has acted throughout the development of this essay in the role of a critical friend, and his own interest in autoethnography has developed through our joint collaborations in disseminating autoethnography as drama. In this essay, we promote the idea of the writing self as researcher.

In general terms, recording and documenting subjective experience were championed some time before the more recent qualitative commentaries offered by Sparkes (1998, 2002a, 2002b) and others. In 1983, Schön suggested that there was a role for the subjective in research and argued that the knowledge base of professional expertise is founded on "subjective reflection on experience" rather than on what he termed "objective science." More than 25 years later, autoethnographic articles in qualitative journals (e.g., Stone, 2009; Douglas, 2009) are still introduced with references to the inadequacies of science. Personally, I am not overly convinced that such sentiments are likely to gain any converts (not from a committed qualitative readership, at any rate). To my mind, there seems to be little value in arguing how limited scientific research is or how it might have failed to do this or that. Within the domain of sport and exercise psychology, scientific approaches to research in terms of hypotheses, statistical analyses, and author-evacuated texts (Sparkes, 2002b) are here to stay and will doubtless produce excellent and indifferent scholarly works as the years go by (as qualitative research might also do).

So, the case I am trying to make here for writing as research is not predicated on the supposed weaknesses of another genre; rather, it promotes a type of writing that delivers a certain kind of insight—one that emphasizes the complexities of personal experiences and of context. To my way of thinking, autoethnography offers the potential for insight and, on that basis, I feel it has value. Many readers may wonder why an essay like this is deemed necessary, particularly since autoethnographic texts are appearing more regularly in journals and textbooks. My case is straightforward. Given that autoethnographic texts are now in the public domain, I take some comfort in the fact that autoethnography enjoys some degree of acceptance. That said, a personal concern remains, which is founded on the possibility that engagement with autoethnography, in terms of both reading and writing, risks developing a niche audience. Put another way, published autoethnographies might suggest that all in the garden is rosy, yet this view might overlook the relative scarcity of the genre and the scale of engaged readership. With those sentiments in mind, the qualities of autoethnography are revisited here with the hope of expanding participation in terms of the number of researchers who write and the number of readers who consume this form of work.

Following on from this critique, and central to the present essay, is an associated view that, in writing terms, the discipline of applied sport psychology has only just begun to embrace a range of different texts such as sport-based autoethnography (Gilbourne, 2002; Jones, 2006; Douglas, 2009, Stone, 2009). In relative terms, and particularly within applied sport psychology, autoethnographic texts remain rare, and I suggest that this is due in part to the ongoing dominance of the post-positivist qualitative text. I champion the case for the autoethnographic text through reference to the personal experiences that such texts reveal and the ways in which contextual factors are also explored. These qualities, I argue, describe personal experiences as multilayered and complex phenomena. This essay also considers how an autoethnographic text might embrace a creative approach to writing and contrasts these literary developments with assumptions associated with traditional scientific and realist tales (Sparkes, 2002b). As the essay progresses, I associate autoethnography with the notion of the researcher as writer.

THE EMERGENCE
OF NEW EPISTEMOLOGIES

During the 1990s, I was working as a sport psychologist in the UK higher education system, writing occasionally, and doing my PhD research part-time. My doctoral studies were founded within the methodology of action research (Gilbourne, 1999, 2000), and so the gradual acceptance of qualitative inquiry in sport psychology was quite exciting for me. Around the time of my research, a number of qualitative publications emerged that provided me with guidelines for collecting qualitative data (e.g., Dale, 1996; Gould, Jackson, & Finch, 1993), and other sources presented me with ideas about undertaking analysis of qualitative material (e.g., Côté, Salmela, Baria, & Russell, 1993). Beyond these technically oriented texts, I was also drawn toward other literature that focused on the underlying philosophical and paradigmatic positions that supported qualitative research in sport (e.g., Bain, 1989, 1995). It is perhaps unsurprising that as qualitative research started to appear more frequently in peer-reviewed journals, critical (yet constructive) observations also emerged. For example, Krane, Andersen, and Strean (1997) encouraged qualitative researchers to become more confident in the protocols they used, questioned the security of claims to inductive analysis, and queried the coziness of certain triangulation procedures. In another groundbreaking critical review, Sparkes

(1998) challenged the consistency with which notions of validity were represented in qualitative research texts (in sport psychology, that is). These different articles influenced my thinking and encouraged me to develop a critical mindset.

I recall being fascinated by the prospect of a new qualitative landscape—one that appeared tantalizingly close. Sparkes (1998) acted as my particular catalyst. He argued that different ways of writing allow new ways of knowing and challenged the applied sport psychology community to broaden the epistemology, and I liked those sentiments. At the time, I viewed the previously mentioned calls for change and later ones (e.g. Biddle, Markland, Gilbourne, Chatzisarantis, & Sparkes, 2001) as early beginnings from which the writing of research, and so the communication of knowledge, might embrace a range of writing styles. Despite such optimism, a good deal of qualitative research over the last 20 years has stayed within the broad protocol of deductively derived questions followed by deductively oriented analysis (although deductive notions tend not to be readily acknowledged in the literature). This critique formed the cornerstone of my own contribution to the review of qualitative research in the domain of sport psychology (Biddle et al., 2001). In more specific terms, the review argued that qualitative research papers, when viewed as a "body of work," demonstrated a certain dependence on theory-led, semistructured interviews and deductive content analysis protocols. This view suggested that such procedural dominance could restrict the representational aspirations of both researcher and reader.

The realist tale (Van Maanen, 1988, 1995) has come to be closely associated with qualitative research in sport psychology. In Biddle et al. (2001), we took critical risks in arguing that the definitions and assumptions of the realist tale align with much of the qualitative research that has been published within the domain of sport psychology, and in providing a definition we explained that

> as a genre, the realist tale has a number of compositional conventions, which, according to Van Maanen (1988, 1995), include the following. First there is a swallowing up and almost complete disappearance of the author in the final text. Once the researcher has finished the job of collecting and analysing the data he or she simply vanishes. As such, there is a marked absence of the narrator as a first person presence in the text. (p. 801)

I have always (reluctantly) considered realist tales or protocol to be a gold standard of sorts and have come to see the realist tale in book chapters, journal papers, and conference abstracts as a genre that has dominated qualitative inquiry within applied sport psychology through the 1990s. In fact, a cursory glance at published qualitative texts suggests that the realist tale remains the dominant writing form to the present day.

A FRACTURE IN CONVENTION

It is difficult to be definitive about a point of change—a time in research history from which there seems no line of retreat, a moment of release, of emancipation. I will, however, suggest here that permission to write differently within the domain of applied sport psychology can be associated with two events: first, the arrival of *Telling Tales in Sport and Physical Activity* (Sparkes, 2002b), which promoted the idea that research might be represented through a range of different stylistic tales, and second, the launch of *Qualitative Research in Sport and Exercise* in April 2009. My own role in this latter event forces the following debate to concentrate on the first event.

Sparkes (2002b) begins by considering the scientific tale and the realist tale. Clear differences exist; for example, hypothesis testing and statistical analysis are scientific processes that would never appear in a qualitative realist text. Nevertheless, I have always viewed these two tales as being similar in stylistic terms and, more covertly, in aspiration. When reviewing the conventions that underpin what he termed the scientific tale, Sparkes made reference to the *Publication Manual of the American Psychological Association* (4th edition, 1994). He highlighted aspects of the manual that dealt with issues such as the expression of ideas, writing style, grammar, and the reduction of bias. Sparkes observed that the manual makes an overt distinction between scientific prose and creative writing (something of particular significance for the arguments developed later) and emphasized the need to avoid literary devices such as "inserting the unexpected" or "shifting the tense," which might "confuse" or "disturb" readers (p. 29). The corollary to those concerns is that writers of the scientific tale should strive to deliver a clear and logical text. This style would also be expected to be housed in a framework that establishes a problem or research question, reviews past literature, states hypotheses, outlines methodology, presents results (often statistical in form), and, finally, discusses findings in light of established thinking. To my way of thinking, both quantitative and qualitative researchers in the field of applied sport psychology are secure in APA territory.

Sparkes (2002b) brought the underlying conventions of the realist tale into sharper focus, and in doing so he reiterated several of Van Maanen's views. For example, Sparkes noted that Van Maanen highlighted the tendency for realist texts to marshal quotations from participants in such a way as to promote a theoretically laden, and thus factual, landscape. In Biddle et al. (2001), we had proposed that any such tendencies in sport psychology research might be partly explained through reference to a range of personal and technical factors. For example, Krane et al. (1997) had earlier argued that a researcher's prior knowledge of salient theory is likely to result in published work housing deductive qualities. We had built on that view and argued that deductive tendencies could also be mediated by the degree to which interviews were structured around contemporary theoretical positions and depicted a qualitative research community bound, de facto, to the established theory-laden landscape of the time (Biddle et al.).

The arrival of *Telling Tales in Sport and Physical Activity* (Sparkes, 2002b) certainly added energy to the debate over how qualitative researchers might tell a research story, and I sensed at that moment that Sparkes had awakened many sport psychologists to the notion of writing in different and creative ways, themes he had rehearsed in a journal text both earlier and in that same year (Sparkes, 2000, 2002a). His texts, in combination over the years, have supported calls for epistemological expansion that have included references to processes such as autoethnography (Sparkes, 1996) and writing styles such as creative nonfiction (Agar, 1995). The interface between autoethnography and creative nonfiction are explored in the discussion that follows, thus moving the focus away from the dominant deductive processes and realist templates discussed so far.

AUTOETHNOGRAPHY: A NEW FORM OF WRITING

The emergence of autoethnographic texts might suggest the emergence of a new generation of communicators who undertake writing as research process in itself, and this is a theme I warm to later. However, when standing back for a second or two, writing about one's experiences may not be as radical as at first it appears. For example, we have long acknowledged writing as a reflective and reflexive process across a number of embedded methodologies, such as action research and ethnography, and through reflective practice in applied training. For researchers and practitioners engaged in such methods, the writing of field notes is central to the evolution of the knowledge building process. What I am keen to consider here is the notion of writing as research that stands independent of the established methods and processes previously highlighted.

Sparkes (2000) cites Frank (1991), who writes with great clarity and humility on this issue and through his own experiences of illness:

> *I want what I have written to be touched as one touches letters, folding and refolding them, responding to them. I hope ill persons will talk back to what I have written. Talking back is how we find our own experiences in a story someone else has written. The story I tell is my own, but readers can add their own lives to mine and change what I have written to fit their own situation. These changes can become a conversation between us…My own experiences are in no sense a recipe for what others can expect or should experience. I know of no exemplary way to be ill.* (pp. 4–5)

Such sentiments house aspirations to reach out and communicate, and for such ideals to be realized a text requires certain qualities. Such texts do not necessarily seek to advance theory; they offer, instead, personal depth and contextual detail, and so insight is gained through an understanding of a lived world or through being introduced to context as rationale for why someone's life was cast in a particular manner.

Examples of autoethnographic writing in sport have dealt with challenging topics, such as sport injury (Gilbourne, 2002), dysfluency and coaching (Jones, 2006), applied sport psychology practice (Lindsay, Breckon, Thomas, & Maynard, 2007), anorexia and exercise (Stone, 2009), and the motivations behind elite sport performance (Douglas, 2009). All of these authors offer readers personal and, in places, emotive accounts of their own experiences, and some elements of their work are illustrated later in this chapter. In terms of style, these texts attempt to draw readers in, to paint pictures of certain events, in the hope that readers will be able to share and feel what the authors themselves experienced. In terms of epistemology and style, they break away from the interview–analysis cycle outlined earlier and, just as the common qualitative template foregrounds theory, these storied accounts tend to allow context to emerge as the primary thematic. I have always considered the capacity of autoethnography to explore both self and self-in-context as a central recommendation for the genre. The capacity of an autoethnographic text to provide insights into the multilayered nature of context is a point overtly raised by Jones (2006), who emphasized the importance of texts reflecting the everyday nature of people in context.

I accept that for many people the process of "doing" research through writing about one's own experiences might seem untidy and ill-defined, particularly when it is contrasted with the systematic and distal structures of the scientific protocol and postpositivism generally. Despite these worries, I suggest here that applied qualitative research in the domain of sport psychology could benefit from an expansion in autoethnographic texts (appropriate quality, of course, being a caveat) and also from radical developments in associated forms of writing that engage with the messy and multilayered nature of personal experience.

AUTOETHNOGRAPHIC ILLUSTRATIONS: PERSONAL SELECTIONS

In the final phase of this essay, I offer some brief illustrations from autoethnographic texts that I have found to be engaging, informing, and moving. Autoethnographic writing is based on the author's recollections of self, of others, and of the interrelationships between self and others across different settings and differential timelines. In the first example, Smith (1999) associated his own autoethnography (on the topic of depression) with a process of introspection: "In order to explore my on-going process of embodied depressions, I used Ellis's (1991) introspection method of inquiry. This offers the opportunity to look at inquirers' lived experiences of emotions and is particularly suited to the study of depression" (p. 267).

Here is a short sequence to illustrate how Smith introduces his work:

> *The digital radio alarm reads 5:37 a.m. The day doesn't matter. Days merge into darkness. Darkness lives in my life. Enough of this babbling. Come and join me. Join my pulsating body. Join my fragmented self. Join my life. Join a story. Feel a statistic. Enter into my world. You become me. Two become one.* (p. 264)

I see Smith as writer-researcher, someone undertaking research through the process of writing and thinking and writing and thinking. Consider also the following extracts from Stone (2009):

He ate little and was up at six most days. Sewing, or reading, or walking. In the thin spring light. It was always spring in his memory…His mother was witness to this activity. Sometimes now, as he looked back, he saw her as collusive—as if she could have stopped it happening—that relentless slide into chaos. But she was weak and full of grief herself, he said to himself: it was not her fault…She had said nothing because she did not understand. Or because she was so inured to her own misery that his behaviour did not strike her as strange. Or because her engulfment in grief rendered her oblivious to his decline…His memory, so cloudy now, was of cars arriving, of doctors, of his mother. Of a bed, of sedation. And the next day, of the drive to the hospital. On the way they had stopped and he had bought chocolate…He remembered, or thought he remembered, his mother's pleasure at this purchase. So perhaps she had noticed…after all. (pp. 69–70)

In a foreword to his own work on anorexia, Stone argued that traditional academic discourses on mental illness had a tendency to "exclude the unsettling truths of those who have known that strange country" (p. 68). And so he supported what he termed *artistic* creative modes of discourse as "valuable methods for the doing of research." I would argue that such texts get at issues from a different perspective; they implore the reader to empathize and understand in ways that move the boundaries and extend what readers might come to expect from an academic text.

In the stories of Smith (1999) and Stone (2009), I am, as reader, taken to places that I can see, to clips of film that spool and rewind to be spooled all over again, and so I am taken to understand depression and mental illness in new ways. Clearly, authors who write such texts on such difficult topics do so at a price to themselves, and to a greater or lesser degree they also take risks professionally. Yet this form of communication, this form of research, is dependent on the openness of the conversation between reflective self and self as writer and, in time, between self as writer and reader.

This point is emphasized by Douglas (2009) in her autoethnography "Storying Myself." She describes her own approach to telling her own story as a writer who is acting in the role of "artful persuader." In deciding to story herself, Douglas has attempted to influence applied thinking in the domain of sport through her subjective account of her own life:

> Daily Telegraph *reporter Marie Clark then asked a question. This one, however, came as a shock to the young champion. "Wouldn't your father have been proud of you now?" Clark asked, as much a statement or assumption as a question... The reply was as much a shock to the journalist as the question had been to the player: "No." Faces looked up from notebooks, pens stopped, earnest expressions, and eyes pinned attention on the relative unknown. "No," she said firmly shaking her head and waiting for words. "My father was proud of me, not what I did today, not hitting a golf ball around the golf course."* (p. 178)

Douglas (2009) provides readers with a challenging and scholarly debate situated alongside various segments of her story. She suggests, and I hope I have understood her correctly, that for storytellers as writers and researchers, the key is understanding the self through association with threads of opportunity or existence that somehow weave into a timeline of moments or events that, together, unearth personal understanding and meaning. If this is not a definition of research, then I don't know what is!

I suspect that, for the applied sport psychology community, one of the most challenging facets associated with the slow emergence of autoethnographic writing based in sport and exercise is the associated movement toward the creative or literary. These sentiments are more readily associated with fiction and theater than with research, and some unease and caution are understandable. Autoethnographic texts seek to engage, to involve, to tempt readers into the mind's eye of the author, to invoke reflection in the reader, and to promote change through that reflection. These are challenging aspirations that require a text to paint pictures (the phrase "promoting imagery" might be a more colloquial way of describing the process).

Creative writing techniques can, therefore, be used to generate images in the mind of the reader. For example, readers might be invited (through the nature of the writing) to picture themselves in the classroom, stadium, or gym or on the training ground. In the following illustration from my own work (Gilbourne & Richardson, 2006), I sought to use creative nonfiction techniques to draw readers into the changing rooms of a professional soccer club: "In the changing rooms, 20 players wait to hear who will play. Most are sat down staring straight ahead. A few are stood up talking quietly in the corner[…] someone is bouncing a football on the floor" (p. 330). The text develops by positioning the psychologist within the changing rooms: "Peter, the psychologist, is leaning against the back wall, hands in pockets[,] he surveys the scene" (p. 330). The vignette progresses to explore an applied moment involving a sport psychologist and a player, and the next few lines outline the antecedents for what is to follow: "The manager walks in[;] all conversation stops. The whole room straightens up. He begins reading out the team. As the names are read out Peter realizes a big name has been dropped from the squad. He glances across. The player's eyes are focused on the tiled floor, his arms folded tight across his chest" (pp. 330–331).

This vignette is presented in an uncompromising, matter-of-fact style. The intention was to capture the anxieties and (in one case) the loneliness that descended upon a group of professional players as they waited to hear the names of those selected to play. The piece also invites the reader into the mind's eye of the sport psychologist, who, with "hands in pockets…surveys the scene." The vignette carries on to explore how the dropped player and the psychologist interact and, more specifically, how the psychologist dealt with the situation. The player's body language ("arms folded tight across his chest") may give some indication of the applied challenges that the sport psychologist faced. As the paper develops, it explores the possible consequences of not being selected and sketches out a number of applied skills and philosophical standpoints. In this example, I hope that the vignette helps readers visit the harsh context from which the later skill-based observations are drawn. Readers of creative nonfiction can safely presume that the event being described actually happened. So researchers who opt to write in these terms turn to alternative techniques in a desire to thaw out frozen memories and draw a reader into their own "mind's eye." The value in such works extends to the applied training domain by allowing younger researchers and practitioners to reflect on and debate applied moments before they are exposed to applied situations themselves. In that sense, if writing does somehow "paint a picture," then it follows that others (readers) can access that scene and consider how they might have reacted had they been an actor in the scene themselves.

CONCLUSION

I have sought here to revisit and reinforce the value of autoethnographic writing and associated creative forms as a means for progressing knowledge and understanding in applied sport psychology. The essay also develops an emphasis on the notion of writer as researcher; more specifically, the autoethnographic writer as researcher is presented as someone who uncovers the authentic nature of his or her personal experience and foregrounds the context in which the experience has taken place. In establishing this case, I recognize that autoethnographic texts have emerged but also suggest that they are small in number (relative to the available literature more generally). Consequently, I have argued that a need remains to promote this form of communication in order to sustain the progression of an alternative to the dominant historical and contemporary qualitative genre that foregrounds theory and places writers into an evacuated, distal role. Although I have emphasized the capacity of autoethnographic texts to engender empathy and sensitivity, as opposed to developing theory, I do not discount the possibility that the depth and clarity with which autoethnographers explore context could encourage readers to identify a particular feeling or reaction or behavior with elements of a macro theory such as attribution, self-efficacy, or achievement goal theory. Indeed, such associations might be seen as inevitable rather than possible given that readers bring their own history and training to bear on any text. Arguably, it is the engaging way in which context is explored—one that sustains interest and encourages a further bout of self-reflection—that makes possible such connections between context and theory. This form of theory connection, in which the reader recognizes, applies, or discerns theoretical patterns, is very different from papers that headline theory from title to conclusion. In the former, the reader decides on the degree of theoretical fit; in the latter, the researcher determines theoretical parameters. I think we need more of the former.

IDEAS FOR REFLECTION AND DEBATE

1. Autoethnography is sometimes criticized for being self-indulgent. Consider this critique as something that might be used to dismiss *all* autoethnographic works or something that might be reasonably applied to certain texts.

2. Reflect on the possible connections between writing autoethnographically and engaging with critical social science.

3. How might research methods curricula in undergraduate and postgraduate programs introduce, encourage, and develop auto-ethnographic writing for students?

4. Consider what source materials might help student writers to embrace an autoethnographic style.

5. How might autoethnographic sources influence applied sport psychology practice in the future?

REFERENCES

Bain, L.L. (1989). Interpretive and critical research in sport and physical education. *Research Quarterly for Exercise and Sport, 60,* 21–24.

Bain, L.L. (1995). Mindfulness and subjective knowledge. *Quest, 47,* 238–253.

Biddle, S.J.H., Markland, D., Gilbourne, D., Chatzisarantis, N.L.D., & Sparkes, A.C. (2001). Research methods in sport and exercise psychology: Quantitative and qualitative issues. *Journal of Sport Sciences, 19,* 777–809.

Côté, J., Salmela, J.H., Baria, A., & Russell, S. (1993). Organizing and interpreting unstructured qualitative data. *The Sport Psychologist, 7,* 127–137.

Douglas, K. (2009). Storying myself: Negotiating a relational identity in professional sport. *Qualitative Research in Sport and Exercise, 1,* 176–190.

Ellis, C. (1991). Sociological introspection and emotional experiences. *Symbiotic Interaction, 14,* 23–50.

Frank, A. (1991). *At the will of the body.* Boston: Houghton Mifflin.

Gilbourne, D. (1999). Collaboration and reflection: Adopting action research themes and processes to promote adherence to changing practice. In S.J. Bull (Ed.), *Adherence issues in sport and exercise* (pp. 239–263). Chichester, England: Wiley.

Gilbourne, D. (2000). Searching for the nature of action research: A response to Evans, Hardy, and Fleming. *The Sport Psychologist, 14,* 207–217.

Gilbourne, D. (2002). Sports participation, sports injury and altered images of self: An autobiographical narrative of a lifelong legacy. *Reflective Practice, 3,* 71–88.

Gilbourne, D., & Richardson, D. (2006). Tales from the field: Personal reflections on the provision of psychological support in professional soccer. *Psychology of Sport and Exercise, 7,* 325–337.

Gould, D., Jackson, S.A., & Finch, L. (1993). Sources of stress in national champion figure skaters. *Journal of Sport and Exercise Psychology, 15,* 134–159.

Jones, R.L. (2006). Dilemmas, maintaining "face," and paranoia: An average coaching life. *Qualitative Inquiry, 12,* 1012–1021.

Krane, V., Andersen, M.B., & Strean, W.B. (1997). Issues of qualitative research methods and presentation. *Journal of Sport & Exercise Psychology, 19,* 213–218.

Lindsay, P., Breckon, J.D., Thomas, O., & Maynard, I.W. (2007). In pursuit of congruence: A personal reflection on methods and philosophy in applied practice. *The Sport Psychologist, 21,* 335–352.

Richardson, L. (2000). New writing practices in qualitative research. *Sociology of Sport Journal, 17,* 5–20.

Schön, D. (1983). *The reflective practitioner: How practitioners think in action.* San Francisco: HarperCollins.

Smith, B. (1999). The abyss: Exploring depression through a narrative of the self. *Qualitative Inquiry, 5*(2), 264-279.

Sparkes, A.C. (1996). The fatal flaw: A narrative of the fragile body-self. *Qualitative Inquiry, 2,* 463–494.

Sparkes, A.C. (1998). Validity in qualitative inquiry and the problem of criteria: Implications for sport psychology. *The Sport Psychologist, 12,* 363–386.

Sparkes, A.C. (2000). Autoethnography and narratives of self: Reflections on criteria in action. *Sociology of Sport Journal, 17,* 21–43.

Sparkes, A.C. (2002a). Fictional representations: On difference, choice, and risk. *Sociology of Sport Journal, 19,* 1–24.

Sparkes, A.C. (2002b). *Telling tales in sport and physical activity: A qualitative journey.* Champaign IL: Human Kinetics.

Stone, B. (2009). Running man. *Qualitative Research in Sport & Exercise, 1,* 67–71.

Van Maanen, J. (1988). *Tales of the field: On writing ethnography.* Chicago: University of Chicago Press.

Van Maanen, J. (1995). *Representation in ethnography.* London: Sage.

ESSAY 6

THE PRACTITIONER AND CLIENT AS STORYTELLERS:

Metaphors and Folktales in Applied Sport Psychology Practice

Mark B. Andersen
Victoria University, Australia

Harriet D. Speed
Victoria University, Australia

In the sport psychology literature, recent attention has been paid to the stories, or narratives, or life histories, that athletes relate to their practitioners. But what of the stories the sport psychologist tells? Mark and Harriet ask whether sport psychologists can use their clients' and their own metaphors, stories, and tales (from their cultures and other cultures) to promote athletes' self-understanding. Myths, folktales, and metaphors have been used for centuries to instruct, warn, delight, pass on values, and even enlighten. In this essay, the authors focus on sport psychologists and clients as metaphor creators and storytellers and on how telling stories, both ancient and modern, may be a type of activity that contributes to the therapeutic alliance and helps athletes see and feel their worlds in new and salubrious ways.

The greatest thing in style is to have a command of metaphor.
    Aristotle, *Poetics* (XXII)

INTRODUCTION

Aristotle was writing about Greek drama and lyric and epic poetry, but we think his suggestion of having a command of metaphor also applies to applied sport psychology practitioners. The more we (Mark and Harriet) both practice, the more we find that metaphors, folktales, and illustrative stories become central to the therapeutic process. One could say that we both practice a kind of metaphoric therapy. I (Mark) have Buddhist leanings, as one can read in essay 11 in this book, but I am not a Buddhist. Nevertheless, I find that Buddhist metaphors and parables are often useful in applied sport psychology practice. Some of my clients who have interests in Buddhism come up with their own metaphors for their psychological conditions or states of being, and I sometimes tell them Buddhist stories (or Sufi, or Jewish, or Christian stories) and use a short narrative or an image to encapsulate what might be going on for them. For example, I have worked with a karate athlete who also happens to be a registered psychologist in Australia. When she is doing karate in competition and practice, she uses the metaphoric image of herself driving a red Ferrari with the Dalai Lama riding shotgun. When she is with her psychotherapy clients, she is driving a Volvo. The Ferrari represents a quick, powerful, and finely tuned instrument, and the Dalai Lama is her state of being in equipoise, in present time, and open to anything that happens. While doing therapy, she and her clients are in one of the safest cars in the world, steady, comfortable, and secure, and even if there is a crash, they both will survive the bumps and bruises of the therapeutic process. When things were going well in her sport, she would say, "I was hangin' with the Dalai Lama (DL)." And when things had fallen apart she would say, "The DL was nowhere in sight." My client generated the Ferrari, Dalai Lama, and Volvo metaphors herself, and she and I have used them, in some fashion, during many of our sessions.

In this essay, we are interested in both the metaphors and stories clients tell us and those that applied sport psychologists tell their clients. These valuable personal and cultural representations probably do not receive the attention they deserve in applied sport psychology practice.

THE POWER OF METAPHORS AND FOLKTALES

There are dozens of books and hundreds of journal articles about metaphors and storytelling in psychotherapy (e.g., Battino, 2005; Burns,

2001, 2007; Gordon, 1978; Hammond, 1990; Kopp, 1971). In the applied sport psychology literature, metaphors and storytelling are mentioned in a wide variety of texts and journal articles, but it is relatively rare to see analyses of how and why they are used in treatment. Hanin and Stambulova (2002) studied Russian athletes' self-generated metaphors and how they fit within the individual zones of optimal functioning model. Ruiz and Hanin (2004) examined the self-generated metaphors that Spanish karate athletes used for performance. Curry and Maniar (2004) described an academic program for enhancing student-athletes' sport performance in which one of the teaching methods was narrative storytelling. Efran, Lesser, and Spiller (1994) gave self-protective metaphors (e.g., bubble, cocoon, chrysalis) to tennis players to help them deal with distractions, negative thoughts, and off-task cognitions. Jones (2003) briefly discussed the use of metaphors and storytelling to control emotions in sport settings. Simons (2000) took a different slant on metaphors and imagery and how they can be helpful in broader contexts. He suggested that metaphors and images

> *have a powerful way of reflecting perspective and philosophical concepts. They connect with the richness of experiences and the complexity of beliefs and feelings. . . . [Images] may be literal, such as the experience of great performance, or they may be more metaphorical, such as feelings of connectedness induced by a striking scene in nature. We may develop emotionally charged images of inspiration, challenge, freedom, joy, or uniqueness, or images of calmness, acceptance, serenity, or satisfaction.* (p. 88)

Simons' suggestions take metaphors and imagery into the realm of deep personal experience, connectedness, what it means to be alive, and even the possibility of transformation.

In mainstream performance psychology, there is also Holmes and Collins' (2001) work on the physical, environment, task, timing, learning, emotion, perspective (PETTLEP) approach. Although they suggested that mental imagery of performance should be functionally equivalent to the actual task, there is latitude to use metaphoric imagery (e.g., the peacefulness and beauty of a mountain meadow in early summer) to evoke emotional states of calmness and serenity, if such an affective state is desired. If an athlete's history of performing contains many negative emotions, then evoking a performance image may bring about detrimental anxiety, and metaphoric images connected to positive emotions may help counteract a history of maladaptive emotional responses.

All of the works just cited have helped bring the power of metaphor to the attention of applied sport psychologists, and they constitute a good start. Our interests, however, involve the metaphors and stories told by both clients and practitioners in the working-relationship context of psychological treatment.

The study of stories, or narrative analysis, has become quite popular in the past decade and is the subject of a growing number of journal articles and book chapters (see essay 1 in this book). Smith and Sparkes (2009a, 2009b) have written extensively about narrative analysis, but their research addresses the stories people tell as research participants. We do not believe that the context of research diminishes the importance and meaningfulness of the stories and their analyses, but such stories and analyses seem to be one or two steps away from tales told in the relatively long-term intimate working relationships of practitioners and clients in treatment. Our therapy-oriented focus revolves around the following questions: (a) Why did the athlete tell this particular story to this particular practitioner at this particular time? (b) Why did this practitioner tell this particular story or use this metaphor at this time? (c) What purpose are the stories and metaphors serving? (d) In what ways might the stories or metaphors be symbolically connected to the therapeutic alliance? (e) How might the stories and metaphors that both athletes and practitioners use be therapeutic? In Carless and Douglas' (2008) study of sport and men with mental illness, they have provided some solid evidence of the therapeutic value of telling stories. What they have done looks close to narrative therapy, even though they are not therapists. Leahy and Harrigan (2006) and Mascher (2002) have combined narrative therapy, metaphor, and sport and have pointed the way to use these aspects of clinical practice in working with athletes.

Why are metaphors and stories so powerful and useful? One reason is that our brains make metaphoric connections all the time. In dreams, for example, the images, events, and representations are often stand-ins (metaphors) for what is happening (or has happened) in a person's life. A dreamer who finds himself alone in a frozen wasteland may be constructing a metaphoric image for feeling lost, lonely, unloved (cold), and unable to move in any human contact direction (frozen). We (Mark and Harriet) have both had the experience in therapy of discussing a client's current problems and difficulties when suddenly some memory neurons fire in the client and she says, "I just remembered something that happened when I was 12." Such sudden memories and images from a relatively distant past are almost always intimately connected to what is happening in therapy. They are usually metaphoric representations of what is currently going on for the client. For example, I (Mark) was working with a swimming coach in his 40s, and we were discussing how he didn't feel close to his family, that his siblings were much more successful than he was, and why he felt like he didn't matter much to them. Then suddenly he said, "I just flashed on something that happened when I was about 8 years old. The family was going to a football game, and I didn't want to go. I wanted to stay home. So the whole family got in the car and drove away, leaving me at home alone." The image of him watching his family drive away, of an abandoned 8-year-old boy, was a poignant and painful metaphor for his current feelings.

In describing how metaphors and stories work, Lankton (2005) wrote:

> *metaphors work because the mind is metaphoric. It [metaphor or story] holds attention due to drama—material presented out of sequence. It creates experience because people live in a world of ambiguity. It leads to change when properly conducted, because experience can be elicited, associated, linked, and eventually conditioned to occur in novel ways and in novel situations. Consciousness will generally follow the plot line and stick to the need for resolution of the drama of the story (no matter how minimal), and yet the mind listens to plot while the unconscious responds to the experiences retrieved. As a result, images, ideas, affects, and urges can be elicited and basically brought into play to better assist a client in personal or interpersonal adaptation.* (p. xiii)

For much of this chapter we show how client-generated and practitioner-generated folktales, images, and metaphors can be used to help those we serve. We start with a tale from Islam.

THE WISE FOOL: MULLAH NASRUDDIN

There is a wonderful historical and legendary character in the Sufi tradition of Islam. He is the satirical figure Mullah Nasruddin, and his "wise fool" stories are told throughout the Islamic world. He was born in Anatolia (Turkey) near the beginning of the 13th century, but he is claimed by many cultures and countries (e.g., Iran, Iraq, parts of Western

China). Many of the humorous tales of Nasruddin also contain deeper meanings that may help sport psychologists communicate concepts, processes, and knowledge in an age-old fashion. For example, there is a tale of Nasruddin losing his ring in the dark basement of his house. Nasruddin thought he couldn't find his ring in all that darkness, so he went out in the daylight outside his house and began searching for it there. A neighbor passing by stopped and asked, "Mullah Nasruddin, you seem to be searching. Are you missing something?" Nasruddin replied, "Yes, my ring. I lost it in my basement." Rather baffled, his friend said, "But Nasruddin, you should look for it down in the basement where you lost it." As if it were self-evident, Nasruddin said, "That won't work. How do you expect me to find anything in all that darkness!? Out here there is much more light."

I (Mark) have used this tale of Nasruddin with many clients in different contexts. It is often one of the first tales I tell clients, usually in an intake session, when explaining the process of psychotherapy. I say, "Most of us are like Nasruddin, searching in the light for something that is missing (or not right). We stay in the light and on the surface where the search is easier (and safer) but not too fruitful. What we don't do is explore the darkness and the subterranean (Nasruddin's basement, a client's suppressed or repressed emotions, the unconscious). We may find some interesting and useful things out in the light, but often what we are looking for, like Nasruddin's ring, lies in a darkness that is uncertain and possibly scary. The process of psychotherapy often involves moving from the light to the darkness and searching there, but I will be with you in both the light and darkness as we go on this search together." Many of my clients respond with something like "I've never heard of Nasruddin, but I like that story. I sort of feel like him. I've been looking around for a long time, but I am not finding any answers."

As I (Harriet) was reading this Nasruddin tale, I was reminded of an athlete (a basketball player in her early 20s) I worked with at the Australian Institute of Sport. After her first session in a flotation tank without lighting and background music (which she had always used in previous sessions), she commented that in the darkness and stillness and silence of the flotation tank she experienced something like never before: the experience of herself, just herself. At first, she experienced an uncomfortable absence (that is, of external stimuli), but a point came when the experience changed dramatically to one of a presence, the presence of herself, someone she had never experienced before. She felt the presence of her body and an unusual sensation of being deeply connected to it, and she was flooded with feelings of love and warmth. This young woman had struggled with poor body image and low self-esteem for as long as she could remember. When we talked about her flotation tank experiences in the next counseling session, and compared her experiences with and without external stimulation (and in particular the light), she commented that she had always kept the light on in her life so she could see what others thought of her (she was extremely sensitive to how others responded to her and, not surprisingly, had often misinterpreted their responses) and hear what they had to say about her. Usually, what she saw and heard (i.e., her interpretation) reinforced her sense of self-loathing (particularly about her body) and feelings of inadequacy. Turning the light off in the flotation tank not only turned off all this external input but also provided the quietness for her to experience, as she stated, just herself. We used the flotation tank thereafter to help her get to know her newly discovered self and, as this self found its voice, she began to challenge many of the negative perceptions that she had held of herself, as well as her reliance on (perceived) external evaluations. She eventually learned how to "turn the lights off" without the flotation tank. She learned that she could find what was missing, first in an actual darkness and later in the metaphoric darkness of "lights off."

METAPHORS IN POPULAR MEDIA

The popular media supply rich sources for metaphors and images. Clients often pluck images or stories from movies or television shows that metaphorically fit their current situations. In the year before I (Mark) started my doctoral studies in psychology (with a doctoral minor in exercise science and sport psychology), I saw the profoundly moving (for me) motion picture *Gallipoli* (Gannon, Lovell, Stigwood, & Weir, 1981). It tells the tale of two Australian athletes (runners) who bond with each other in classic Aussie mateship and go off to Turkey to the World War I horror and tragedy that was Gallipoli. Early in the film, when the action is still in Australia, the central character, Archy Hamilton, is being prepped by his Uncle Jack (also his coach) for a footrace. They engage in an intense dialogue before the race:

Jack: What are your legs?

Archy: Springs. Steel springs.

Jack: What are they going to do?

Archy: Hurl me down the track.

Jack: How fast can you run?

Archy: As fast as a leopard.

Jack: How fast are you going to run?

Archy: As fast as a leopard!

Jack: Then let's see you do it!

The power of language and images is palpable. There are the steel springs, coiled energy ready to hurl Archy down the track. There are the speed, grace, power, and strength of a leopard. I tell all my applied sport psychology students to rent the movie and watch that scene. It has everything. There is the strong working and personal relationship between Archy and Jack (as both coach and uncle). There are love, respect, and trust between them, and then there are explosive and elegant metaphors. Part of the power of metaphors, in working with athletes and coaches, stems from their connection to the working alliance. Athletes' metaphors and practitioners' metaphors become *our* metaphors. A shared metaphor or image enables a shared understanding of something important for the client and no doubt helps fuel, preserve, and possibly deepen the therapeutic relationship.

In the film *Crouching Tiger, Hidden Dragon* (Schamus, Linde, & Lee, 2000), the character Yu Shu Lien is a master of qing gong ("light body skill"), a traditional Chinese martial art form that consists of two main skills: the ability to perform seemingly impossibly high vertical jumps and the ability to travel long distances with a flitting, continuous motion as if flying. In one spectacular scene in the film, Yu Shu Lien pursues Jen Yu (another master of qing gong) who has stolen the legendary Green Destiny sword. The two characters possess seemingly magical powers, literally flying through the air as they vault across roofs, running up walls, and moving with superhuman ease. In the end, they battle aloft in the beautiful and lyrical bamboo trees in a sequence that almost resembles a complex dance rather than a fight. For me (Harriet), the qing gong scenes, although imaginary and fantastical, were as powerful as they were enchanting. They were enchanting because they were elegantly beautiful and magical. They were powerful because they awakened in me a kind of kinesthetic imagining, both vivid and realistic, of what it might feel like to engage in such feats of superhuman movement.

Some time after viewing the film, I happened to work with a female high-jump athlete in her late teens who was having difficulty with the takeoff component of her jump. She said that her legs often felt heavy toward the end of the run-up and that her planting foot felt like dead weight at the point of takeoff. To address these feelings of heaviness, she had incorporated a number of physical and mental training techniques. For the most part, the mental techniques involved conjuring up metaphorical images of animals such as a lion accelerating and pouncing on its prey or a horse powerfully leaping up and forward over a jump. Unfortunately, the use of these images had made little, if any, difference in the heaviness she felt in her legs. In discussing these images with me, she described feeling that they were all wrong. She was able to relate, to some degree, to the visual images of the animals, but because they were quadrupeds, their movements were unlike what she actually experienced when running or jumping, and as a consequence she was unable to get any sense of the internal feeling of the animals' movements. I told her about my experiences watching the qing gong scenes in *Crouching Tiger, Hidden Dragon,* and she was quite eager to view the scenes. I suggested that she watch the entire film to get a sense of the mental discipline and practices that are fundamental to performing the fantastical qing gong feats—and because it is such a great film. When we next met, she delighted in telling me that she got it. What had awakened in me when I had first watched the scenes had also awakened something in her. She sensed immediately that this internal image (or representation) would see her flying over the bar, and with practice, both on and off the field, she was able to replace the heaviness in her legs with lightness and strength. As she later declared, she now had "a tiger in the tank."

I mention the delight that she took in telling me about her experience of getting it because it underlies an important point in the development of our therapeutic relationship. My suggesting that she watch the film was a type of metaphoric gift. I was giving her something that had moved me, something meaningful that was part of my aesthetic world, and she got it. The giving and receiving of such personal gifts (understanding, empathy, even love) are part of building the therapeutic alliance, and the stronger the alliance, the more likely it is that there will be positive outcomes of treatment (Horvath & Bedi, 2002). Shared metaphors, stories, and images can reinforce and deepen the client–practitioner relationship. We say more about metaphoric gifts at the end of the chapter. For now, we turn to some tales and metaphoric concepts from Buddhism and how they might be useful in treatment.

AN ATTACHMENT METAPHOR: TWO MONKS, A RIVER, AND A LADY

An older and a younger monk were walking on a journey, and they came to a river that was flowing quite swiftly. There was a young lady on the bank, and she was fearful of not making it across the river, of falling and drowning. The older monk picked her up in his arms and carried her safely across the river. The monks left the young lady on the far riverbank to continue her journey. After about an hour, the older monk started to notice that the younger monk was becoming agitated. The older monk asked, "Is something the matter?" The younger monk burst out, "How could you do that back there at the river?! You know we are not allowed to touch women. It's against our vows!" The older monk replied, "I left the young lady on the riverbank; why are you still carrying her?"

When my (Mark's) clients talk to me about past hurt, injustices, insults, shameful acts, and regrets, we usually try to examine what those events mean, but when clients keep repeating those stories, I want to help them explore what purpose their ruminations are serving. Telling them the story of the two monks, the river, and the young woman may start a process of looking at how clinging to hurt usually serves the purpose of making us feel bad, often confirming our secret opinions that we deserved such hurt. The story captures the futility and pain of holding on to unpleasant events. It is also a starting point for a discussion on how a client may begin to learn to let go.

A STORY OF ATTACHMENT: HUNGRY GHOSTS

In Buddhism's wheel of life, there are six realms or states of being. I (Mark) find that telling the story of the hungry ghosts realm is often helpful for my clients. This realm is populated by beings with narrow necks and the swollen bellies of the malnourished. They want to eat and drink, but when they try, it is painful. They are in a constant state of craving. They believe that if they fill themselves up, then they will be happy and satisfied, but they can never be filled. Examples in sport would be athletes who first want to make it to the national team; if they get on the team, then they will be happy. But once there, they find that making the team doesn't fill their emptiness: "If I can just make the Olympic team, then I'll be happy." But that also is not enough. Then it becomes "If I can win an Olympic medal," then "win a gold medal." It never stops.

A society that equates acquisition of material goods with happiness is a culture of hungry ghosts. In his book *Affluenza,* Oliver James (2007) used the metaphor of a virus to capture the problems of materialist-capitalist societies where more and more acquisitions (e.g., wealth, looks, fame) lead not to happiness but to despair and further feelings of emptiness as the new acquisitions fail to fill our psychic voids. His virus is a hungry ghost writ large. It is probable that many athletes who come to sport psychology practitioners for performance enhancement are in the hungry ghost realm. They want that extra edge so they can succeed in sport, or make Daddy proud, or make their empty lives meaningful, or gain love, or feel worthy of love. Better sport performance won't actually do any of those things; or if it does, the momentary happiness gained from better performance will be fleeting, and the hunger will set in again. Major aspects of this realm include the attachments of addiction and dependency.

Being a hungry ghost keeps one out of present time. One becomes future oriented, focused on acquiring something (e.g., a medal, a car, a new sexual partner), on feeding that metaphoric empty belly. In my therapy room, I have a powerful painting depicting two hungry ghosts. When I tell my clients about hungry ghosts, I have them look at the painting so they have both a story and a strong image. Usually within a few weeks of my telling this story, a client will come to therapy and say something like "Man, at the tournament I was hungry ghosting all over the place, but then I started focusing on my breath, and . . ." They use the story and the image to help recognize when they are clinging and craving to make a shift back to moment-to-moment awareness and stay in present time.

A STORY OF SELF-PROTECTION: HERMIT CRABS

When working with athletes, I (Harriet) often provide them with an opportunity to describe the metaphors, images, and mental narratives they generate to represent and understand the world as they experience it. My motives are usually twofold. First, for athletes who have difficulty identifying and analyzing problem areas and issues (performance or otherwise), this technique is less threatening and confronting than direct questioning, and it helps them find their voices. Second, in almost all cases, the use of metaphor helps me understand the nature and context of an athlete's experiences and the range (and magnitude) of effects that those experiences have on the athlete. In some ways, I find that metaphors are like projective tests, providing not only a channel for communication but also a sensitive (and safe) mechanism for exploring meaning at both the conscious and unconscious levels.

Earlier this year, I began working with a junior athlete (female, 16 years old) who presented with generalized anxiety and sleep disturbance, which later progressed to a diagnosis of post-traumatic stress disorder. The athlete had experienced prolonged sexual, verbal, and physical harassment by a male of similar age when at school and when engaging in activities in the general community (a small rural township). Discussing the specific details of the harassment, particularly those of a sexual or otherwise physical nature, was a no-go area for this athlete, as is common for people who have PTSD; reliving the traumatic experiences is too distressing for the individual and usually detrimental to the therapeutic process and the client's progress, particularly in the early stages of treatment.

As treatment continued and our therapeutic alliance grew, I gently broached the issue of her experiences of harassment, suggesting that it could be beneficial if we started to explore ways that might make it safe for her to share with me some of her experiences, either directly or indirectly. Her response was a mixture of compliance and ambivalence as we proceeded to discuss the pros and cons of keeping a journal, drawing pictures, conjuring up images, and making up fictional stories to represent the real stories that were so difficult for her to tell. In the counseling session that followed this discussion, the athlete turned up with a brightly decorated shoebox and invited me to meet her new pets. When the lid was taken off the box, there lay three hermit crabs, curled up safe and sound under their seemingly oversized protective shells. When I commented on these unusual-looking pets, she proclaimed that hermit crabs were the ideal animal creation and the best pets she could imagine. They were perfectly created because of their highly protective shells and their ability to remain still and virtually unnoticeable. They were the ultimate pets for her because she understood them and related to their need to be highly protected. For me, being introduced to these pets carried with it a clear message; it was a powerful metaphor by which the athlete conveyed to me how she was feeling about the prospect of addressing some of her traumatic experiences in future sessions with me. She was prepared to go there but needed to know that she would have protection, that I would protect her. Although I was initially unsure about the precise process we would employ, her own use of a metaphor in this case provided some clues and a starting point. What I was clear on was how she felt about proceeding and the safeguards (protection) I needed to have in place if we were to do so.

HEARING AND LISTENING TO OTHERS AND OURSELVES

How does one hear a story? I (Mark) remember attending a presentation on a qualitative study of commitment in professional sport. The researcher was giving examples of what some athletes said that illustrated high commitment. One quote went something like this: "Becoming a Titan (not the real team name) has been a lifelong dream. This team is my life, and I am giving 110 percent. I can't even think of not being a Titan." The researcher was using this quote to illustrate (and applaud) commitment. Well, it does sound highly committed, but I heard a story about anxiety: "I can't even think of not being a Titan; just the thought of not being a Titan brings up anxiety, so I have to avoid such thoughts. If I weren't a Titan then I would be nothing, and that scares me, so I don't think those thoughts." The researcher heard positive commitment, and I heard a story of distress and suppression because the researcher and I were bent in different ways.

In using metaphors, folktales, and images we need to remind ourselves constantly that we are all bent in different ways. Therapists have different theoretical orientations. Clients (and practitioners) have different life histories that will influence the strength or weakness of a metaphoric or storytelling intervention. Client-generated metaphors are probably the best place to start because they have obvious personal relevance, as in the case of the hermit crabs. Later, as practitioners gain knowledge and understanding of their clients' worlds, they may grow to feel confident in introducing therapeutic metaphors and stories. If the therapeutic relationship is a strong one, then even if the story or metaphor doesn't work for the client, there is usually no harm done. We (Mark and Harriet) both have the not uncommon experience of introducing a metaphor that we think captures what is happening for the client, only to have the client say, "Not really, I don't feel that way at all." Our metaphors can't all be winners. Our usual response to this scenario is "Well, that one didn't work. Let's see if we can come up with something that does."

In helping athletes and coaches develop their own metaphors and images, listening is the key, and sport psychologists can hone their skills at picking up on metaphoric language. For example, after a good performance, an athlete might say, "I was so pumped at the start. It was great." Then, the practitioner could reply with "When you say the word 'pumped,' what sort of images come to mind?" The reply might be "It was like I was Thor, and my javelin was a thunderbolt." And there we have a wonderful metaphoric image generated by the client with a little help from the psychologist. This technique is at least as old as Freud and is called free association. Asking clients what's on their minds (and assuring them that whatever comes up might be useful, no matter how silly or embarrassing or fantastical it may be) can go a long way in helping them generate useful and powerful metaphors for themselves. Free association is a central process in psychodynamic psychotherapy and has many other uses besides metaphor generation. We do not, however, see much application of free association in the mainstream sport psychology literature.

Sport psychologists may also need some help with their own metaphors. The story at the beginning of the chapter included a metaphor in which the athlete-psychologist sees herself driving a Volvo when working with her psychotherapy clients. In self-reflective practice, the psychologist's own metaphors, images, and free associations may help explore questions such as the following: "Who am I in this therapeutic relationship?" "What images come to mind when I think about this client?" "What metaphors or stories pop into my head as my client and I start the termination process?" A supervisor can assist in working through these questions. In psychodynamic supervision, we constantly ask supervisees about what is going on for them right now (in terms of thinking, images, emotions). For example, a supervisee might say, "I feel I am not getting anywhere with this client." A supervisor might respond with a request for a simile: "So, what is that going nowhere like for you?" The supervisee might say, "It's like I am trapped in a box and can't find a way through, a way to open the box." The supervisor could then use the supervisee's metaphor by saying, "Well, let's sit in that box for a while together; it may be a bit cramped, but let's see what comes up. Maybe we'll find a way through. We could possibly start with you remembering other times when you have felt stuck with no way out." Supervisors and supervisees, like clients and practitioners, form working alliances, and the development of that bond can be nurtured through shared metaphors. Sitting in a box together and working things out are a fine metaphor itself, both for the working alliance in supervision (see essay 10 in this book for a discussion of assisted self-reflection) and for the therapeutic relationship between client and practitioner.

A FINAL METAPHOR

A few years ago I (Mark) wrote the following (Andersen, 2006) passage; we include it here to illustrate how we use metaphors in teaching the next generation of applied sport psychologists and how the whole process of working with athletes is often deeply metaphoric:

> *An athlete comes to a sport psychologist with a gift wrapped in a box. In that box, there are hopes, fears, dreams, desires, frustrations, secrets, joys, and unhappiness. The athlete can do a lot of things with that gift. She can keep it hidden in her pocket. She can place it on her knee and talk about it, but never put it out on the table. It is an odd package, this gift; it does not adhere to the laws of physics. If the gift is opened, it can suddenly become quite large and scary, almost filling the room with threat and pain (e.g., a history of sexual abuse). Or, it can, once it is opened, become quite small and manageable (e.g., a misinterpretation of coach communication that can be easily resolved). Even so, the gift, and the giving of the gift to another, usually involves some level of risk, and often the gift is set on the table but never opened fully and only talked about in a superficial (and safe) manner. Sometimes the gift has a card on it that says "performance," but the contents say much more. Too often, sport psychologists only read the card or look at the colourful wrapping. For example, the athlete may say, "I get so nervous before each match that I throw up every time." Metaphorically, the athlete has made a small tear in the gift's wrapping paper. The sport psychologist then brings forth a bit of sticky tape (e.g., relaxation exercises) and proceeds to repair the rip in the wrapping without actually taking the paper off and looking into the box to find what is behind the anxiety (e.g., the horrible equation that good performance = good person, fears of losing parental love). When the rip in the wrapping is made by the athlete, the sport psychologist could also say, "OK, let's slowly start to take the paper off this gift and see what there is here. I'll be with you all the way."*

The sport psychologist also has a gift (cf. Yalom, 2003). And that gift contains her expert knowledge, her personality, her genuineness, care, empathy, appreciation for beauty, compassion for human frailty, the ability to handle the athlete's gift with unconditional positive regard, and, yes, even love. The handling of both gifts between these two people can be a model for the finest there is in human relationships. The core of the working alliance, the collaborative empiricism between athlete and sport psychologist, is how both these metaphoric gifts are presented, examined, and accepted. (pp. 696–697)

CONCLUSION

The metaphors of gifts, of working alliances and collaborative empiricism, are what we use to help our psychology students come to grips with, understand, and appreciate the gravity, the joys, the frustrations, the "ah-ha!" moments, the confusions, the seriousness, and the tenderheartedness of the work they do when they sit down with athletes and talk. We encourage them to gather stories and metaphors from all over the world, to read myths and folktales, to ask their athletes to exercise their imaginations and free-associate, to use their own creative faculties to create new metaphors, and to tell their own stories to help athletes see, understand, and feel in new and healthier (and happier) ways.

Pass your stories on.

IDEAS FOR REFLECTION AND DEBATE

1. What stories, images, or metaphors from your culture or religion do you have that you could possibly use in practice?

2. How do you (if you do) help your clients develop their own metaphors or images?

3. In terms of your own stories and metaphors, how much do you disclose to clients, and what principles guide those disclosures?

4. Do you and your clients ever examine the images, metaphors, and story lines in your clients' dreams? If so, how do you go about exploring those dreams and what they might be saying?

5. One metaphoric Zen proverb goes like this: "First there is a mountain; then there is no mountain; then there is a mountain again." One

might draw a corollary regarding the training of sport psychologists: First there is Dave; then there is no Dave (he has become a *sport psychologist*); then there is Dave again. How might the metaphor of mountains, viewed in terms of graduate students such as Dave (or Sally, or Fred, or Pippa) becoming sport psychologists, be helpful for your students?

REFERENCES

Andersen, M.B. (2006). It's all about performance . . . and something else. In J. Dosil (Ed.), *The sport psychologist's handbook: A guide for sport-specific performance enhancement* (pp. 687–698). Chichester, England: Wiley.

Battino, R. (2005). *Metaphoria: Metaphor and guided metaphor for psychotherapy and healing.* Norwalk, CT: Crown House.

Burns, G.W. (2001). *101 healing stories: Using metaphors in therapy.* New York: Wiley.

Burns, G.W. (2007). *Healing with stories: Your casebook collection for using therapeutic metaphors.* Hoboken, NJ: Wiley.

Carless, D., & Douglas, K. (2008). Narrative, identity and mental health: How men with serious mental illness re-story their lives through sport and exercise. *Psychology of Sport and Exercise, 9,* 576–594.

Curry, L.A., & Maniar, S.D. (2004). Academic course for enhancing student-athlete performance in sport. *The Sport Psychologist, 18,* 297–316.

Efran, J.S., Lesser, G.S., & Spiller, M.J. (1994). Enhancing tennis coaching with youths using a metaphor method. *The Sport Psychologist, 8,* 349–359.

Gannon, B. (Producer), Lovell, P. (Producer), Stigwood, R. (Producer), & Weir, P. (Director). (1981). *Gallipoli* [Motion picture]. Australia: Paramount.

Gordon, D. (1978). *Therapeutic metaphors: Helping others through the looking glass.* Capitola, CA: Meta.

Hammond, D.C. (Ed.). (1990). *Handbook of hypnotic suggestions and metaphors.* New York: Norton.

Hanin, Y.L., & Stambulova, N.B. (2002). Metaphoric description of performance states: An application of the IZOF model. *The Sport Psychologist, 16,* 386–415.

Holmes, P.S., & Collins, D.J. (2001). The PETTLEP approach to motor imagery: A functional equivalence model for sport psychologists. *Journal of Applied Sport Psychology, 13,* 60–83.

Horvath, A.O., & Bedi, R.P. (2002). The alliance. In J.C. Norcross (Ed.), *Psychotherapy relationships that work: Therapist contributions and responsiveness to patients* (pp. 37–69). New York: Oxford University Press.

James, O. (2007). *Affluenza.* London: Vermilion.

Jones, M.V. (2003). Controlling emotions in sport. *The Sport Psychologist, 17,* 471–486.

Kopp, S.B. (1971). *Guru: Metaphors from a psychotherapist.* Palo Alto, CA: Science & Behavior Books.

Lankton, S. (2005). Foreword. In R. Battino, *Metaphoria: Metaphor and guided metaphor for psychotherapy and healing* (pp. v–xv). Norwalk, CT: Crown House.

Leahy, T., & Harrigan, R. (2006). Using narrative therapy in sport psychology practice: Application to a psychoeducational body image program. *The Sport Psychologist, 20,* 480–494.

Mascher, J. (2002). Narrative therapy: Inviting the use of sport as metaphor. *Women & Therapy, 25*(2), 57–74.

Ruiz, M.C., & Hanin, Y.L. (2004). Metaphoric description and individualized emotion profiling of performance states in top karate athletes. *Journal of Applied Sport Psychology, 16,* 258–273.

Schamus, J. (Producer), Linde, D., (Producer), & Lee, A. (Director). (2000). *Crouching tiger, hidden dragon* [Motion picture]. Taiwan, Hong Kong, USA, China: Asia Union Film & Entertainment.

Simons, J. (2000). Doing imagery in the field. In M.B. Andersen (Ed.), *Doing sport psychology* (pp. 77–92). Champaign, IL: Human Kinetics.

Smith, B., & Sparkes, A.C. (2009a). Narrative analysis and sport and exercise psychology: Understanding lives in diverse ways. *Psychology of Sport and Exercise, 10,* 279–288.

Smith, B., & Sparkes, A.C. (2009b). Narrative inquiry in sport and exercise psychology: What can it mean, and why might we do it? *Psychology of Sport and Exercise, 10,* 1–11.

Yalom, I.D. (2003). *The gift of therapy: Reflections on being a therapist.* London: Piatkus.

PART II

ISSUES IN PROFESSIONAL DELIVERY

In this part of the book, the contributors share their experiences in their roles as deliverers of professional services with an eye toward some of the major issues they have encountered on their diverse paths. The territories they describe are colorful and varied landscapes of practice and training. The authors move through multidisciplinary teams and political institutions. They challenge us with what can be learned from deviant practices and social work and social justice models. They remind us that multiculturalism is not just about interactions between people of different ethnicities and cultures but is ubiquitous in most applied settings. Many sport psychologists view reflective practice as an essential part of service delivery, but this part of the book reveals some of its pitfalls and limitations. As a complement or alternative to reflective practice, the supervision of applied work makes a hefty appearance in two of the essays, and there is a call for a depth of supervision and training that, though not constituting therapy, is therapeutic for the practitioner's growth and development.

One major theme in this part of the book involves alternative ways to conceptualize and do applied work in sport psychology. In North American and European models of applied practice, we find that concepts of the self (e.g., self-esteem, self-efficacy, self-determination) seem to dominate the discourse around athletes, coaches, and service delivery. The essay on Buddhism in this part offers an ancient and different way to look at ourselves, our athletes, and our interactions, and it challenges our often unquestioned notions of self.

Above all, the authors in this part (and especially in the last essay) offer their personal experiences and their elations, joys, frustrations, despairs, and hopes for their athletes, for themselves, and for the profession of applied sport psychology. They are a passionate lot, and we have learned much from them. We hope you will too.

COLLABORATIVE PRACTICE:
Multidisciplinary Support Alongside Multiagency Engagement

Dearbhla McCullough
Roehampton University, United Kingdom

Michael Korzinski
Private practice, United Kingdom

In this essay, Dearbhla and Michael reflect on the challenges of working with an elite athlete as he sought asylum in the United Kingdom. This moving and intensely human essay outlines elements of his traumatic history alongside the challenges he faced in a new country. The authors also discuss their experiences of collaborative practice (between the disciplines of clinical and sport psychology) and offer insights into the work carried out in both domains.

INTRODUCTION

In many cases . . . the patient who comes to us has a story that is not told, and which as a rule no one knows of. To my mind, therapy only really begins after the investigation of that wholly personal story. It is the patient's secret, the rock against which he is shattered.

Jung (1963, p. 117)

One such story is imbedded in the hearts and minds of the people whose lives were touched and enriched through their relationship with a certain extraordinarily gifted but deeply troubled young athlete. His life was tragically cut short just 5 years after he arrived in the United Kingdom; in this chapter, we share elements of that story with you.

We are never sure when a person will come along who will test our assumptions and the boundaries of our professional practice. We can rest assured, however, that such a day will come for all of us. For the authors, that test came in the guise of a young international middle-distance runner who had been tortured in his country of origin and was seeking asylum in the United Kingdom. The sheer complexity of this young man's problems defied traditional solutions and tested the limits of both practitioners in the areas of service delivery, intervention, and professional boundaries.

This young athlete presented a unique opportunity for two people from different professional backgrounds—one an expert in the field of psychological trauma, the other a chartered sport psychologist—to work together. I (Michael Korzinski) have been providing care and treatment to victims of torture and other forms of gross human rights violations, such as human trafficking and genocide, since 1990. I am the cofounder and clinical director of the Helen Bamber Foundation, a voluntary organization that specializes in working with such victims. I was a member of the U.S. national cycling team in its lead-up to the 1984 Olympic Games in Los Angeles. My aspirations for becoming a world-class cyclist were ended when I sustained an injury in an accident while training. I (Dearbhla McCullough) am a sport psychologist chartered by the British Psychological Society and accredited by the British Association of Sport and Exercise Sciences. I am employed at Roehampton University as a senior lecturer in sport psychology. I have been running since the age of 10 and have competed for Northern Ireland at both the junior and senior levels. My interest in, and subsequent passion for, becoming a sport psychologist was fueled by my personal experience of burnout as a junior athlete. I have been providing support to competitive athletes, across various sporting backgrounds and levels, since 1998.

Under normal circumstances, it is unlikely that our professional paths would have crossed. The rehabilitation needs of this client, however, required the combined skill sets that we both possessed. Our appreciation and mutual respect for each other's perspective fostered a spirit of cooperation that enabled us to combine these skill sets effectively in supporting this vulnerable young man.

In telling this story, we highlight the many challenges that the athlete's cultural background, traumatic history, and asylum status presented. Much of the work we did involved simple and often pragmatic methods, which serve to illustrate processes and actions that expand what might be understood by the term "support." We believe that our work with this talented but troubled young athlete is well described by Corlett's (1996) statement that "the most difficult counselling situations often illuminate the difference between curing and caring" (p. 91). We also believe that this story touches on issues that may be worthy of further consideration by the reader, including the following questions:

- When should professionals work independently, and when is it beneficial for practitioners with different skills and attributes to work collectively to find solutions?

- Should we always stick to the boundaries of expertise that our ethical codes dictate to us?

- What are the limits of cognitive–behavioral interventions and trauma-focused therapy?

K'S HISTORY

K, a pseudonym, was part of a five-man team that won gold at a world championship running event. The smiles in the team's victory photograph, however, masked the unfolding of a political drama that would lead K and another highly acclaimed national team member to claim political asylum in the UK.

K's decision to seek asylum did not happen spontaneously. It was the culmination of years of oppression that began in early childhood. K was the eldest child in a family of five, which also included a mother, a father, a younger sister, and a brother. His family worked a small farm, raising cattle, sheep, and chickens. K identified his profession as that of a farmer, but running was a way of life for him. He ran to school. When he was shepherding the animals and one went missing, as often occurred, he would run to find it. Livestock were extremely important to the family's life, and the loss of a cow could have a significant economic effect. K once described running for days in search of a prize cow. He was elated when he found it alive and well. Thus running was a way of surviving, a way of life: "I ran everywhere. It was normal."

Many great runners have come from the region where K was born. Running is woven into the landscape and into the fabric of life. A combination of altitude and a pristine arid climate create the ideal environmental conditions for a person's cardiovascular capacity to grow and develop. The people of this region, however, have been systematically oppressed for centuries. People who speak up for their rights are often persecuted. Torture, imprisonment, sustained harassment, and murder by death squad are not uncommon occurrences (Human Rights Watch, 2007). K's father was a spokesperson for the community. He tutored the young K in the culture of his people and did not spare details of their suffering. His father was arrested for advocating on behalf of the community. The first arrest took place in 1991, when he was seized by armed soldiers, held for 4 months, and tortured. K remembered being terrified by the marks on his father's back.

K also recalled his father being arrested on two other occasions. In one of his sessions with me (Michael), K described witnessing his father get punched, slapped, kicked with military boots, and beaten with the butt of a Kalashnikov rifle. Research has shown that exposure to violence or violent threats of an interpersonal nature, such as seeing a parent rendered helpless through physical violence, can profoundly affect a child's emotional and psychological development (Herman, 1992). According to Herman, the associated symptoms are complex and enduring. The victim loses his or her sense of safety, trust, and self-worth. This finding is supported by my research and work as a psychotherapist with the Helen Bamber Foundation (Korzinski, 1997). And in the case of K, who had witnessed his father being arrested, beaten, and tortured, these experiences instilled a deep sense of insecurity and worry that his father could be taken from the home at any time. On one of the occasions, K himself received a savage blow to the head as he tried "to protect my father from the soldier." K's mother informed him that he was unconscious for several minutes. Afterward, K began to have seizures.

In a later incident, K did not know that when the soldiers dragged his father from the family home it was the last time he would see his father alive. Several weeks later, his father's body was found in a nearby forest with two bullet wounds to the head. K was 11 years old. The image of his father's body haunted K for the rest of his life.

After the death of K's father, the continuing persecution of his mother forced her to flee the family home and ancestral farmland. K saw it as his duty as the eldest son to honor his father's memory and protect the family's home and land. He refused to accompany his mother, who implored him to abandon the home and come with her. For her own safety and that of her other children, she left K behind. He stayed in the house alone but was supported and assisted by sympathetic neighbors.

One month after his mother fled, K was arrested outside his school and taken to the local police station. He was asked of his mother's whereabouts and other questions about his deceased father's political activities. The authorities instructed him to report weekly to the police station. K was subjected to harassment, beatings, and, on two other occasions, detention and torture.

At the end of the academic year in 1994, K went into hiding. He continued to run, and running began to hold a different meaning for him. He found that it became a way of making the pain go away. It helped him forget the torment that plagued his daily life and the nightmares that haunted him.

Upon his return to school, K was arrested again and taken to the same police station. He was detained in a cell, handcuffed, and tortured for almost a month. He was punched, kicked, burned with cigarettes, and stomped upon as he lay on the ground. He was interrogated about his mother's whereabouts, his own activities, names of people who used to attend his father's meetings, and his own allegiances. For most of us, enduring such hardship would be unimaginable, but it became something of a way of life for K. He was not going to let it break him.

K continued to run. He began to wonder whether his running might be a way out from the grinding oppression. He knew of other runners from his region who, through their athletic excellence, had been able to rise above the political and ethnic divides. He truly realized his talent for running, however, only when he won a national student event. After this success, K became dedicated to running and invested everything of himself in it. He had never thought about his running in this way and regarded it as a gift from God. K also felt that running somehow made his life safer. Through his athletic talent, he was able to prove his worth to the government and the society in which he lived. He was spotted by a well-known running coach, and his future as a member of the national running elite was set in motion.

K mentioned that the runners from his country often talk about two faces: one face they present to the world and another they carry in their hearts and minds. The athletes are told that they must not involve themselves in politics. The best runners must run for the officials. Through a combination of fear and intimidation, on the one hand, and a system of financial and social rewards on the other, the runners learn to comply or carry on their activities in secret.

K had no choice. If he were to find an outlet for his developing capacity as a runner, he would have to run for the very system that persecuted his people, that tortured him, that had tortured and murdered his father, and that had destroyed his family. K learned to split off the feelings he had about the government's involvement in his father's murder. In his mind, he imagined that he was running for his father and his people. Each race he won became an unspoken moral and political victory. Nonetheless, he found it difficult to reconcile this approach with his underlying hatred for the government. He continued to involve himself in politics. Even as a member of the national team, he was not above being taught a lesson. When he was told that his life hung in the balance if he failed to perform well at an upcoming world championship, he sought asylum in the UK.

PSYCHOTHERAPY SUPPORT: MICHAEL KORZINSKI

When I first met K, he was still wearing his national team running kit as he sat with a teammate in the crowded drop-in unit of an organization that specialized in working with victims of torture. Years later, K would laugh about this meeting. He said, "We did not have any other clothes. Usually we would have to hand in the national team uniform after the competitions, and if you damaged or lost it you would have to pay for it. It felt good not to give it back." I was asked to provide an initial assessment of his social, psychological, and legal protection needs. A proper understanding of rehabilitation begins with seeing the individual person in the context of the environment. How a person functions invariably results from an interaction between the capacities and dispositions he or she possesses as an individual and the environment in which he or she lives. Rehabilitation does not occur in a vacuum. It is not just what happens between the clinician and the client within the confines of the four walls of the consulting room; rather, the larger social, cultural, and political context can play an enormous part in an individual's recovery. Therefore, understanding K's needs as an asylum seeker was interconnected with his aspirations as a runner and as a victim of torture.

K presented as a traumatized, seriously depressed man who found it extremely difficult to speak about his experiences. There was little spontaneous movement and rarely any smile. There was a vagueness to his answers. For example, when asked what he thought about, he would say, "I think about what happened." It took time before K felt able to build the trust he needed to speak about his experiences. He was not convinced that he should speak about them at all. He tried hard to block out the past, but his memories seemed to push back as if they had a life of their own.

K was suffering from severe post-traumatic stress disorder (PTSD; American Psychiatric Association, 2000, *Diagnostic and Statistical Manual* IV-TR). He experienced typical symptoms, such as intrusive memories, flashback phenomena, anxiety and suspiciousness, disturbances of attention and concentration, volatility of mood, feelings of depersonalization (the self not feeling real) and derealization (the world not feeling real), typical nightmares (in which episodes of the traumatic experience are repeated in a stereotypical way), and relatively undisguised hypervigilance and hyperalertness. He was also going through a severe depressive disorder (APA, DSM-IV-TR) and showing symptoms of pervasive depressed mood, fixed posture sleep, appetite disturbance, feelings of inner deadness, self-blame, and guilt. K clearly needed help. The question, however, was what form that help should take.

The concept of psychotherapy was alien to K, as it is for many asylum seekers who come from different cultural backgrounds. Asylum seekers often arrive in the UK with some basic understanding of certain aspects of Western health services, including psychological therapies, but many people from non-Western cultures find the disclosure of intimate material to someone who is perceived as a stranger (the therapist) to be highly unusual (Davies & Webb, 2000; Savin & Martinez, 2006). People from K's country of origin, for example, have a concept known as active forgetting, which is considered the normative means of coping with past difficulties within that culture (Burnett & Peel, 2001). For them, the Western concept of working through the trauma is both strange and potentially retraumatizing. In addition, the person's distress is often communicated in the language of the body. Much has been written and published about how in certain cultures the somatic communication of psychological and emotional distress is not only the expected form of presentation but the accepted one as well (Davies & Webb, 2000). I specialize in working cross-culturally and have an advanced understanding of the way in which images and experiences of catastrophic violence and loss influence a person's identity and sense of one's body. At the Helen Bamber Foundation, we have found that a person's traditional way of coping with psychological trauma and loss begins to break down when confronted by an alien culture with little or no prospect of returning to their home country due to the person's fear of future persecution there. Western psychological therapies often fail because they appear to be unable to bridge the gap between the cultural, social, and psychological traditions that people bring from their homelands and the treatments offered in the host culture (Korzinski, 1997). The person must cope not only with the extreme trauma associated with previous experiences of persecution and torture (Friedman & Marsella, 1996) and the loss of loved ones and culture (Eisenbruch, 1991; Silove, 1999) but also with adjustment to a culture in which much of what the person has learned about how to be in the world may no longer apply (Silove, 1999).

What this account of K does not convey is the complex manner in which these symptoms were interwoven with his identity as a runner. His running had political, cultural, and symbolic meaning. Through his running, he was able to process his feelings psychologically and make something of his life. His running also had hidden inner meaning. He ran for his father, the victims still in detention, and his tribal people. He communicated through language of the body—the language of running. It was his way of coping. If something were to interfere with this process, K would be at risk of developing more serious mental disorders than he already had. Running was an integral part of his psychophysical development and was fundamental to the way in which he coped with his problems. His need to run, however, was on a collision course with the realities of being an asylum seeker in the UK.

When K first arrived in the UK, he was filled with hope and belief that he would shortly be running for Great Britain and Northern Ireland. He spoke in lofty terms about "running for freedom." He had fantasies that his asylum claim would be quickly sorted and that he would return to training at altitude, something he was obsessed about. Countless sessions were spent exploring this fantasy's meaning and importance to him. In his mind, the clock was always ticking. Every day he remained at sea level was another day in which he could not perform at the level he expected of himself.

K arrived in the UK at a time when the government was struggling to restructure the national asylum system. The government's aim was to create a firmer, faster, and fairer asylum policy that would be able to delineate between so-called bogus asylum seekers and those who were genuine. The government was also targeting, through legislative changes, so-called pull factors, such as an asylum seeker's access to mainstream benefits and housing. There was also a concerted campaign in various sectors of the media that were openly xenophobic to asylum seekers and other so-called outsiders. K's dreams of running for freedom ran into the realities of being an asylum seeker in the UK. He once said, "Dr. Michael, I am running to nowhere." From a rehabilitation standpoint, I was working within extremely restricted parameters. His identity as a runner was central to his sense of self but also connected to his traumatic experiences. The opportunities open to him as a runner and an asylum seeker, however, were severely limited compared with what he had grown accustomed to as an athlete in his native country. For example, he could not leave the UK to train at altitude. He could not leave the UK to compete; he could not leave the UK, period. He was required to live in accommodations supported by the NASS (National Asylum Support Service) on £30 a week. He was not allowed to work to supplement his income. He was moved seven times into different accommodations throughout London. Each time, he would need to reregister with local services such as medical care. Indra (1993, cited in Korac, 2003, p. 53) highlights the "asymmetry of power and voice between the state . . . and refugees." Throughout the 1990s and into the early part of the new millennium, the Home Office decision-making processes were characterized by long delays. It could take years for a person to receive an initial decision, and this process was impossible to influence unless there were some extreme or compelling reasons to do so. One's Olympic dreams did not fall into this category. More often than not, the decision was a refusal. The person then entered into a lengthy appeals process. All of these processes took time, which K felt he could not afford to lose. Time has a special meaning for athletes; it is the benchmark by which their performances are judged. It had now taken on added meaning for K as an asylum seeker.

K's sense of anger, frustration, and bitterness began to grow. He had lived his entire life under a repressive regime and now sought asylum in the UK not only for his own protection but also because of his motivation to run for freedom and democracy. The current situation compounded his trauma and mirrored past experiences in which his rights as a human being had been violated. K had thought that he had reached a safe haven, but his life as an asylum seeker in the UK was anything but safe and secure. He found the current situation a continuation of past humiliation. He had fled one form of persecution only to find another. Rather than improve, things had become (in his mind) worse. He was no longer training in the rarefied air of his homeland but pounding the backstreets and parks of London while trying to survive on £30 a week. He continued to train and compete whenever he could. In one race, he lapped the entire field. His training, however, began to have an increasingly desperate and manic quality. It was as if his identity were slipping away and he was running with all his power just to hold on to his sense of who he was. K's friend who had defected with him had given up running for a variety of reasons that included leg damage deliberately inflicted on him during an interrogation session in his country. This situation was painful for K because he admired this man as one of the great runners from his country. K could not accept that his friend had given up. His friend told K that he could not train the way he did back home. He needed to adapt. But K seemed to drive himself even harder.

At one point, K announced proudly that he had found a running manager who would take care of him. K said that his manager would support K financially and that he could live in the manager's house. However, once the manager realized that K could not travel internationally and that his asylum status was unresolved, the manager found a polite way of withdrawing his offer. K was devastated. It became increasingly clear to me that unless I somehow addressed the outer chaos that was beginning to dominate K's life as a runner, there would be no possibility of addressing his survivor's guilt, PTSD, and depression. His running is what bound all these experiences together.

The weekly sessions now involved my phoning on behalf of K to various people in the UK's running community. The aim was to help K integrate effectively into the new community in which he found himself, but as soon as the person on the other end of the phone understood that K was an asylum seeker, he or she would withdraw. Some would offer helpful advice and suggest another person to phone or even (occasionally) a place to train. Others were far more cynical about his motivation for claiming asylum: "They just come over here because they think it's easy to make money." I informed this particular person that K was currently supporting himself on £30 a week and politely put down the phone. The bottom line, however, was that without clarity regarding K's asylum status, it was difficult to move ahead.

One day, K came to the office in an acute state of crisis. He had missed several sessions. He resurfaced to say good-bye and that he was giving up running. For K, giving up running was the equivalent of giving up on life itself. K said he wanted to run off London Bridge into the river: "I felt that I must say good-bye to you, but I was afraid to come because I knew that you would try and stop me. I just want it to be over."

"K," I asked, "what has happened?" He could barely speak. Tears began to well up in his eyes. He said that he had watched the eighth annual International Amateur Athletic Federation world championships in Edmonton, Canada. He had been transfixed by seeing runners, many of whom he knew, performing on the world stage. One runner he had previously beaten in his country did exceptionally well: "We used to joke about the guy. It was unbelievable. Now I have become the joke. The government will say, 'See, he left and now he is nothing.' Time is going for me, Dr. Michael." K felt trapped. He could not return to his country, and the hardships of his life in the UK were unexpected and overwhelming. He spoke with great love and affection for the runners from his country: "We all have secrets. Each one of us has a story, which we mostly keep to ourselves. I could only see their pain."

"Are you speaking about your own pain?" I asked. K burst into tears and sobbed inconsolably.

K had never fully grieved the death of his father. He remained haunted by the memories of his torture and the images of his dead father's brutalized body. Now, when he ran he felt guilty and ashamed. He felt responsible for his father's death. He was tormented by thoughts that he had betrayed his father by having run for a system that had tortured and murdered him. He still felt, however, that his father supported him, and K would hear his voice encouraging him: "Grow up, my son; keep doing well." For K, doing well meant achieving his goals and becoming the great man and runner he had the potential to be, but he no longer saw the possibility of doing well. He felt he was dying as a runner—dying inside as a person.

For a therapist, being confronted by a suicidal patient always raises questions. Will I do the right thing? How real is the threat? How does one assess the risk? What can I do, if anything, to help prevent someone from taking his or her own life? The standard risk assessment that we are all familiar with as mental health professionals helps us evaluate the situation, but it felt to me that going through a list of questions or phoning the psychiatrist or GP was not what was needed at this moment.

K seemed to be looking to me for a reason to live, at a moment in time when he could not find the answer within himself. It did not feel right to challenge or confront his suicidal wish directly. I felt that K was being driven by a profound need for someone to recognize and understand his pain. "K," I said, "you must be feeling so desperate to have reached this point. The pain must be unimaginable. I am grateful that you have come to speak with me today to come and say good-bye. You have lost so much, and it must feel that you will never get it back." K said, "Thank you, Dr. Michael. Thank you for understanding." When K saw the other runners on television, he saw himself—the self he could have been, should have been, would have been, if not for the tragic circumstances that had characterized his life since childhood. He now felt worthless and broken inside.

We sat in silence for several minutes. I was filled with feelings of worthlessness and failure. It didn't seem to matter at this point whether these feelings belonged to me as a therapist who was on the verge of losing a patient or constituted an identification with K's own despair that I was picking up in the countertransference. Perhaps a part of my unconscious surfaced, and then I remembered what it was to have a dream crushed by forces beyond one's control. It connected with my own Olympic aspirations. I felt the need to acknowledge his talent when there was no one else to do it. I thought, and spontaneously said, the following: "K, it has always been my dream to learn to run. How to train properly. I was an athlete once and really loved training. I was wondering if one day we could run together. You could show me the way." For a moment K looked genuinely surprised. On the surface, the comment seemed completely out of sync with what was happening, but it was exactly what needed to happen. He replied, "Dr. Michael, do you really want to learn to run?" "Yes," I replied, "it is something that I have wanted to do. I want to get healthy. Also your running means so much to you. It has brought you so much joy and pain. Maybe it would help me to understand things better." K suddenly straightened up in his chair. Eyes focused, he became animated. "Do you think so, Dr. Michael?" K asked. "What do you think?" I asked. "Yes, running is very good to be healthy," he replied. "I want to show you my running." K paused again, then said, "Dr. Michael, do you really want to learn to run?" "Yes, I do . . . as long as we don't go too fast." K burst out laughing. It was a deep, genuine, infectious laugh that would make anyone who heard it want to join in. We both laughed together. Once again, his eyes filled with tears. "No, no, Dr. Michael, not too fast. Step by step. When do you want to start?" "How about this Sunday," I said. K replied, "OK, this Sunday at 7 o'clock. We must start early." I thought to myself, *Well, here we go.*

This unorthodox intervention in therapy marked a dramatic shift in our working relationship. Many months later, on one of the training sessions, K commented on this particular moment. "I didn't think that I had anything to give. But when you asked me teach you, I felt like a human being again, that I had something to give to somebody else. It was a great honor for me. You are my doctor. I could not say no. It is good to run with someone whom I can trust and who knows my secrets. I ran in the past with music to try and drown out my thoughts with the sound. Now when we run together, we talk about many things. We laugh because sometimes you are very funny, Dr. Michael."

What I had done at that moment was affirm to K that he was not worthless, that in my eyes he had value and something important to give. Words would not have been enough. It was through showing up early that Sunday morning that I demonstrated to K that I recognized his gift as both a runner and a person. I also came to appreciate how truly gifted he was as an athlete and a teacher. From a cultural point of view, K considered it an honor to teach me. I was "Dr. Michael." The title bestowed on me, whether I was worthy of it or not, a certain status that commanded respect. During our training sessions, however, K was the expert. The power relationship achieved some balance. He gave me my weekly training schedule. Everything was carefully written down in broken English. Running on grass, doing "hillys," running through the forest. Fast, slow, long, short, up and down, and everything in between. He could tell the level of my fitness just by listening to the sound of my breathing. During those training sessions, I respected K's authority and status as a person who had devoted his life to his craft. Asylum seekers rarely have the opportunity to demonstrate their capacity to contribute to the quality of life for others. During those training runs, K was able to give something he valued within himself back to his doctor. His gifts were received with the greatest respect and in the spirit in which they were given. We both finished those early Sunday morning runs feeling empowered.

A new team began to take shape around K. It was a different team from what he had known before. All the members of this team were committed to fighting for his human rights. There was Helen Bamber, who gave evidence at his asylum appeal; two doctors, one of whom had documented K's scars and submitted a medical report, and the second who had identified that K suffered from temporal lobe epilepsy; and a psychotherapist, who was involved in helping K integrate into the community when he was granted his status. When K went to court, he told his story. He said, "I do not care what they decide. I have told my story, and people will now know the truth." K was recognized as a refugee. In all, it took 3 years for K's claim to be decided—an eternity in the life cycle of a runner. K paid a heavy price to run for freedom.

There was also growing recognition that K needed to find a way of building new relationships within the UK running community, relationships with people who could understand what it means to be a runner of his caliber, how to work with him, and, perhaps more important, how to help him regain his dignity as an athlete. I contacted the Sport Performance Assessment and Rehabilitation Centre (SPARC) at Roehampton University, and they agreed to assess him.

SPORT PSYCHOLOGY SUPPORT: DEARBHLA MCCULLOUGH

I was approached to work with K by the director of SPARC. All I knew at that stage was that Michael had contacted SPARC in the hope of obtaining support for K from consultants with expertise in sport science. Michael expressed that such support was critical to the reestablishment of K's social identity (see Amiot, Sablonniere, Terry, & Smith, 2007) as a runner and to the achievement of his goal of competing at the Beijing Olympics in 2008. The initial objectives of the sport psychology support staff were to assist K with his training and race goals.

I was aware from the outset that K was unable to pay for my support because of his refugee status. Michael had chosen not to disclose the full details of K's history beyond this information, fearing I would become overwhelmed and hence be put off becoming involved. K's status, however, together with the knowledge that he had been undergoing psychological treatment since his defection, gave me a clear indication that he had almost certainly experienced some level of trauma leading up to his defection. I felt compassion for his plight, which influenced my decision to offer my support pro bono. A further influencing factor was that he had been a successful international athlete from a sport in which I have been competing since the age of 10. I have a deep passion for running, and my involvement to this day is an important part of my own identity. I admired K for what he had achieved in my sport and for his commitment in trying to get back to that level despite his adverse circumstances. I also understood the difficulty in being able to achieve K's dreams without support and guidance. As a sport psychologist and fellow athlete, I felt a compulsion to help. I believed that my professional background, coupled with my knowledge, experience, and contacts within the running world, would be valuable in facilitating K's integration into the UK running community and to the subsequent achievement of his goals. I also thought my own background experiences and running identity would be advantageous in building a trusting alliance between us despite our cultural differences, because we would hold in common something that was near and dear to us both (Amiot et al., 2007). Running would become our common language.

My first encounter with K proved to be a greater challenge than I was prepared for. It was conducted, as are the majority of my first consultations, as a classic one-to-one interview. In something of a mirror of Michael's initial experience with K, he presented as an extremely nervous and apprehensive individual, and he made no eye contact with me throughout the session. My questions centered on his running experiences, but I managed to glean very little from him. He responded simply yes to almost every question I asked, even those that required an open response. K's standard of English was not something I had discussed with Michael, so I was unsure about whether he was struggling to understand me or was intimidated by the situation. Whatever the reason, I was feeling at a loss and doubtful about how to progress. Despite this feeling, I was moved by K's genuine willingness to be present and by the fact that he appeared to be working as hard as I was in trying to connect and make sense of what was happening. So, in the end, I resorted to writing distances from 1500 meters to marathon on paper in the hope that he would communicate his personal best times and dates in written form. This tactic proved to be a small breakthrough, and I felt it best to end the session at this point.

I was quite unprepared for the effect that this meeting would have on me. For the first time in my life, I had come face to face with the reality of what it means to be an asylum seeker in the UK, and it was a remarkably humbling experience. I was truly overwhelmed. My overriding feeling toward K was one of sadness for a man who, only a few years earlier, had been such a successful athlete but was now struggling to identify with a new culture and with his identity as an asylum seeker. Homelessness, poverty, fears for the future, insecurity, attachment difficulties, and identity crises have been highlighted as consequences of being a refugee (Silove, Steel, & Psychol, 2006). These problems were not something that I had fully appreciated until this point. In defecting, K had lost so much—his family, home, culture, lifestyle, running identity, and prospects for the future. He was suffering psychologically from these losses. My discussions with Michael after this first consultation were invaluable in helping me gain a better perspective on K's life. I understood how he had dealt with the UK protocols for asylum seekers, which had resulted in his life being put on hold for the past 3 years. He could neither work nor compete internationally without UK citizenship, and the lack of income and the poor living conditions were severely compromising his health and affecting his ability to train and compete at the level he was accustomed to. I also was made aware that K was experiencing psychological trauma as a result of his untold experiences prior to his defection.

I spent quite a bit of time questioning my capacity to help K. After the first consultation, I considered walking away on the basis that I saw no role for me at this stage of his rehabilitation. Despite my feelings of helplessness, I decided to continue supporting K. I just wanted to help in any way that I could. Michael's reassurance that everything was "going fine" was also fundamental to this decision. I was uncertain about how or where I could begin after what was evidently a poor start, but it was apparent that I needed to reevaluate my approach and the focus of support. K's sporting issues interconnected with the issues surrounding his life history and current situation. Thus his overall well-being was an important area to address. It seemed entirely inappropriate and futile, especially at this point, to focus solely on K's running needs by using a classic cognitive-behavioral performance-enhancement framework. So, rather than focusing on techniques such as goal setting, my priority became the life issues that were impinging on K's ability to race and train. In essence, Michael and I shared the same objectives but approached them in different ways. As a team, we were now focused on trying to improve the quality of K's overall life experience.

As with any client–practitioner alliance, my effectiveness in supporting K first hinged on developing a trusting relationship. At the same time, building a working alliance presented a major challenge in light of the complexity of K's situation and life experiences. I had learned from Michael about K's suspiciousness. He often doubted people's intentions—a state of mind that resulted from encounters both before and after his defection. Knowledge of his wariness, together with the language and cultural differences I had to confront in communicating with K, led me to question the efficacy of meeting with him in a formal one-on-one interview situation. I decided to take a more culturally sensitive (Davies & Webb, 2000) and flexible (Savin & Martinez, 2006) approach in my interactions with K by meeting him in locations where I thought he would feel most comfortable and in control, namely his sport and home environment.

My initial method for gaining trust from K was via Michael who, as the main provider of support, had developed a strong bond with him. If K saw me supporting him alongside Michael, whom he trusted whole-heartedly, then this connection might facilitate the development of our relationship. Therefore, I accompanied Michael to some of K's races. We were able to observe and discuss K's behavior and performance outcomes in light of his preparation and ongoing life issues. Michael became an important figure of support for me, especially in these initial months. He became the means by which I communicated with K, and he assisted in my understanding of K the person as well as K the athlete.

Two major turning points in gaining trust and acceptance from K stand out in my mind, and recalling them is emotive. They are the images I choose to remember K by rather than a different image of the agitated, distant, and vague individual I had previously encountered. The first was a chance meeting at the track where I complete a weekly training session. Although K was aware of my involvement in running, he had never seen me in this role. This coincidental meeting, which came about when K joined the track squad where I also trained, pro-vided him with an opportunity to view me beyond my role as his sport psychologist. His behavior toward me in this environment was mark-edly different than in our previous encounters. For the first time, he asked me questions and inquired about my training. He even offered me some coaching advice. Having a common social identity between practitioner and client has been identified in the cultural psychology literature as beneficial to the building of a trusting alliance (Amiot et al., 2007), and this common ground may explain why K's perception of me as a fellow athlete helped to cement our relationship.

The second occasion, which marked the most significant turning point in our relationship, occurred when a fellow sport scientist and I visited K's flat to help him decorate. This decision was a difficult one to make in view of the boundaries of applied sport psychology practice. Never-theless, having researched the cultural refugee literature on crossing therapeutic boundaries (Kroll, 2001; Savin & Martinez, 2006) and upon seeking advice from Michael, I decided that it would be of benefit to K and to the development of our professional relationship. However, in spite of Michael's having prepared us for what we would encounter, I was again confronted by the brutal reality of what it means to be a refu-gee in the UK. It was much worse than I had imagined. I found myself shocked and almost moved to tears by the depressing conditions that K was living in. I struggled to contain my feelings of pity toward him.

Papadopoulos (1999) drew attention to the difficulty for practitioners in working with clients who have experienced extreme adversity beyond being victims of trauma. In an attempt to prevent these feelings from clouding my perception of K, I tried to reappraise my view of him as a normal person in abnormal circumstances. This shift enabled me to appreciate more of his qualities as a person beyond his status as a refugee. K was a very proud host, and it was important to our relationship that I accepted his cultural hospitality. Savin and Martinez's (2006) research on cross-cultural boundary dilemmas highlights that such acceptance can be an indication to the client that the relationship is valued. K responded well to our visit, in which he disclosed much more of himself. This visit marked the first occasion where I saw him openly laugh. Later, we visited K's flat on a number of occasions, continuing to help him decorate, which further grounded our relationship. Michael brought to my attention that these visits were significant in facilitating K's adaptation and integration into UK society, because we had been the only White female UK guests to visit his flat.

The provision of tangible, informational, and emotional social support (Hardy & Crace, 1993) exemplified my role as sport psychologist over the course of my 2 years of working with K. Amiot et al. (2007) highlighted the significance of social support in facilitating the social identity integration process of immigrants. Moreover, Haslam, O'Brien, Jetten, Vormedal, and Penna (2005) provided evidence that social support has a "positive effect in attenuating stress when . . . provided by in-group members rather than out-group members" (p. 380). Even though in many ways I was an out-group member, it is my belief that sharing a common social identity with K as a runner was significant in facilitating his process of adaptation into the UK running community. In an attempt to ameliorate some of K's life and sporting issues, my social support centered on continuing to help him organize his flat, educating him about the structure of UK athletics, identifying races, and contacting race organizers to get race fees waived.

CONCLUSION

K was found dead in his flat 5 years after arriving in the UK. He was 25 years old. The most likely cause of death was a severe epileptic fit while sleeping. News of his untimely death came as an immense shock to all those who had known him. The members of the rehabilitation support team were no exception; we all found it tremendously difficult to accept. The tragedy of the situation was magnified in that life had become more stable for K in the months leading up to his death. He had at last been awarded UK citizenship, which meant that he was able to seek employment. More important, however, K was able to compete internationally. Time was no longer standing still! During this period, K had expressed an interest in becoming a personal trainer or coach for children and had found himself a girlfriend (something we only became aware of after his death). The direction of sport psychology support provided to K had reflected this stability as the focus had shifted toward guiding K with his competition goal setting and planning in the lead-up to selection for the Beijing Olympics.

It is poignant to remember throughout this case that no matter how much progress we had made with K in terms of his adaptation and integration into UK society, his traumatic history and refugee experiences were ever-present with him. His untimely death left us with overwhelming feelings of disbelief, sadness, anger, despair, and guilt. How can one come to terms with the loss of an exceptional human being and athlete, who had overcome so much adversity only for his life to be cut short at a time when it was becoming more coherent and fulfilling? Could we have done more to help him or indeed to prevent his death? Would he have achieved his ultimate goal of running in the Beijing Olympics in 2008? Evaluating the effectiveness of our interventions does not really get close to finding the answers to such questions. However, even an evaluation of effectiveness is difficult in a case as complex as K's. If effectiveness is measured in terms of sport performances, we can consider the fact that K had two exceptional races in the months before his death. Otherwise, though, his performances remained inconsistent. Since our holistic approach was aimed at improving the quality of K's overall life experience, a more appropriate measure of our effectiveness would involve his interpersonal skill development. K was beginning to contemplate life outside of running, which demonstrates his level of adaptation and ability to feel part of a new community. To us, K had come far in his capacity to cope with the complexities of ordinary life and appeared to have started to find some happiness in life. This is how we choose to remember him.

IDEAS FOR REFLECTION AND DEBATE

1. Consider the ethical challenges uncovered in this essay and reflect how you might have dealt with the situation yourself.

2. Working alongside a psychologist from a different disciplinary background is central to the story. Consider how the two approaches house different techniques and processes, then reflect on how those differences might be shared with other sport psychologists through training and pedagogy.

3. Both practitioners took risks as part of their interventions, and in both cases the risks appeared to bear fruit. Where in the story do you identify risk, and what ethical considerations do you feel might be invoked by such actions?

REFERENCES

American Psychiatric Association. (2000). *Diagnostic and statistical manual of mental disorders* (4th ed., text rev.). Washington, DC: Author.

Amiot, C.E., Sablonniere, R., Terry, D., & Smith, J.R. (2007). Integration of social identities in the self: Toward a cognitive-developmental model. *Personality and Social Psychology Review, 11,* 364–388.

Burnett, A., & Peel, M. (2001). Asylum seekers and refugees in Britain: Health needs of asylum seekers and refugees. *British Medical Journal, 3,* 544–547.

Corlett, J. (1996). Sophistry, Socrates, and sport psychology. *The Sport Psychologist, 10,* 84–94.

Davies, M., & Webb, E. (2000). Promoting the psychological well-being of refugee children. *Clinical Child Psychology and Psychiatry, 5,* 541–554.

Eisenbruch, M. (1991). From post-traumatic stress disorder to cultural bereavement: Diagnosis of Southeast Asian refugees. *Social Science and Medicine, 33,* 673–680.

Friedman, M.J., & Marsella, A.J. (1996). Post-traumatic stress disorder: An overview of the concept. In A.J. Marsella, M.J. Friedman, E.T. Gerrity, & R.M. Scurfield (Eds.), *Ethnocultural aspects of post-traumatic stress disorder: Issues, research, and clinical applications* (pp. 11–30). Washington, DC: American Psychological Association.

Hardy, C.J., & Crace, R.K. (1993). The dimensions of social support when dealing with sports injuries. In D. Pargman (Ed.), *Psychological bases of sport injuries* (pp. 121–144). Morgantown, WV: Fitness Information Technology.

Haslam, S.A., O'Brien, A., Jetten, J., Vormedal, K., & Penna, S. (2005). Taking the strain: Social identity, social support, and the experience of stress. *British Journal of Social Psychology, 44,* 355–370.

Herman, J. (1992). Complex PTSD. *Journal of Traumatic Stress, 5,* 377–391.

Human Rights Watch. (2007). *Ethiopia: Events of 2006.* www.hrw.org/legacy/englishwr2k7/docs/2007/01/11/ethiop14704.htm.

Jung, C.G. (1963). *Memories, dreams, and reflections.* London: Routledge.

Korac, M. (2003). Integration and how we facilitate it: A comparative study of the settlement experiences of refugees in Italy and the Netherlands. *Sociology, 37,* 51–68.

Korzinski, M. (1997). Mind and body: *The treatment of the sequelae of torture using a combined somatic and psychological approach.* Unpublished doctoral dissertation, The Union Institute, Cincinnati, OH.

Kroll. J. (2001). Boundary violations: A culture-bound syndrome. *Journal of the American Academy of Psychiatry and the Law, 29,* 274–283.

Papadopoulos, R. (1999). Working with Bosnian medical evacuees and their families: Therapeutic dilemmas. *Clinical Child Psychology and Psychiatry, 4, 107–120.*

Savin, D., & Martinez, R. (2006). Cross-cultural and boundary dilemmas: A graded-risk assessment approach. *Transcultural Psychiatry, 43,* 243–258.

Silove, D. (1999). The psychological effects of torture, mass human rights violations and refugee trauma: Toward an integrated conceptual framework. *Journal of Nervous and Mental Disease, 187,* 200–207.

Silove, D., Steel, Z., & Psychol, M. (2006). Understanding community psychosocial needs after disasters: Implications for mental services. *Journal of Postgraduate Medicine, 52,* 121–125.

PLAYFUL DEVIANCE

William B. Strean
University of Alberta, Canada

DJ Williams
Idaho State University, United States

Play is an exultation of the possible.
  Martin Buber

In the training of sport psychologists, and in the sport psychology literature in general, little attention is paid to playfulness and even less to deviance. In this chapter, Billy and DJ undertake a journey of their own through reference to autoethnography and ethnographic explorations of the theme of playful deviance in diverse fields of work and play, including sport psychology, criminology, social work, and the underground world of bondage and discipline and sadomasochism (BDSM).

INTRODUCTION

Our academic and professional lives occur inside many boundaries. The lines and scripts for behavior are often pervasive yet transparent. We forget to notice the guidelines that dictate what is appropriate or acceptable. Are you not fucking convinced? Perhaps that kind of breach of language is a shocking example of how we are always one step away from being outside what is tolerable.

Perhaps the simplest definition of deviance we can offer, and it may be a simplistic one as well, is based on the notion of that which moves away from or is outside of the norm. If we are to grow and progress in the discipline and practice of sport psychology, we might benefit from some deviance. Some garden varieties of deviant behavior may be motivated by a wish to be different for the sake of attention or thrills. We propose that playfully stepping outside of what is currently mainstream can help us expand possibilities and improve the quality of what we do.

In terms of academic undertakings, we are sympathetic to Sparkes' (2002) notion about "displacing (traditional) research tales, but not simplistically discarding [them]" (p. xi). We believe that placing a Mona Lisa smile on your face and exploring novel and uncharted ways of pursuing new ideas and understandings are both refreshing and beneficial for the growth of the field.

Similarly, when doing applied work, we see great value in looking beyond the typical menu of interventions and experimenting with adaptations from the wide world of methods and concepts that have been used to help people find greater satisfaction and results. Rather than deepen the conceptual rationale for playful deviance, we elect here to share some examples of our own musings and trials in hope of demonstrating the outcomes.

> *Play seems to be the essential feature in productive scientific thought—before there is any connection with logical construction in words or other kinds of signs that can be communicated to others.*
>
> Albert Einstein

PLAYFUL RESEARCH DEVIANCE

Just as Elton John asked us to remember when rock was young ("Me and Susie had so much fun"), we recall when qualitative research was deviant. Perhaps it is still somewhat deviant, but it has certainly come to occupy a much larger part of the scope of sport psychology research than it did in 1990, as a graduate student at Illinois, I (Billy) organized a symposium on qualitative research at the North American Society for the Psychology of Sport and Physical Activity with Tara Scanlan and Harold Levine, both of UCLA. My foray into qualitative research involved a desire to pursue what rang true for me based on my background in general philosophy, philosophy of science, and research methodology. I also liked challenging the status quo in hopes of creating new possibilities. There are many ways to diverge from what is tried and true. It is easy to be argumentative, belligerent, or aggressive in attempting to justify an alternative. I found that a more playful and possibility-oriented approach was more productive and fun. I credit some of my qualitative research cohorts at Illinois in bringing forward the ideas that led to a paper by my mentor (Peshkin, 1993) and my sport psychology–specific paper (Strean, 1998) on the possibilities of qualitative research.

In addressing how to be playfully deviant, we might do well to consider personal and environmental variables. My dad was something of an iconoclast, and as I developed I'm sure I was rewarded when I questioned authority and traditional approaches to solving problems. An environment that supports such play is important for fostering an ability to draw outside the lines. My doctoral supervisor, Glyn Roberts, also enjoyed provocative questions and was supportive of my interest in doing something relatively untried in sport psychology research at the time.

As I moved from graduate school to my early phases of life as an academic, I continued to stray from the beaten path (though using such a cliché suggests conformity). I continued to pursue various qualitative methodologies, and I encouraged graduate students working with me to do the same. Sometimes, deviance includes returning to what was once mainstream but had fallen out of vogue; my exploration of psychodynamic psychotherapy applications to sport psychology (Strean & Strean, 1998, 2005) certainly was not following along with what I was hearing at conferences or reading in journals. This kind of playful deviance can resurrect useful ideas that have been discarded prematurely or excessively. My openness to new approaches and perspectives has helped graduate students move into narrative inquiry and autoethnography (Olsen, 2008; Williams, 2004).

Just as qualitative methods were once considered deviant, autoethnography, specifically, may be considered by many to be a deviant form of research. Unlike many traditional methods, autoethnography is an experience-near form of research. The researcher highlights multiple roles and identities within a single individual (the researcher) rather than insist on neutrality or objectivity. It is precisely the creative use of narrative, however, blurring identities and constructed social boundaries, that gives autoethnography its utility and power as a research approach. Although many methods lead to the construction of categories and the reinforcement of boundaries, autoethnography speaks to the other and emphasizes our common humanness. It is beyond the scope of this chapter to delve into a full presentation regarding the methodology of autoethnography, and we refer readers to the work of others for a more thorough discussion of this approach (i.e., Boch-ner, 1997; Ellis, 2004; Ellis & Bochner, 2000; Giles & Williams, 2007; Sparkes, 2000, 2002, 2003). Suffice it to say that autoethnography is now being applied within a number of social science disciplines. Once again, academics are witnessing the normalization of a deviant research approach.

WHAT BDSM CAN TEACH US ABOUT SPORT PSYCHOLOGY

After discovering and using autoethnography as a doctoral student mentored by Billy, I (DJ) wondered about how it might further knowl-edge on various unconventional topics. I had discovered that autoeth-nography helps bridge the "us versus them" chasm between offenders and law-abiding citizens (Williams, 2006), and Billy had encouraged making both research and practice playful and fun. Still, I wondered about marginalized people who live unconventional lives that centered on noncriminal forms of playful deviance. Could autoethnography be applied to further knowledge about alternative erotic lifestyles? What might I learn about being an embodied person? Are there discoveries yet to be made from practices that center on unconventional ways of relating to one's body and how we are socialized to understand our-selves and our bodies?

Some of my research focused on sexual offenders and their leisure patterns, but what about those who engaged in specific erotic forms of noncriminal and consensual deviance, such as bondage–discipline, dominance–submission, and sadism–masochism (BDSM)? A thorough review of the literature convincingly demonstrates that although BDSM participants commonly are perceived as having psychopathology, which according to traditional psychiatry apparently causes their unusual practices, these people don't seem to be any more psychopathological than the general population (e.g., Baumeister, 1991; Connelly, 2006; Richters, de Visser, Rissel, Grulich, & Smith, 2008; Sandnabba, Santilla, Alison, & Nordling, 2002; Weinberg, 2006). Despite research show-ing that many BDSM participants are not psychologically disturbed, researchers who investigate such phenomena tend to study from a distance without participating (or without acknowledging it if they do participate). It seemed to me, however, that insights might be gained by studying BDSM as a participant. Taking Billy's perspective that research can be fun, I gave myself permission to enter the unfamiliar world of BDSM, potentially to explore it autoethnographically. From a scholarly perspective, I figured it might be interesting and rather enjoyable to explore carefully my own physical and psychological reactions to getting tied up, spanked, whipped, "tortured," and so forth by a sexy expert (my subjective view of what is sexy) in that business. Now, I'm a little embarrassed that I didn't think of it sooner.

Over the past few years I have worked with several professional mistresses and masters and attended numerous BDSM community play parties. Rather than simply observe, I have often been a willing participant. The activities I have chosen to engage in were carefully evaluated and selected with an emphasis on safety and mutual consent.

I have learned some interesting lessons, including coming face to face with the common fallacy rooted in religion and psychiatry that BDSM practitioners must be particularly dangerous, psychopathological, and perhaps necessarily immoral. Through exploring BDSM firsthand, I have more appreciation for my body and seem to be in better tune with it. I am more aware of the tremendous diversity of acute sensations that my body can feel and how I may respond to them. At the same time I am far more aware of the depth and pervasiveness of my socialization. Some sensory experiences that are often thought of as being painful can simultaneously be intense but pleasurable; thus pain doesn't seem to be an adequate description of such experience. Fakir Musafar (in a film by Gary & Jacobsen, 2005) maintains that "there is no such thing as pain, only intense physical sensation." In many common social spaces, discourse with roots in Western, Judeo-Christian culture doesn't seem to map personal BDSM experience very well. And I have wondered how well I really understand what others, particularly those with backgrounds different from my own, are trying to communicate. I have also found that BDSM activities powerfully link various personal identities to embodied experiences, and many of these experiences I describe as being spiritual. They have served to nourish an appreciation for human creativity, deep interpersonal connections, social diversity, and self-expression.

BDSM practitioners are common people who seem to value creative play that involves controlled sensory manipulation (stimulation or deprivation) and the acting out of fantasies. Such activity entails the adult responsibility of maintaining physical and psychological safety among participants even as it is infused with the nature of childhood in that creative play is valued and embraced. BDSM practitioners often recognize that people feel sensations differently and that behaviors may be experienced and interpreted differently.

As people in our society approach adulthood, they are socialized away from participation in the childhood world of play. At the same time, our culture teaches us to avoid discussion of sexuality and eroticism, despite the fact that these are important aspects of our humanness. Both of these social messages can be damaging to people, yet constructed boundaries are tightened and reinforced.

Understandably, many BDSM participants remain in the closet regarding their participation in their worlds of playful deviance. For a time, I struggled with the question of whether or not to reveal my participation, and I have been cautioned by some academics against writing about my experiences. No doubt there have been some repercussions, but there have also been positive effects. Still, I believe that progress does not occur unless there are people who speak out, and as a scholar on deviant leisure I am in a position to do so (unlike participants in many other professions). At a recent workshop I gave to a large group of BDSM practitioners on the subject of BDSM and social psychology, I asked members to raise their hands if they would be willing to disclose their lives to a clinician, such as their medical doctor, psychotherapist, counselor, or social worker. Not one hand went up. Several participants expressed concerns about facing discrimination by helping professionals, which is a legitimate fear.

BDSM participants represent a wide range of people and occupations. They work as business people, educators, laborers, lawyers, doctors, nurses, and architects. The motivations for participation in BDSM seem to be varied and complex. I am aware of one professional athlete who sees a mistress, apparently to help him better focus his mind through the distractions of carefully administered pain. I doubt that his sport psychologist is aware of his unorthodox supplementary training, yet he insists on its effectiveness. Of course, the work of professional athletes directly involves use of their bodies, and they tend to be acutely aware of various sensory experiences. Athletes may also have access to potential erotic play partners and the financial means to obtain alternative erotic psychological and sensory experiences; it would not surprise us if BDSM participation in one form or another is a little more common among top-level athletes than it is in the general population. Perhaps this topic is a future research project.

Outside of professional sport, I am also aware of a clergyman who sees a mistress from time to time as a means of playing out specific aspects of his Christian beliefs, and it is important to this client that actual physical sensation be a part of the role play. For him, BDSM seems to help deepen the meaning and purpose in his life. For him, adding carefully planned sacrificial pain through BDSM seems to add a physical (sensory) dimension to his religious understanding. My experiences with BDSM communities and professional mistresses and masters suggest that many individuals apparently use BDSM for enjoyment and self-expression and as a way to relieve stress. Others sometimes use it as a reward when certain personal and professional goals are achieved (behavioral reinforcement).

The examples I have included illustrate different ways in which some people already use BDSM as a component of performance psychology. Sport psychology may benefit by recognizing the tremendous range of human beliefs and practices, by reevaluating practices that are assumed to be psychopathological but are probably not, and by considering creative interventions to help specific clients achieve their goals. If sport psychologists are to become increasingly effective in helping diverse clients, we may need to be more open, flexible, and supportive for people whose lives may be nontraditional.

We have offered here some of our own examples of playful deviance in our research lives. What we advocate is that our field grows, expands, and moves forward more quickly when we are willing to have some fun and try new things. Academia is infamous for its conservative nature, and we are all familiar with Kuhn's notions of the structure of scientific revolutions. It takes maverick scientists to break out of a way of thinking that has nearly exhausted its usefulness. George Bernard Shaw suggested, "The reasonable man adapts himself to the world. The unreasonable one persists in trying to adapt the world to himself. Therefore all progress depends on the unreasonable man" (Cohen & Cohen, 1998, p. 388). In this sense, we advocate being unreasonable, which can mean freeing ourselves from reasons not to try something new. It seems much of our research activity as a field shows a reluctance to embrace newer methodologies and divergent ways of considering what constitutes knowledge. Injecting some more monkey business into our cerebral practices and investigative adventures may serve us well in seeking out new ideas and understandings. We encourage you, in the spirit of *Star Trek,* to muster both the fearlessness to split an infinitive and the courage to move into uncharted research territory: "To boldly go where no one has gone before." (If you are still reading this chapter after tales of BDSM, you have gone boldly and will be rewarded with some tales of our work with clients.)

APPLIED PRACTICE

As in the research realm, we have discovered much value in straying from the norm in our work with athletes and coaches. For starters, like many of my (Billy's) friends and colleagues who pursued sport psychology because of a passion to work with athletes, I found myself in a graduate program that almost exclusively prepared me as a researcher while doing little to aid my development as an applied practitioner. For a variety of reasons, including expanding my armamentarium of methods to intervene with athletes, I completed a program to become a certified professional co-active coach with the Coaches Training Institute. The co-active model (Whitworth, Kimsey-House, Kimsey-House, & Sandahl, 2007) holds that clients are creative, resourceful, and whole and that they have or can find answers to most of their own problems and challenges. The paradigm also involves addressing the client's whole life and taking the approach that the client brings the agenda. Such concepts are not unique, but they expanded the mental skills approach and the orientation of sport psychology practice that provides answers to client-athletes, which I had learned in graduate school. Co-activity formed a new umbrella for my applied work. It also brought new skills that enabled me to work with athletes on nonperformance issues with greater ease and grace.

A further step from the tried and true in sport psychology practice emerged for me in my pursuit of studies in somatics at the Strozzi Institute. A detailed account of how somatics (from *soma*, thus approaching, examining, and working with the *body* in its wholeness) can be applied in sport psychology is covered in a recent article (Strean & Strozzi-Heckler, 2009). For our purposes here, we offer a synopsis of the approach with a focus on how it may exemplify playful deviance. Although some areas in sport psychology discourse consider emotions and the body in useful ways, much of what we do as a field reproduces dualistic approaches to body and mind or heavily privileges cognition as a means for intervention. Part of playful deviance entails having a notion that either something isn't quite right or something better is possible. In my studies of professional (life) coaching, I came across some somatic methods and ways of thinking about the body and working with and through the body that held great promise. By studying somatics, learning somatic sensibilities, and using specific techniques and practices (e.g., somatic bodywork, centering, new forms of attention training), I found more powerful and effective ways to help athletes enhance performance. I also found these methods especially effective in working with other areas of clients' lives.

Somewhere along my deviant path, I came to see that much of what I had learned and seen in sport psychology was transactional. That is, we did something to help athletes do something differently. What I saw through the combination of coaching and somatics was how to take a more transformational approach and help athletes to *shift the self that they are.*

Another element of what may influence the playful deviance of your two authors here is a shared background in social work values. Billy sometimes says, "I would not be here today if it were not for social work. Both of my parents were social workers." DJ picked up a master's degree in social work prior to his doctoral studies and has taught in the field of social work as a nascent academic. At the heart of our playful deviance, then, there may well be some deep abiding sense that the purpose of our research and practice is fundamentally to help make life better, especially for those who may be disadvantaged. We have researched topics such as fun in kids' sports, solution-focused physical education, recreation with juvenile delinquents, and promotion of physical activity within social work because we wanted to help reduce some suffering and enhance quality of life for people with challenges.

LESSONS LEARNED FROM SOCIAL WORK, FORENSICS, AND PLAYING WITH BAD GUYS

The strong influence of social work values such as social justice, self-determination, the importance of human relationships, and service to help make life better for others were taught and modeled to Billy by his parents. Although my (DJ's) work is interdisciplinary, most of my university teaching has been in social work departments.

One of the salient features of social work is its overt reliance on a generalist approach. Although most disciplines focus on specialization, social work begs, borrows, and steals (i.e., crosses boundaries) from related disciplines. The field of social work incorporates knowledge from multiple disciplines to inform specific social work issues. Of course, other fields also incorporate outside knowledge to some degree. We like this flexibility. We believe sport psychology can retain key purposes and functions that distinguish it as a profession even as we increase our openness to incorporating knowledge from a broader range of fields. People (including athletes) and their issues are complex, and knowledge from multiple sources may be useful in understanding and effectively addressing diverse human problems and issues.

My practice experience as a forensic social worker has taught me that, contrary to media and movie portrayals of offenders as something akin to monsters or animals, people in the criminal justice system are also diverse and complex. My clinical work with hundreds of people in the criminal justice system has taught me that offenders tend to be regular people and that rigid boundaries constructed to categorize people are just that—rigid, constructed categories. Although "us (law-abiding citizens) versus them (criminals)" distinctions are commonly assumed as valid, social psychology research, including the classic Stanford Prison Experiment, shows that ordinary, asymptomatic people can quickly dehumanize others. Despite such research, prison policy within the United States has become more punitive (Haney & Zimbardo, 1998).

Perhaps nowhere are "us versus them" barriers greater than with respect to sexual offenders, who are commonly portrayed as predators motivated primarily by deviant fantasies. Interestingly, the term "sexual predator" began to appear in print in 1987 and its use drastically increased during the 1990s (Jenkins, 1998). Of course, incidences of sexual offending are disturbing and unacceptable, yet this social issue has turned into a moral panic (see Neuilly & Zgoba, 2006). Sex offenders are assumed to be a homogeneous group who are incapable of avoiding reoffense. Such myths about sexual offenders are pervasive, even among clinicians and law enforcement professionals, and strongly influence public policy (see a thorough review in Quinn, Forsyth, & Mullen-Quinn, 2004).

Research shows that sex offenders do not have particularly high rates of reoffense. For example, Alexander (1999) conducted a meta-analysis that included 79 studies and represented nearly 11,000 sex offenders. Results showed that offenders who participated in relapse prevention treatment had a re-arrest rate of 7.2%, compared to 17.6% for untreated offenders. In their comprehensive review of the sexual offender treatment literature, Marshall, Marshall, and Serran (2006) concluded that, consistent with other reviews, sex offender treatment is effective in reducing recidivism. They also suggest that increased beneficial effect might be achieved by improving therapeutic relationships with offender clients and developing innovative treatment strategies.

As a forensic social worker, I have seen many clients, both sex offenders and other classifications of offenders, develop empathy for others and change their own lives. I have had more success in working with clients in correctional settings as I have become more empathic toward them and more creative in applying a broader range of potential interventions. Several times, I have used examples from sport and physical activity to help clients who have such interests in understanding rehabilitation concepts. I have also suggested participation in specific leisure activities, including physical activity and sport, for specific clients who were motivated to participate and were working through clinical issues that might be partially resolved through meaningful leisure and physical activity. Several of these cases resulted in psychotherapeutic success. Applying leisure programming and exercise psychology principles to mainstream correctional therapy, however, is considered by many to be quite deviant.

I am convinced on the basis of both research and clinical experience that working to understand the diverse needs of others, applying creative interventions that address specific needs of individual clients, and nurturing empathy are far better strategies for reducing crime and victimization than are building more prisons and incarcerating large numbers of people.

LABELING AND OTHER INSANITY FROM DR. DEVIANT

I (DJ) have been fortunate in my career to spend considerable time in a wide range of social settings and communities. Of course, a number of scholars have spent time learning about criminal deviance, but probably few have had the privilege of receiving training from highly respected professional mistresses and masters or hanging out (both figuratively and literally) with radical body modification artists. It's been an educational experience, and I've had lots of fun. Still, outsiders may refer to members of several deviant groups, me included, perhaps somewhat jokingly, as "insane." Nevertheless, the colloquial distinction of "sane–insane" does not hold credibility when simple social convention is assumed to be the distinguisher.

As noted earlier, "normal" and "deviant" tend to be embedded, but we often see them as being separate. Rather than pair deviance with insanity, psychological instability, or some similar term, it is more useful to consider issues involving ethics, safety, mutual consent, and empathy in evaluating the tolerance of what we see as normal and deviant behaviors and practices. I don't perceive jumping out of an airplane while wearing a parachute and being connected to an experienced jumper to be insane or crazy. Nor is it necessarily crazy to hang a few feet off the ground from flesh hooks safely and carefully inserted by experienced modifiers. For some, it can be freeing, enlightening, and fun. Personally, it seems crazier to avoid participating in activities that, although unusual, are secretively and genuinely desired and may be meaningful and enriching. Taking some calculated risks—for clients, practitioners, and researchers—can be a good thing.

Finally, we remind readers of strong tendencies toward "othering" those who do not fit the norm. Perhaps as a pun, "other insanity" might refer to a rigid insistence on marginalizing people we perceive as being radically different from ourselves. Although each of us is unique, human beings still have much in common. Billy's wise dad liked to paraphrase Harry Stack Sullivan by saying, "People are far more human than otherwise." We and our clients can be unique, diverse, and interesting, but we're all a complicated mix of light and dark.

CONCLUSION

As we asserted with respect to research, we have given examples in which we have seen different approaches to applied work pay dividends for our clients. Given the uniqueness and artistry necessary to be effective practitioners, we hope to encourage our readers to swing out and try some approaches that are distinct from what has been previously done.

We admit to finding (perverse) pleasure at times in standing outside of the norm. DJ perhaps has demonstrated this stance in the extreme. We want to be clear that our advocacy is not essentially about being devilish but being grounded in Wittgenstein's bottom line of "what does this accomplish?" We believe that your life as an academic and as a practitioner will be a lot more fun if you play and try new ideas and practices. We are unabashed proponents of fun and we contend that our field will be more vibrant and will contribute more to the health and happiness of those we serve if our members are having a good time and being inventive. Furthermore, we suggest that our progress depends on people having the moxie to delve into the unpopular and unsupported regions of knowledge and practice.

IDEAS FOR REFLECTION AND DEBATE

1. What were your initial intellectual and emotional responses when the topic of BDSM came up in this essay? By the end of the essay, what did you think?

2. The authors could have easily have written about voodoo and voodoo dolls. Such fetish objects are most commonly made for positive purposes rather than for the Hollywood version of sticking pins in them to cause others pain. They were made for protection, love, health, and many other positive purposes. What are some variations of voodoo dolls that you might use in applied sport psychology, and why? Or why not?

3. The Roman playwright Terence wrote, "*Homo sum, humani nihil a me alienum puto*" (I am a man, and nothing human is alien to me). How do you respond to this statement as a professional (and as a person) in light of this essay?

4. How do you play with your athletes and coaches? What purpose does that play serve?

5. How might you be deviant in your practice? How would you defend that deviance?

REFERENCES

Alexander, M.A. (1999). Sexual offender treatment efficacy revisited. *Sexual Abuse: A Journal of Research and Treatment, 11,* 101-117.

Baumeister, R. (1991). *Escaping the self.* New York: Basic Books.

Bochner, A.P. (1997). It's about time: Narrative and the divided self. *Qualitative Inquiry, 3,* 418–438.

Cohen, J.M., & Cohen, M.J. (Eds.). (1998). *The new Penguin dictionary of quotations.* London: Penguin Books.

Connelly, P.H. (2006). Psychological functioning of bondage/domination/sadomasochism (BDSM) practitioners. *Journal of Psychology and Human Sexuality, 18,* 79–120.

Ellis, C. (2004). *The ethnographic I: A methodological novel about autoethnography.* Walnut Creek, CA: AltaMira Press.

Ellis, C., & Bochner, A.P. (2000). Autoethnography, personal narrative, reflexivity. In N.K. Denzin & Y.S. Lincoln (Eds.), *Handbook of qualitative research* (pp. 733–768). Thousand Oaks, CA: Sage.

Gary, J. (Director), & Jacobsen, G. (Director). (2005). *Modify* [Motion picture]. United States: Committed Films.

Giles, A.R., & Williams, D.J. (2007). Are we afraid of our selves? Self-narrative research in leisure studies. *World Leisure, 49,* 189–198.

Haney, C., & Zimbardo, P. (1998). The past and future of U.S. prison policy: Twenty-five years after the Stanford Prison Experiment. *American Psychologist, 53,* 709–727.

Jenkins, P. (1998). *Moral panic: Changing concepts of the child molester in modern America.* New Haven, CT: Yale University Press.

Marshall, W.L., Marshall, L.E., & Serran, G.A. (2006). Strategies in the treatment of paraphilias: A critical review. *Annual Review of Sex Research, XVII,* 162–182.

Neuilly, M.A., & Zgoba (2006). Assessing the possibility of a pedophilia panic and contagion effect between France and the United States. *Victims and Offenders, 1,* 225-254.

Olsen, K.R. (2008). *Transcending fear and personal barriers: A narrative inquiry into the lived experience of skydiving.* Unpublished master's thesis, University of Alberta, Edmonton, Canada.

Peshkin, A. (1993). The goodness of qualitative research. *Educational Researcher, 22*(2), 23–29.

Quinn, J.F., Forsyth, C.J., & Mullen-Quinn, C. (2004). Societal reaction to sex offenders: A review of the origins and results of the myths surrounding their crimes and treatment amenability. *Deviant Behavior, 25,* 215–232.

Richters, J., de Visser, R.O., Rissel, C.E., Grulich, A.E., & Smith, A.M.A. (2008). Demographic and psychosocial features of participants in bondage and discipline, "sadomasochism" or dominance and submission (BDSM): Data from a national survey. *Journal of Sexual Medicine, 5,* 1660–1668.

Sandnabba, N.K., Santilla, P., Alison, L., & Nordling, N. (2002). Demographics, sexual behavior, family background and abuse experiences of practitioners of sadomasochistic sex: A review of recent research. *Journal of Sexual and Relationship Therapy, 17,* 39–55.

Sparkes, A.C. (2000). Autoethnography and narratives of self: Reflections on criteria in action. *Sociology of Sport Journal, 17,* 21–43.

Sparkes, A.C. (2002). *Telling tales in sport and physical activity: A qualitative journey.* Champaign, IL: Human Kinetics.

Sparkes, A.C. (2003). Bodies, identities, selves: Autoethnographic fragments and reflections. In J. Denison & P. Markula (Eds.), *Moving writing: Crafting movement and sport research* (pp. 51–76). New York: Lang.

Strean, W.B. (1998). Possibilities for qualitative research in sport psychology. *The Sport Psychologist, 12,* 333–345.

Strean, W.B, & Strean, H.S. (1998). Applying psychodynamic concepts to sport psychology practice. *The Sport Psychologist, 12,* 208–222.

Strean, W.B., & Strean, H.S. (2005). Commentary on chapter 10. In M.B. Andersen (Ed.). *Sport psychology in practice* (pp. 193–198). Champaign, IL: Human Kinetics

Strean, W.B., & Strozzi-Heckler, R. (2009). (The) Body (of) Knowledge: Somatic contributions to sport psychology. *Journal of Applied Sport Psychology, 21,* 91–98.

Weinberg, T.S. (2006). Sadomasochism and the social sciences: A review of the sociological and social psychological literature. *Journal of Homosexuality, 50*(2/3), 17–40.

Whitworth, L., Kimsey-House, K., Kimsey-House, H., & Sandahl, P. (2007*). Co-active coaching: New skills for coaching people toward success in work and life.* Mountain View, CA: Davies-Black.

Williams, DJ. (2004). *Release from the "us vs. them" prison: Granting freedom by giving voice to multiple identities within physical activity and offender rehabilitation.* Unpublished doctoral dissertation, University of Alberta, Edmonton, Canada.

Williams, DJ. (2006). Autoethnography in offender rehabilitation research and practice: Addressing the "us vs. them" problem. *Contemporary Justice Review, 9,* 23–38.

ESSAY 9

SPORT PSYCHOLOGY SERVICES ARE MULTICULTURAL ENCOUNTERS:

Differences as Strengths in Therapeutic Relationships

Stephanie J. Hanrahan
University of Queensland, Australia

In this essay, Stephanie argues that cultural applied sport psychology research and practice have some serious limitations. Her case is built on the notion that whenever a sport psychologist and athlete sit down together (regardless of whether they come from different cultures or the same culture), two different worlds start to approach each other. Stephanie develops this theme by offering examples and illustrations relating to race, gender, and sexuality; she explores these issues in building rapport and forming relationships, which she views as "the core of any sport psychologist–athlete encounter."

INTRODUCTION

Cultural sport psychology research is limited, often superficial, and prone to sensitive and respectful stereotyping. Cross-cultural research in sport psychology typically compares questionnaire responses from athletes identified as being from culture X with responses from athletes identified as being from culture Y. Although it is heartening to see researchers in the field recognize that not everyone is the same and that culture can influence how we think, feel, and behave, this structure of comparing X to Y inaccurately suggests that all members of a given culture are generally similar to each other and measurably different from people in other cultures. The official viewpoint of the American Anthropological Association is that "evidence from the analysis of genetics (e.g., DNA) indicates that most physical variation lies within so-called racial groups. This means that there is greater variation within 'racial' groups than between them" (1998). This same argument can be applied to groupings of individuals by religion, nationality, gender, sexual orientation, disability, sport, or level of competition (e.g., "elite athletes"). The variability between individuals from a given culture is assuredly greater than the differences between groups.

How does one even determine to which culture a given individual should be compartmentalized? A simplistic example is one of Black and White. When a child has one parent who is Black and the other who is White, is the child Black or White? What happens when that person grows up and has a child with someone who had an Asian mother and a Hispanic father? Based on an Australian High Court ruling to describe and define an Australian Aboriginal person (Dean, 1984), people are members of a particular culture if they identify themselves as such and are recognized by that cultural community as being a member.

Race and ethnicity are only two aspects of culture. Cultural diversity also involves age, gender, national origin, religion, sexual orientation, (dis)ability, language, and socioeconomic status. Culturally competent (and ethical) practitioners collect and then apply information "about client differences to help develop an effective consulting relationship and to implement interventions that will likely be useful to the person(s) with whom [they] are working" (Watson, Etzel, & Loughran, 2006, p. 25).

CULTURAL AWARENESS: SELF AND OTHER

Some practitioners may consider themselves to be "enlightened" because they are not racist or sexist or homophobic; they do not believe that race, gender, or sexual orientation accounts for differences in human character or ability or that a particular race, gender, or sexual orientation is superior to others. They believe it is good practice to treat everyone the same, because all people are alike regardless of culture. Being color or culture blind, however, ignores the effect that culture can have on norms, values, beliefs, and behaviors. One could argue that racists or homophobes are culturally aware. They are aware that people are different, but they negatively stereotype all individuals they identify as being part of a cultural group as having specific characteristics or abilities that are inferior to their own. Aside from the inferiority bit, this stance is no different from practitioners who assume that most all clients' problems come from membership in a (probably oppressed) cultural or racial minority group.

Yes, as practitioners we need to be culturally aware—aware of the culture of our clients as well as aware of our own cultural values, stereotypes, and biases. For some of us, self-awareness also means being aware of the benefits of belonging to the dominant culture (e.g., White privilege). Members of a dominant culture may not know what it is like to feel out of place, to have one's occupation or sport of choice questioned, or to have athletic performance attributed to natural ability with no recognition of effort just because one looks different than the majority. Nor might they recognize the value of being able to freely work, study, or play without being considered exotic or being looked at with suspicion as if they might commit a crime. The next time you go to the grocery store or are sitting at a bus stop (i.e., have the opportunity to "people watch"), ask yourself how you would feel if the different people you see were the partner of a loved one or arrived at your house when you called a locksmith. To what do you attribute any variance in feelings? What judgments might we all be making when interacting with others? Are these judgments suspended (or suppressed) when we work with clients?

To be a culturally sensitive practitioner, one needs to be aware of and responsive to the attitudes, feelings, and circumstances of people from other cultures. We have the responsibility of developing the necessary skills to be competent when working with people from cultures other than ours or to make appropriate referrals. We all are, or will be, working with people from a variety of cultural backgrounds. With the globalization of society, there are few (or, I would argue, no) sporting teams with members from only one culture. To be effective practitioners, we need to be aware of factors that are part of clients' (and our own) cultural identities. Objective elements of culture are often the most obvious. We have all made cultural references when discussing where to go out for dinner (e.g., Chinese, Italian, Mexican). Other objective elements include eating utensils (e.g., pointy chopsticks, blunt chopsticks, fingers, knife and fork, spoon and fork), dress, and language (although one could argue that English is indeed multicultural if the origins of words are considered).

Norms are standards, models, or patterns regarded as typical within a particular group or culture. If broken, norms can make people feel uncomfortable or even angry. When a client is culturally different than the practitioner, the practitioner needs to consider the extent to which relevant norms of the client might be adopted within the session. For example, in Western psychological service, physical contact with clients (beyond handshakes) is usually considered to be questionable or poor practice. In some cultures, however, it is common to make physical contact when communicating (e.g., a hand placed on the arm of the person with whom one is speaking). Greetings might involve no contact, a handshake, a hug, or one or more kisses. The interpersonal space that is considered to be comfortable in different situations (e.g., the zone of personal distance) also can vary across cultures. In mainstream North America, 18 inches to 4 feet (0.5 to 1.2 m) is usually considered a comfortable distance. The distance is considerably less in some Latin American countries and considerably more in some North African and Asian countries. The distance between client and practitioner is not the only spatial consideration. In some cultures, it is standard for clients and practitioners to sit face to face (albeit at varying distances). In some cultures, however, this seating arrangement would be viewed as confrontational or aggressive; in these cultures, it may be more appropriate to sit alongside or at a slight angle to the client.

Additional cultural norms that can affect communication include eye contact, the meaning of specific words and of silence, and the structure of the conversation. Making eye contact can be considered polite, aggressive, or even an attempt at seduction. Avoiding eye contact can indicate either respect or a lack of interest. Saying yes as a statement rather than a question or exclamation can indicate agreement, approval, or consent; it might also mean that the person is obliging and wants to be thought well of or that the person doesn't understand what is being said but does not want to appear stupid. The obvious way to avoid possible misunderstanding with the meaning of yes is to stick with open-ended questions.

Cultural norms can affect the flow of conversation in both social and professional situations. Some cultures favor a regular exchange of questions and answers. Even if someone is telling a story, it may be considered suitable to interrupt to ask questions for clarification. Asking questions may indeed be indicative of interest and therefore considered polite behavior. In other cultures, narration is the norm. The individuals speaking are given the opportunity to tell their stories in their own time without interruption. Silence is likely to be perceived as indicating genuine interest rather than indifference. Interrupting to ask questions would be rude. In these cultures, the typical intake interview that some practitioners use might result in clients' shutting down, and asking multiple questions could actually decrease rather than increase the amount of information shared.

Culture can also affect how likely people are to state a firm opinion. In some cultures, it is completely expected that people will voice their opinions and that they feel comfortable doing so even when their opinions may not be fully formed or match the opinions of those around them. In other cultures, people tend to be reluctant to state firm opinions because they may feel that they are not in a position to make a comment, they do not want to disagree with others, or they have no opinion. On one occasion, a professor from China sat in on one of my graduate classes in which students were presenting orally. He was surprised that I (the "expert") allowed them (the "neophytes") to present information in class. He was even more shocked when a lively debate took place in class. He told me that in China, students were in class to learn, not to think for themselves (for practical reasons, I avoided getting into a debate about the possibility of learning from engaging with the material). Another related example is in Japan, where athletes are considered to be at the bottom of the team hierarchy and coaches are at the top. Athletes (i.e., those of low status) tend to be reluctant to express opinions in front of coaches (i.e., those perceived to be of higher status). By association, sport psychology practitioners seen to be close to the coach will be identified as members of the higher echelon, meaning that athletes may hesitate to open up to them (Kozuma, 2009).

People sometimes tend to believe that the way in which they live and experience life is normal and that it is "foreigners" who are exotic and have interesting cultures. I have heard multiple middle-class, heterosexual, White adults who are members of the mainstream culture where they live mention their envy of minorities because of their rich and vibrant cultures. They seem to believe that as part of the mainstream they have no identifiable culture; they feel that culture is something other people have.

We all, however, have been enculturated. We have gone through the process of learning to live within a particular culture. Some of us have also engaged in the process of acculturation, adopting the culture of another group (to varying degrees). We all usually try to learn to be participating members of society by learning the ways of a given society or social group so that we can function effectively within it. If we move, either through forced relocation (e.g., famine, war) or through personal choice, we are confronted with different ways of doing things. Sometimes the exposure to multiple cultures results from being a minority member of society within a different mainstream culture. Knowledge about general cultural practices does not take into account whether, and to what extent, individuals practice their original culture, particularly when it is not the mainstream one (Kontos & Breland-Noble, 2002). Because of this variance in the adoption of a culture, we cannot effectively generalize and group people by culture. Exploring how people integrate culture(s) into their lives and which aspects of culture are pertinent to a given situation provides a useful starting point for developing awareness of individual cultural differences.

RELATIONSHIPS: MULTICULTURAL AT THE MICRO-LEVEL

The majority of this essay so far has focused on macrocultures at national (e.g., Japanese) or ethnic (e.g., Hispanic) levels, but we are also influenced by microcultures. Neighborhoods, schools and universities, employment organizations, sporting clubs, and even families develop values and norms that are shared (at least to some extent) within subgroups. These microcultures may differ widely even within the same macroculture. For example, if you found a small town or an inhabited yet isolated island where everyone had the same ethnicity and nationality, you would still see variance in roles, beliefs, values, norms, and traditions within subgroups of that society. For example, families may differ on aspirations, love, abuse, how and what secrets are kept, what is and is not allowed to be discussed, and what family lies are told and retold. Similarly, within the same macroculture, the norms relating to punctuality and standard of dress may differ across employment organizations. Cultural norms also differ by sport—for example, the importance of appearance, the level of acceptance of marijuana use or drinking, and the number of hours per week that one is expected to train. Just take a moment to reflect on these three factors in terms of sumo wrestling, surfing, gymnastics, swimming, equestrian, and rugby. The values and norms vary depending on the sport. The issue of microcultures is made even more complex because clubs and teams within the same sport and macroculture will have their own microcultures and may vary in factors such as the importance placed on winning, having fun, or socializing.

Within each of these microcultures, individuals will vary in the degree to which they adopt or accept the ways of that microculture.

We are all products of macro- and microcultures. Nevertheless, given the variability of acculturation, even if we were able to find two people of the same ethnicity and nationality, who lived in the same family (and neighborhood), went to the same school and university, worked the same job, and participated in the same sport in the same club, they would probably still differ to some extent in terms of culture because of the variance in how much of each micro- or macroculture each one adopted. Many client–practitioner relationships are multicultural at the macro-level. All client–practitioner relationships are multicultural at the micro-level.

Whenever a sport psychologist and athlete sit down together (regardless of their cultural backgrounds), two different worlds start to approach each other. Sometimes they whiz right by each other and make only fleeting contact. Sometimes they collide with painful results for both parties. Sometimes they start to orbit each other, and good work begins. There is an assumption that the orbits for sport psychologist and athlete will be much larger if the two parties come from different cultural backgrounds. Maybe, maybe not. For example, say a White gay male psychologist from Chicago sits down with a straight Black male middle-class athlete from Los Angeles. The psychologist's next athlete is a straight White Iowa farm boy. The White psychologist may have more in common with the urban Black athlete (experiences of urban living, discrimination, hate, and violence) than with the Iowa boy, but both encounters are multicultural.

DEVELOPING CULTURAL AWARENESS

Parham (2005) suggested that prior to working with clients, consultants should reflect on the degree to which their own cultural background (e.g., ethnicity, gender, age) might influence the work they do on behalf of their clients as well as how the cultural backgrounds of clients might affect client–practitioner relationships. Parham also encouraged consultants to consider the bigger picture of a client's situation. Instead of focusing only on the sport performance challenge that brought the athlete to the psychologist's office, Parham recommended that consultants also gather data on the athlete's overall functioning within the nonsport domains relevant to that person. I agree that these steps are necessary for effective multicultural practice (i.e., all practice). I think it is often beneficial, however, to go further and therefore suggest that the psychologist can help build rapport (and knowledge and sensitivity) by directly asking the athlete from another culture to be the psychologist's "teacher" (decreasing power dynamics and introducing some balance to the therapeutic relationship) with a statement such as "I have read some things about where you come from and the traditions you may have grown up with, but it would be helpful if you could tell me about growing up in Cuba, your family and cultural traditions, how people relate to each other, such as coaches and athletes, men and women, parents and children, and so forth." It's a simple and direct approach that gets to the heart of the matter—the building of a mutual working alliance (transforming "you" and "me" into "us"), which is the core of any sport psychologist–athlete encounter. A practitioner can gain understanding of the athlete's world by inquiring about family, school, or neighborhood traditions; how the athlete fit, or did not fit, into those microcultures; what the athlete internalized from those microcultures; and so forth.

Finding out about the athlete's cultural background and experiences is only part of the equation. As I alluded to previously, practitioners also need to engage in self-reflective examinations of the ways in which their own macro- and microcultures influence how they view the world and interact with others. We often live in ignorance of how cultures influence our thoughts, behaviors, and expectations. It may not be until we place ourselves in other cultures that we recognize that our way of doing things is not the only (or even standard) modus operandi. As Martens, Mobley, and Zizzi (2000) recommended and Silva, Metzler, and Lerner (2007) seconded, cultural awareness and sensitivity can be enhanced by experiencing culture shock through immersion in alternative cultural gatherings. One obvious way to experience cultural immersion is to travel to foreign countries. Many travelers, however, never come close to experiencing the cultures of their seemingly exotic destinations. One does not get immersed in the local culture by staying in up-market chain hotels, eating in hotel restaurants, spending days in hotel pools, or lounging on sanitized beaches and perhaps taking an organized trip to a tourist-oriented market to buy a trinket and get a glimpse of the locals. One does not necessarily need to go to the extreme of staying with a local family or volunteering at a local orphanage, refugee camp, or the like; but to experience culture, one needs to do more than look out the window of a tourist bus or hired car. For those with an interest in sport, one way to experience culture is to visit a local sporting competition—whether it be the local Friday night fights (Thai boxing) in Thailand, *fútbol rápido* (soccer played on a cement court) in Mexico, *sepak takraw* (somewhat similar to volleyball but played with a cane ball that cannot be touched by the hands) in Malaysia, or curling (similar to shuffleboard on ice) in Sweden. Alternatively, playing a recreational sport that is popular in many countries (e.g., soccer, volleyball) can be a more hands-on (or feet-on) way of interacting with locals when traveling.

Even if time or money limitations prohibit international travel, most cities and towns provide opportunities for varied cultural experiences. Cultural festivals, performing arts groups, religious organizations, and social clubs can all provide opportunities for us to challenge ourselves with experiences beyond our typical day-to-day lives. Examples of intentional culture shock might include a straight man going to a gay nightclub, a White person going to an African cultural fair, an Asian or Hispanic person going to the local Polish club, or anyone attending a religious service outside of her or his own belief system. Whether one is traveling to another country or another neighborhood, however, the behavioral norms of the culture, especially those that denote respect or taboo, need to be understood. If these norms are unknown, do a bit of web surfing or ask someone!

By intentionally immersing ourselves in other cultures, we can learn to recognize that not all cultures have the same view of the world. It is helpful if we can be open to new ideas and be prepared to reevaluate our own values, attitudes, and behaviors. Little personal or professional growth will occur if we automatically judge alternative ways of doing things as wrong and stick to a belief that our own culture offers the one true and correct way of being. Some politicians have argued that our society needs to be multicultural tolerant. I don't think that is good enough. Being tolerant means being willing to put up with others. I think we need to go much further and become appreciative of other cultures. After all, how boring would life be if everyone were exactly the same!

As practitioners, we need to attempt to leave our conscious expectations at the door when meeting athletes and coaches from new cultures (or, for that matter, from our own culture). We all, however, have many hidden expectations, prejudices, and biases that we cannot access because they are unconscious. Supervision is an excellent place to try to uncover those buried prejudices and biases. A skilled supervisor can help practitioners explore their subtle thoughts, behaviors, and emotions that may be indicative of underlying stereotyping based on race or ethnicity. Also, because we do not know the degree of a client's acculturation, we should make no assumptions about others based solely on the identification of their cultures. In the same way, we should not jump to cultural assumptions based on looks. There are Black Scandinavians, blonde Hispanics, and Asian Germans.

ADAPTING BEHAVIORS TO SUIT THE CULTURAL CONTEXT

When working in another culture, we need to modify our communication styles to suit the prevailing cultural context. To some extent, we adjust all the time when we work with athletes from different sports. One way we make adjustments in different sporting contexts is by changing our verbal behavior. Hopefully, we don't talk about "playing sport" when working with swimmers (ever heard of someone "playing backstroke"?) or "starters and nonstarters" when working with individual sport athletes. Similarly, we hopefully alter our terminology when referring to the court, field, track, pool, gym, ice, or arena relevant to the particular sport.

We need to accept that methods that work well in some cultural contexts are simply unsuited to others. For example, in North America, Europe, and Australia, it is common for sport psychologists to focus on the self—self-determination, self-talk, self-confidence, self-efficacy, self-esteem, self-concept, self-actualization. In Arab cultures, however, the common saying *insha'Allah* (God willing) suggests that the self is not the main determinant of performance or well-being. In some cases it may be culturally contradictory for sport psychologists to encourage individual athletes to believe that they determine their own performance outcomes. Many traditional sport psychology interventions that promote internal control and self-regulation may be in opposition to religious practices and philosophies where faith in various outcomes is placed outside the self (Galloway, 2009).

Practitioners do not need to disregard what they have learned and effectively used with clients in the past, but familiar professional practices may need to be adapted to new cultural contexts. For example, Peters and Williams (2006) found that larger proportions of negative to positive self-talk were associated with poorer dart-throwing performance for European Americans but with improved performance for East Asians. Although this study clumped people into groups by ethnicity and geography, the findings do suggest that practitioners should be cautious in using interventions to change negative self-talk into positive self-talk when working with clients with East Asian backgrounds. The commonly held assumption that positive self-talk is a desirable skill in all athletes is in question. Even if the findings of Peters and Williams are supported by additional research, however, practitioners would not need to avoid all self-talk interventions, but instead modify the techniques they may currently use depending on the cultural identity of the client. For some clients, helping them increase their negative self-talk may be motivating and beneficial to performance.

CONCLUSION

This idea of modifying interventions to suit clients should be the standard mode of operation for all sport psychologists. When sport psychology was a relatively new field located primarily within the domain of physical education, the status quo entailed a psychoeducational approach of teaching mental skills to athletes and coaches. Many consultants had their standard bag of interventions that they taught to most all participants regardless of level, situation, culture, or need. Now, although psychoeducational sessions designed to help athletes develop psychological skills can help athletes enhance their performances and their enjoyment of participation, these approaches no longer constitute the be-all and end-all of the field. Now that some of the basic tenets of counseling and psychotherapy have been widely accepted (and expected) in the field of sport psychology, we have recognized the role of rapport development and communication. As discussed in this chapter, every encounter between a sport psychologist and a client is a multicultural encounter, meaning that culture will affect these interactions. We need to be open to others having different ways of doing and being that are in some ways determined by the micro- and macrocultures in which they have lived.

IDEAS FOR REFLECTION AND DEBATE

1. One can roughly divide a person into several facets: universal factors (common to almost all humans, such as the desire to be loved), sociocultural variables, and unique features (the individual as a one-of-a-kind phenomenon). Within your practice or research, which of these aspects takes the prominent position, and why? (No fair saying they all get equal attention!)

2. We are all some combination of sexist, racist, homophobic, xenophobic, ageist, weightist, and so forth. What are your "ists" and other prejudices, and how have you reduced them?

3. In most Western cultures, the White, heterosexual male is at the top of the heap. In what ways are White, straight, male sport psychologists advantaged and also disadvantaged as professionals?

4. It is impossible to be knowledgeable about all the cultures in the world. What steps do you actively take when you start working with someone whose culture is relatively unknown to you?

5. How do you respond, overtly and covertly, when working with clients who express cultural biases and prejudices (e.g., sexism, homophobia) that clash with your cultural values?

REFERENCES

American Anthropological Association. (1998, May 17). *Statement on "race."* www.aaanet.org/stmts/racepp.htm.

Dean, J. (1984). Tasmania v. Commonwealth. 158 Commonwealth Law Review 243.

Galloway, S. (2009). A Canadian sport psychologist in Kuwait. In R.J. Schinke & S.J. Hanrahan (Eds.), *Cultural sport psychology* (pp. 153–164). Champaign, IL: Human Kinetics.

Kontos, A.P., & Breland-Noble, A.M. (2002). Racial/ethnic diversity in applied sport psychology: A multicultural introduction to working with athletes of color. *The Sport Psychologist, 16,* 296–315.

Kozuma, Y. (2009). Samurai and science: Sport psychology in Japan. In R.J. Schinke & S.J. Hanrahan (Eds.), *Cultural sport psychology* (pp. 211–223). Champaign, IL: Human Kinetics.

Martens, M.P., Mobley, M., & Zizzi, S.J. (2000). Multicultural training in applied sport psychology. *The Sport Psychologist, 14,* 81–97.

Parham, W.D. (2005). Raising the bar: Developing an understanding of athletes from racially, culturally, and ethnically diverse backgrounds. In M.B. Andersen (Ed.), *Sport psychology in practice* (pp. 210–215). Champaign, IL: Human Kinetics.

Peters, H.J., & Williams, J.M. (2006). Moving cultural background to the foreground: An investigation of self-talk, performance, and persistence following feedback. *Journal of Applied Sport Psychology, 18,* 240–253.

Silva, J.M., III, Metzler, J.N., & Lerner, B. (2007). *Training professionals in the practice of sport psychology.* Morgantown, WV: Fitness Information Technology.

Watson, J.M., II, Etzel, E.F., & Loughran, M.J. (2006, Fall/Winter). Ethics and cultural competence. *Association for Applied Sport Psychology Newsletter, 21*(3), 25.

PROBLEMS IN REFLECTIVE PRACTICE:
Self-Bootstrapping Versus Therapeutic Supervision

Jack C. Watson
West Virginia University, United States

John R. Lubker
West Texas A&M University, United States

Judy Van Raalte
Springfield College, United States

Reflection is an optical term concerning the redirection of photons, and the most common example of the process is that of light hitting a mirror. Depending on the quality of the mirror, the information in the light can be more or less clear, but the information always gets changed in that left becomes right. If the surface of the mirror is distorted (not perfectly flat), the image can be broadened and take up the whole mirror or be flattened and thinned. In this essay, Jack, John, and Judy consider how optical metaphors involving mirror, light, and reflection provide useful frameworks for describing the process of examining the psychologist in service. They note that the reflective practitioner should hold in mind that what one sees in the self-examination process may be manifested back to front or left to right, exaggerated, diminished, or even upside down. The quality of the mirror—that is, the density of the medium through which the information is passing (e.g., the darkened metaphoric lens of depression)—stems from the ontogenetic psychosocial histories and cultures of each practitioner. The authors argue also that if our lenses and mirrors are damaged, then a sort of self-bootstrapping reflection will usually result in repeated retelling of the same distorted story.

INTRODUCTION

What does it take to be a competent sport psychology practitioner? Knowledge is a good place to start. Sport psychologists can develop knowledge by reading literature, attending professional conferences, and completing coursework to stay current with evidence-based interventions. Many sport psychologists also strive for clarity of vision. Their goal is to understand what is really going on and to find the truth as the client sees it. But is finding or seeing the truth essential to competent practice? In many cases, athletes' and coaches' circumstances are complex. There may be many truths to discover. We believe that excellent practitioners not only are gifted visionaries but also should be reflective professionals. Further, we contend that although self-reflection is a beneficial process, it is not sufficient, and interpersonal supervision is also necessary. In this chapter, we identify the differences between reflective practice and supervision, present a critical overview of current supervision practice, and provide suggestions for promoting supervision in the field of sport and exercise psychology.

SELF-REFLECTION

Self-reflection (often called introspection) has a long history in disciplines such as philosophy and psychology. David Hume and John Locke relied on engaging in introspective processes to discover how their experiences influenced their perceptions (Drever, 1968). Self-analysis has been at the crux of psychoanalysis, for both the client and the practitioner, since it was first discussed by Freud in the early 20th century. Self-analysis has been praised as a necessary function in the voyage of self-discovery; it has been defined as a process of internal examination brought about by an experience that leads to a clarification of the self and results in a changed conceptual perspective (Boyd & Fales, 1983).

Self-reflection offers numerous benefits but should not be considered a replacement for supervision. Self-reflection can enhance self-awareness. By reflecting on and processing past events, individuals can become better attuned to their strengths and weaknesses, and engaging habitually in the process of self-reflection helps practitioners approach difficult situations in a thoughtful and insightful manner. Used over time, self-reflection can enable a practitioner to monitor and analyze personal progress with less self-criticism by becoming more focused and intrinsically motivated to self-reflect, which leads in turn to increased enjoyment of the task (Anderson, Knowles, & Gilbourne, 2004; Hanrahan, 1999; Hanrahan & Mathews, 2005; Knowles, Gilbourne, Tomlinson, & Anderson, 2007). What also makes self-reflective practice attractive is that it is a free enterprise. As an internal process, self-reflection can be engaged in at almost any time and place without financial cost. Emphasis on reflective practice is epitomized by the work of Schön (1983, 1987), who recommended that professionals use self-reflection to examine their assumptions, personal theories, and behaviors as practitioners. Although the results of self-examination have been the focus of the self-reflection discussion in the applied sport psychology field, attention needs to be given to why self-reflection as a singular practice is insufficient.

Successful reflection is dependent on the introspective ability of the practitioner. Helping practitioners develop the capacity to self-reflect in action (during a given activity) and on action (after the activity) has become an important feature of professional training programs, and encouraging this kind of development constitutes a central aspect of the necessary supervision of a beginning professional (Atherton, 2005). In Andersen and Stevens' (2007) examination of the reflective practitioner, the optical processes of reflection and refraction are employed metaphorically to address problems in self-reflective practice in sport psychology. Through these optical processes, original information often becomes distorted and bent as it travels. For example, when electromagnetic information makes its way through one's lens and onto the retina, it arrives upside down and turned around. In addition, the interpretation of this information is subject to the receiver's biases and personal histories. For example, a person with narcissistic tendencies might see her practice as brilliant, whereas a person who is dysthymic might view his work through a gray-filtered lens of pervasive unsatisfactoriness. Self-reflection is like pulling oneself up by one's own bootstraps. Unless one is an exceptional person (e.g., the Buddha, Freud), it just cannot be done alone. As when light hits a curved mirror, the same distorted image can occur again and again in self-reflection; as a result, the same biased, self-protective story is told and retold.

Unfortunately, completion of academic and applied requirements is no guarantee of excellence in self-reflection. This problem derives, in part, from challenges associated with self-reflection. Hanrahan and Mathews (2005) found that students who engaged in self-reflection when learning a physical task found it time consuming and experienced reduced enjoyment, increased stress, greater consciousness of their shortcomings, less engagement with the task, and more negativity. There is also the question of what practitioners are reflecting on. The concept of self-reflection is atheoretical or, at best, based on broad models of reflective practice. No guidance for practitioners is available to indicate what frameworks or paradigms they can use to "hold" the self-reflective process. Finally, peculiarities of the sport environment make unbiased self-reflection particularly difficult to achieve.

Athletes and coaches are often focused on outcomes reached by hard work. Many coaches (and sport psychologists) have said that for those who train and prepare correctly, winning will take care of itself. Athletes and coaches who achieve success with the input of sport psychology consultants often credit their winning to their training—and by extension to the sport psychologists who have helped them achieve success. For sport psychology practitioners, then, it is easy to reflect on successful interactions and assume a certain amount of credit for the results. On the other hand, when athletes perform poorly, they and their coaches may attribute the failure to insufficient training or preparation. Here again, it can be easy for sport psychology consultants to agree in the form of this type of thought: "The athlete should have been more thoughtful about our consultation or practiced his or her psychological skills correctly or often enough."

Even the most self-reflective practitioner is subject to cognitive biases such as blaming the victim. Bulman and Wortman (1977) described this bias as based on a motivation to see the world as a fair and just place in which people deserve the misfortunes they receive. When applied to a loss or poor performance in a sport setting, this bias suggests that sport psychologists may have a tendency to sustain belief in a just world by blaming or denigrating the athlete or coach (i.e., presuming that the athlete or coach did something to deserve the loss or that the athlete or coach is not a hard worker and therefore deserved to lose). David Martin, an exercise physiologist at the Australian Institute of Sport, gave a wonderful example of this bias in Richardson, Andersen, and Morris (2008): "The reason you are in this state [poor training form] is because your coach is a dickhead, so there's a big problem. The second thing is I've got a training program, and if you're not responding to it, it's because you are not doing it with intent" (p. 74).

Blame casting and self-serving biases abound in the helping professions, and they color the lenses of self-reflection. We see the same distorted picture over and over again. Practitioners who rely solely on self-reflective practice for guidance—basically, self-supervision—may develop an overly optimistic sense of self and competence, much to the detriment of themselves, their clients, and the field. As Andersen and Stevens (2007) hinted, it is difficult to be unbiased and rational in self-reflection. This difficulty calls into serious question the utility of self-reflection as a sufficient form of professional practice and guidance. It seems that a reflective practitioner would also benefit from consultation with a professional supervisor—someone who can guide and be a devils' advocate in the reflective process. This holds true not only for the student and neophyte practitioner but also for the advanced practitioner with many years of experience.

SUPERVISION

Supervision is an important component of professional training in that it provides an avenue for sport psychology practitioners at all levels to use the experiences and knowledge of others to examine themselves (Andersen, Van Raalte, & Brewer, 2000). Supervision has been defined as a long-term interpersonal relationship designed to foster a greater sense of self-knowledge and a clearer understanding of the therapeutic process through close contact, regular feedback, and communication with a skilled professional (Van Raalte & Andersen, 2000). The purposes of supervision are threefold. First, it should play a central role in the training of new practitioners in applied sport psychology (Andersen, Van Raalte, & Brewer, 1994). Second, it serves as a safe and challenging forum for training ethical behaviors that set the tone for future practice (Andersen, 1994). Finally, supervisors assume a high degree of legal and ethical responsibility for supervisees and their clients (Koocher, Shafranske, & Falender, 2008). Given these qualities, supervision plays a central and gatekeeping role in the training of new sport psychology practitioners (Andersen et al., 1994).

History of Therapeutic Supervision

Supervision as a practice can be traced back to Freud (Bernard & Goodyear, 2009), who is reported to have begun supervising the practice of therapy in 1902 when he met with and supervised a group of physicians interested in using and promoting psychoanalysis. The first recorded psychoanalytic supervision occurred when Freud supervised the work of a father who treated his own son (Little Hans) for a fear of horses (Freud, 1909/1977).

Supervision has been a focus of significant writing and discussion in clinical and counseling psychology for more than 40 years, but it is only since the mid-1990s that it has been seriously written about and discussed in sport and exercise psychology (Andersen & Williams-Rice, 1996). Mentions of supervision had occurred earlier in conference presentations and written work, but the first published research on supervision in sport psychology was conducted by Andresen et al. (1994) and Petitpas, Brewer, Rivera, and Van Raalte (1994). These studies' findings about supervision were somewhat disturbing for the field, given the importance of supervision to high-quality training and the development of practitioners. Only 57 percent of sport psychology supervisors reported having received some formal training in supervision (Petitpas et al.), and 56 percent reported never having received any formal supervision for their own work with athletes (Andersen et al., 1994). Additional findings from Andersen et al. (1994), indicated that students in applied sport psychology were receiving only about 100 hours of supervised training in the field. That figure constitutes just 25 percent of the hours required for certified consultant status granted by the Association for Applied Sport Psychology (AASP), and it amounts to a small portion of the supervised training required of students in counseling and psychology when applying for licensure in the United States. Such experiences often require 700 to 2,000 hours of internship training and 2,000 to 4,000 hours of postdegree supervised practice.

In a more recent study of supervision practices in the United States, graduate students (75 percent) reported being supervised much more frequently for their sport psychology practice than did professionals in the field (18 percent; Watson, Zizzi, Etzel, & Lubker, 2004). Of those professionals who supervised others, 47 percent reported no training in supervision, and 29 percent reported having been trained only through workshops, in-services, and independent study, with no formal academic training. Thus, even though an increasing number of students in sport psychology are receiving supervision, the current status, depth, and breadth of supervision are of concern.

Models of Supervision

Models of supervision vary greatly and are discussed in depth in other places (e.g., Bernard & Goodyear, 2009; Falender & Shafranske, 2004;

Stoltenberg, McNeill, & Delworth, 1998). In the field of sport psychology, supervision often follows one of several common models, and two of these—cognitive-behavioral and psychodynamic—are discussed in the following subsections.

Cognitive-Behavioral Supervision

Given the large number of sport psychology practitioners who use the cognitive-behavioral skill development process in their practice (Van Raalte & Andersen, 2000), it is not surprising that the cognitive-behavioral approach to supervision is also widely endorsed. This model is based on the belief that supervisees need both support and training in the techniques they will use with their clients (Blocher, 1983; Kurpius & Morran, 1988). Supervisors take the perspective that they can use both cognitive and behavioral principles to shape the therapeutic behaviors of supervisees in a way that helps them become more proficient in their work. Supervisors are viewed as expert practitioners who are ultimately responsible for what supervisees learn and for the mastery with which they practice (Bernard & Goodyear, 2009).

From a cognitive-behavioral perspective, positive and negative behaviors and cognitions are learned and maintained through their consequences. It is the role of the supervisor to identify these adaptive and maladaptive behaviors and cognitions in practice and teach and reward those that should continue while extinguishing those that are counterproductive. To accomplish this task, supervisees are guided through and encouraged to practice the skills on themselves (e.g., cognitive restructuring, self-talk, goal setting, anxiety reduction). Identifying these positive and negative behaviors and cognitions is ultimately the responsibility of the supervisor, but the process is done in tandem so that both parties are involved in the exploration (Rosenbaum & Rosen, 1998).

Milne and James (2000) provided evidence that the majority of effective cognitive-behavioral supervision includes "enactive" components such as role plays, behavioral rehearsal, and self-management; "symbolic" components such as prompts and homework; and "iconic" components such as live or video modeling. It is clear that this model places a premium on both preparing practitioners for upcoming consultations and providing feedback following consultations. This form of supervision may also take on a therapeutic function in helping some supervisees confront their own irrational and maladaptive belief systems (Van Raalte & Andersen, 2000).

This type of supervision has some weaknesses in that it focuses almost entirely on the specific client and the strategies being used for improving the consultation with that client. Much less emphasis is placed on improving the practitioner's consultation and relationship style, self-awareness, and personal and professional insight.

Therapeutic Models of Supervision

For some sport psychology practitioners, neither self-reflection nor cognitive-behavioral approaches to supervision will meet their needs. So, what else is available? We strongly propose consideration of a therapeutic model of supervision—that is, a relationship-centered model such as psychodynamic supervision.

The psychodynamic model of supervision stems from Freudian, neo-Freudian, and objects-relations theory. As the first model of supervision to emerge, psychodynamic supervision has had great influence on supervision theory and practice (Bernard & Goodyear, 2009), but in the field of sport psychology it may not be as well known as the cognitive-behavioral models (Andersen & Williams-Rice, 1996).

Psychodynamic models of supervision focus on teaching and learning and on closely examining the supervisee's relationships with the client and the supervisor (Andersen & Williams-Rice, 1996). It is the goal of such supervision to help supervisees become aware of their relationship patterns through exploration of their relationship histories and discussions of how the resulting positive and negative patterns of behavior may affect their current and future interactions with clients (Campbell, 2000). Two important factors in the psychodynamic model are transference and countertransference. In the supervisory relationship, transference refers to the redirection (and projection) of the supervisee's feelings, behaviors, and thoughts from a historical significant other (e.g., mom, dad, siblings) onto the supervisor. Similar (and parallel) processes occur between the practitioner and the client. Understanding and addressing transferential concerns are an essential part of therapeutic and supervision processes. Countertransference is similar to transference but stems from the supervisor's history and projections onto the supervisee. As with transference, countertransference may occur in therapy (between practitioner and athlete) and in supervision (between supervisor and supervisee). Understanding and addressing countertransferential concerns are also an integral part of the supervision process, because knowledge of these feelings is often used in the therapeutic process. Similarly, a supervisee's countertransferential responses to a client speak to the supervisee's own history of relationships. Uncovering those countertransferential responses leads to greater self-awareness, self-understanding, and even self-compassion than might be the case with the more skills-based models of supervision (e.g., cognitive-behavioral models). Analyzing transference and countertransference is a species of deep self-reflection under the tutelage of a knowledgeable other.

In psychodynamic supervision, supervisees are taught to recognize the unconscious thoughts and feelings of their clients and to recognize their own reactions and use them in a therapeutic manner (Lane, Barber, & Gregson, 1998). Psychodynamic supervision often focuses on resistance to self-understanding and on the removal of blind spots that result from unconscious factors. Supervisors help identify and remove blind spots by recognizing and challenging a supervisee's unconscious thoughts and behaviors in both therapy and supervision. Once these unconscious motives are identified, they are put into perspective to help the supervisee be more effective in the therapy setting. This model of supervision goes well beyond that of the cognitive-behavioral approach, and it provides the depth needed for practitioners to understand personal underlying issues that influence how and why they think and act the way they do while also providing insight into underlying themes that may emerge in current and future professional relationships.

Supervision and therapy maintain many similarities (Zaslavsky, Nunes, & Eizirik, 2005). Both processes focus on personal improvement, both require substantial self-involvement, and both foster multidimensional reenactments. Differences also exist, however, and they make these two processes separate. For instance, supervision is not a type of therapy but a didactic process designed to help the supervisee learn. Although therapeutic changes may occur, the primary goal is learning. Most practitioners agree that if student or professional therapists are seeking both personal therapy and professional supervision, their supervisors need to be distinct from their therapists.

SELF-REFLECTION VERSUS SUPERVISION

Unlike self-reflection, supervision involves an interpersonal relationship that is focused on the supervisee's professional growth and development. The supervisee is expected to develop skills, techniques, and self-understanding through counseling and clinical practice and through the process of supervision by an accredited or more experienced supervisor. In this relationship, the supervisor can provide insight and facilitate growth. The supervisor also assumes some responsibility for the well-being of supervisees and their clients. This type of supervisory experience is suitable for any sport psychology consultants, but a supervisee would need to engage in a substantial amount of study of psychodynamic theory before embarking on this journey. In contrast, when practitioners engage in self-reflection without supervision, there is often no voice of doubt or oversight for the client's welfare and no gatekeeper to protect the public and the field. Pulling on our own bootstraps may get us somewhere, but probably not as far as we need to go in order to become self-aware and truly reflective practitioners.

In the supervisory relationship, the supervisor directly influences the supervisee, especially in the ethical practice of sport psychology. In this role, supervisors have the power to guide a supervisee's actions and delivery of service and thus serve as gatekeepers of the field (Feasey, 2002). Supervision does more than help sport psychologists curb counterproductive behaviors. It allows practitioners to learn new skills, try new approaches, get feedback on the work they are doing, and process personal experiences such as successes and disappointments; it also serves as a valuable aspect of self-care and as a foundation for reflective practice.

We should also consider the effect that unsupervised consultants have on our field. Poorly supervised sport psychology consultants are likely to be less effective at their work and thus may lead clients to give up on sport psychology. Unsupervised practitioners may also be more likely than supervised practitioners to slip in terms of behavioral ethics and boundary blurring. Practicing without supervision—without a net, so to speak—leaves practitioners stuck with their blind spots. Such blindness may result in suboptimal or even counterproductive treatment that leaves athlete and coach clients dissatisfied (or even hostile to sport psychologists). These dissatisfied clients may pass along their disappointments to other potential consumers. Thus negative outcomes from sport psychology practice can affect everyone in the field.

So why isn't supervision a fundamental component of all sport psychologists' professional activities? The many reasons range from the practical to the existential. On a practical level, supervision is inconvenient. It requires guided self-reflection and self-awareness, which can be uncomfortable, and calls on practitioners to reveal and consider their weaknesses, blind spots, and failures as well as their successes.

Supervision also takes time and perhaps money. Even with sufficient time and money, the pool of qualified sport psychology supervisors is not large, and not all practitioners who meet the AASP and APA standards believe that supervision is important (Watson, Lubker, & Zakrajsek, 2007). For these and other reasons, some practitioners choose not to take part in regular supervision (Watson et al., 2004; Watson et al., 2007). The circumstances and rationalizations that result in less than full use of supervision may be understandable, but practicing without a net is worrisome for the field of sport psychology. It shows a disregard for the welfare of clients, implies a sense of infallibility and entitlement, and is out of line with the field's ethical standards. As practitioners, sport psychologists need to put clients and the field first by ensuring that they promote the best interests of their clients and serve as strong ambassadors for the field. Career-long supervision is a professional ideal but usually does not occur as often as one would hope.

FUTURE OF SUPERVISION

As a field, sport psychology seems to be caught in a quandary. Should the field push forward by training as many practitioners as possible to reach out broadly, or should training be limited to the highest standards, thus ensuring only a limited supply of the most skilled and effective practitioners? Engaging in self-reflection is a positive step toward developing and maintaining practice skills, but by no means is it a substitute for supervision and peer consultation. We encourage sport psychology practitioners to stop using self-reflective practice as a substitute for supervision. Instead, self-reflective practice should be promoted and used as an integral component of the supervision process for students, supervisors, and professionals (Knowles et al., 2007). Other models, such as phenomenological supervisee-centered and solution-focused supervision, can be effective as well. If psychodynamic supervision does not mesh well with a person's approach to supervision, we encourage that person to find another in-depth therapeutic model that does fit.

Despite the differences that characterize registering, accrediting, certifying, and licensing boards, they tend to share a common assumption that sport psychology practitioners (with minimal training in supervision) are competent to supervise the training of students and young professionals. We recommend that organizations take a strong stance on this issue by working together and developing comprehensive competency requirements for supervisors. Consistent with previous suggestions (Barney, Andersen, & Riggs, 1996; Watson et al., 2004), we hold that all supervisors should be required to be trained in supervision well beyond the level of a workshop at a professional meeting—through, for example, a dedicated graduate course or by means of components in two or three courses—and to have received regular supervision in their practice. Even though it would be ideal to certify supervisors, it is more feasible to establish a minimum set of criteria for supervisors to meet prior to supervising others. Furthermore, if all supervisors should be trained in supervision, then it is essential that programs in the field develop courses in supervision and institute opportunities for metasupervision (i.e., supervision of the supervision that an advanced student provides to a novice student; see Barney et al.). Metasupervision needs to be built into the experiences of practicums, internships, and supervision, and it should be made available to professionals in the field who lack such training.

Organizations involved in registering, accrediting, licensing, and certifying in sport psychology often build into their programs a requirement for minimal coursework, experiences (number of hours of applied contact), and sometimes knowledge (e.g., passing a licensing exam). If the field of sport psychology is to achieve more mainstream acceptance and popularity, it would behoove those in the field to also include required supervision experiences, training in the practice of supervision, and the mechanisms and encouragement necessary to support career-long supervision. If sport and exercise psychology professionals with the status of registration, licensure, or certification are to be given blanket privilege to supervise others by virtue of their professional accomplishments, it is important that they first be trained in supervision and that this training be made a requirement for receiving the registration, licensure, or certification. Training in supervision for all practitioners would undoubtedly help to protect the best interests of the field and of clients.

Sport psychology governing bodies should also consider adopting specific guidelines for the practice of supervision, such as those established by the Supervision Interest Network (1993), and modifying their supervision-related ethical standards and codes of conduct. In addition, governing bodies should consider encouraging or requiring supervision as part of the renewal (recertification, relicensing) process. Although it is not currently an ethical requirement to continue with supervision throughout one's career, we consider it sound ethical practice to experience periodic supervision or consultation with peers. Continuing supervision plays an important part in professional development and offers a great way to stay competent in practice strategies and gain insight into ethical decision making.

CONCLUSION

According to Knowles et al. (2007), the use of self-reflection is part of a "structured and systematic reflection [that] can support applied practice" (p. 121). Although the merits of self-reflection have been discussed, it should be clear that self-reflection is not sufficient to be used as a stand-alone practice in our field. Imagine a parent setting a jigsaw puzzle in front of a child and, just before leaving the room, telling the child that she should complete the puzzle. What is the expectation of what will happen after the parent exits? How will the child act, and what will she think about her experience? In this example, the parent is the graduate training program, the child is the new professional, and the jigsaw puzzle is the consultation situation. Although the child may solve one puzzle effectively, she may still benefit from supervision on puzzle solving. New and more challenging puzzles may appear that cause the child confusion and discomfort. Although the child may appear to solve some of these newer puzzles, further reflection may reveal that they were solved incorrectly, that a puzzle piece was jammed into the wrong spot. The child may not solve some puzzles at all. Through supervision, however, practitioners can gain a broader understanding of the therapeutic process and their roles in it, and, one hopes, they will become more efficient and effective as a result. Supervision is a necessary part of being a professional; it helps ensure the welfare of our clients and the constant advancement of our field. Self-reflection should be used as part of reflective practice supervision, woven into the training of sport psychology graduate students and novice practitioners (Knowles et al.). As consultants, we are stewards of our field, and our actions will dictate how applied sport psychology progresses in the future. It is important that supervision research continue and that practitioners in the field be trained in the art and practice of supervision so that they can effectively train future practitioners.

IDEAS FOR REFLECTION AND DEBATE

1. In your experience, do your practicing colleagues engage in supervision? What are their reasons for doing so (or not)?

2. What role does supervision play in your practice?

3. What are the tensions and congruencies between self-reflective practice and supervision?

4. At times, the lines between psychotherapy and therapeutic supervision become somewhat blurry. How do you personally make the distinction, and what do you do when the lines start to blur?

5. If you are a supervisor, what models have you chosen for supervision, and why? If you are a supervisee, what kinds of supervision have you sought, and why?

REFERENCES

Andersen, M.B. (1994). Ethical considerations in the supervision of applied sport psychology graduate students. *Journal of Applied Sport Psychology, 6,* 152–167.

Andersen M.B., & Stevens, L. (2007). On being a fraud. *Sport and Exercise Psychology Review, 3*(2), 43–46.

Andersen, M.B., Van Raalte, J.L., & Brewer, B.W. (1994). Assessing the skills of sport psychology supervisors. *The Sport Psychologist, 8,* 238–247.

Andersen, M.B., Van Raalte, J.L., & Brewer, B.W. (2000). When sport psychology consultants and graduate students are impaired: Ethical and legal issues in graduate training and supervision. *Journal of Applied Sport Psychology, 12,* 134–150.

Andersen, M.B., & Williams-Rice, B.T. (1996). Supervision in the education and training of sport psychology service providers. *The Sport Psychologist, 10,* 278–290.

Anderson, A.G., Knowles, Z., & Gilbourne, D. (2004). Reflective practice for sport psychologists: Concepts, models, practical implications, and thoughts on dissemination. *The Sport Psychologist, 18,* 188–203.

Atherton, J.S. (2005). *Learning and teaching: Reflection and reflective practice.* www.learningandteaching.info/learning/reflecti.htm.

Barney, S.T., Andersen, M.B., & Riggs, C.A. (1996). Supervision in sport psychology: Some recommendations for practicum training. *Journal of Applied Sport Psychology, 8,* 200–217.

Bernard, J.M., & Goodyear, R.K. (2009). *Fundamentals of clinical supervision* (4th ed.). Upper Saddle River, NJ: Merrill.

Blocher, D.H. (1983). Toward a cognitive developmental approach to counseling supervision. *The Counseling Psychologist, 11,* 27–34.

Boyd, E., & Fales, A. (1983). Reflective learning: Key to learning from experience. *Journal of Humanistic Psychology, 23,* 99–117.

Bulman, R.J., & Wortman, C.B. (1977). Attributions of blame and coping in the "real world": Severe accident victims react to their lot. *Journal of Personality and Social Psychology, 35,* 351–363.

Campbell, J.M. (2000). *Becoming and effective supervisor: A workbook for counselors and psychotherapists.* Philadelphia: Accelerated Development.

Drever, J. (1968). Some early associations. In B. B. Wolman (Ed.), *Historical roots of contemporary psychology* (pp. 11–23). New York: Harper & Row.

Falender, C.A., & Shafranske, E.P. (2004). *Clinical supervision: A competency-based approach.* Washington, DC: American Psychological Association.

Feasey, D. (2002). *Good practices in supervision with psychotherapists and counselors.* London: Whirr.

Freud, S. (1977). Analysis of a phobia of a five year old boy. In A. Richards (Ed.) & J. Stachey (Trans.), *The Pelican Freud library, Vol. 8, Case histories 1* (pp. 169–306). Toronto, ON, Canada: Penguin Books. (Original work published 1909).

Hanrahan, S.J. (1999). Helping students think for themselves: Engaging the brain while you train. *Strategies, 12,* 11–12, 29–30.

Hanrahan, S.J., & Mathews, R. A. (2005). Success in salsa: Students evaluations of the use of self-reflection when learning to dance. In K. Vincs (Ed.), *Conference proceedings. Dance rebooted: Initializing the grid.* Braddon, ACT, Australia: Ausdance.

Knowles, Z., Gilbourne, D., Tomlinson, V., & Anderson, A.G. (2007). Reflections on the application of reflective practice of supervision in applied sport psychology. *The Sport Psychologist, 21,* 109–122.

Koocher, G., Shafranske, E.P., & Falender, C.A. (2008). Addressing ethical and legal issues in clinical supervision. In C. A. Falender & E. P. Shafranske (Eds.), *Casebook for clinical supervision: A competency-based approach* (pp. 159–180). Washington, DC: American Psychological Association.

Kurpius, D.J., & Morran, D.K. (1988). Cognitive-behavioral techniques and interventions for application in counselor supervision. *Counselor Education and Supervision, 27,* 368–376.

Lane, R.C., Barber, S.S., & Gregson, K.J. (1998). Divergent views in psychodynamic supervision. *Journal of Contemporary Psychotherapy, 28,* 187–197.

Milne, D., & James, I. (2000). A systematic review of effective cognitive-behavioural supervision. *British Journal of Clinical Psychology, 39,* 111–127.

Petitpas, A.J., Brewer, B.W., Rivera, P., & Van Raalte, J.L. (1994). Ethical beliefs and behaviors in applied sport psychology: The AAASP ethics survey. *Journal of Applied Sport Psychology, 6,* 135–151.

Richardson, S.O., Andersen, M.B., Morris, T. (2008). *Overtraining athletes: Personal journeys in sport.* Champaign, IL: Human Kinetics.

Rosenbaum, M., & Rosen, T. (1998). Clinical supervision from the standpoint of cognitive-behavior therapy. *Psychotherapy: Theory, Research, Practice, Training, 35,* 220–230.

Schön, D.A. (1983). *The reflective practitioner: How professionals think in action.* London: Temple Smith.

Schön, D.A. (1987). *Educating the reflective practitioner.* San Francisco: Jossey-Bass.

Stoltenberg, C.D., McNeill, B., & Delworth, U. (1998). *IDM supervision: An integrated developmental model for supervising counselors and therapists.* San Francisco: Jossey-Bass.

Supervision Interest Network, Association for Counselor Education and Supervision. (1993, Summer). ACES ethical guidelines for counseling supervisors. *ACES Spectrum, 53*(4), 5–8.

Van Raalte, J.L., & Andersen, M.B. (2000). *Supervision I: From models to doing.* In M. B. Andersen (Ed.), *Doing sport psychology* (pp. 153–165). Champaign, IL: Human Kinetics.

Watson J.C., II, Lubker, J.R., & Zakrajsek, R. (2007, October). Supervision issues in applied sport psychology: An international survey. Paper presented at the annual conference of the Association for Applied Sport Psychology, Louisville, KY.

Watson, J.C., II, Zizzi, S.J., Etzel, E.F., & Lubker, J.R. (2004). Applied sport psychology supervision: A survey of students and professionals. *The Sport Psychologist, 18,* 415–429.

Zaslavsky, J., Nunes, M.L.T., & Eizirik, C.L. (2005). Approaching countertransference in psychoanalytic supervision: A qualitative investigation. *International Journal of Psychoanalysis, 86,* 1099–1131.

IF YOU MEET THE BUDDHA ON THE FOOTBALL FIELD, TACKLE HIM!

Mark B. Andersen
Victoria University, Australia

Joe Mannion
Private practice, St. Louis, Missouri, United States

In Western interpretations of Buddhist principles such as suffering, attachment, and desire, there are many misunderstandings that have probably led to seeing such concepts as alien and not applicable to sport psychology practice. As Mark and Joe argue, Western sport psychologists hold various concepts and constructs of the self as central to applied research and practice (e.g., self-talk, self-image, self-concept, physical self-description, self-efficacy). They also suggest that these psychological views of the self are ingrained in the applied sport psychology canon and that their usefulness is not often questioned. This essay addresses (among other things) the Buddhist concepts of suffering, attachment, and desire, as well as understandings of the self, or, more accurately, "no-self," and how they may be applied to the training of sport psychologists and to the lives and performances of athletes. In Buddhism, all selves are false selves and sources of suffering that are in need of dismantling. The authors also address the Four Noble Truths of Buddhism, and these concepts can be translated relatively easily into sport psychology training and into working with athletes both in and out of the playing arena. For some athletes, destroying the bonds of their constructed false selves may lead to freedom and greater happiness.

INTRODUCTION

Long ago, I (Mark) worked for almost 2 years with a 16-year-old Australian baseball player (until he was 18 years old) named Sammy (not his real name). As Sammy told me his stories of playing, it became clear that during competition he had an incessant running monologue in his head that was fraught with anxiety about making mistakes and concerns over what people (other players, coaches, parents) were thinking about him and what negative judgments they might be making. He was afraid that others would take measure of his performance and that he would be found wanting. His ego, or sense of self, was always under some potential or perceived attack. His worries also extended to other domains such as what his teachers and parents thought of his academic performance.

Sammy deeply loved his baseball. In training and practice he was usually totally engaged in the physicality and decision making of the sport. The running monologue was nearly absent, and the best description of how he was when training would have been *egoless joy of functioning.* One day, I asked Sammy, "Who exactly is that Sammy out there in the game who is doing all this worrying and talking nonstop to himself? What is he?" Sammy paused, then he said, "I'm not sure what you mean." I responded, "OK, I was thinking that there is a big contrast between the Sammy who is out there totally engaged in practice and having a ball and the Sammy who is a bundle of worries and nerves on game day." Sammy's face lit up, and he said, "Oh, you mean the difference between the 'baseball-beast Sammy' and the 'scared-shitless Sammy.'" His naming of the two Sammys was just about perfect.

We then talked about the contrast between the two. We discussed how a beast doesn't really need to think or worry about things; how a beast goes on its merry way, doing the beastly things it knows how to do; and how a beast doesn't really think of itself as a beast. It just is. We talked about how when the beast was out there, there was no worried and scared Sammy around; furthermore, when he was just being, perceiving, acting, and making decisions (e.g., swing, don't swing), there really was no Sammy at all. He liked the idea and said on his own, "It would be cool to be a No-Sammy more often." That name, No-Sammy, became a cue word for him to shift into how he is in practice during game days. Of course, it took a lot of practice to have No-Sammy stick around for most of a game, and his worries and negative thinking emerged again and again. We worked together on some basic mindful walking and mindful running exercises, which he called "No-Sammy walking" and "No-Sammy running." With practice, he worked up to "No-Sammy batting" and "No-Sammy fielding." As he got better at being (mindful in present time), his worries decreased, but he never got rid of them completely (I know of no one who has ever been cured of their neuroses). Sammy's game performance improved to the point that scouts from American universities were looking at him, and he eventually received a scholarship to play and study in the United States. Just as important, and maybe more so, Sammy's happiness increased. He wasn't so plagued by his anxieties and doubts, and when they did arise he was able to be mindful of his worries and emotions and let them rise, fall, and pass. As the Dalai Lama has stated repeatedly in so many of his books, the purpose of life is to be happy. Not once, in all our work together, did I ever mention the words *Buddhism* and *meditation*. Sammy wasn't helped by attempts to build self-esteem, self-worth, self-efficacy, self-belief, self-image, self-narratives (currently quite popular), or any other selfisms. He was helped by learning how to drop the self and its attachments. When his worries appeared, he did not fight them, or try to control them, or cling to them; rather, he would mindfully note their rise and fall as he returned to No-Sammy.

BUDDHISM'S ROLE IN SPORT PSYCHOLOGY

We have obviously stolen our essay title from Kopp's (1974) classic work on psychotherapy *If You Meet the Buddha on the Road, Kill Him: The Pilgrimage of Psychotherapy Patients.* The shocking command to kill the Buddha (or to tackle him) shakes up one's ideas about the proper order of things. In this chapter, we examine some central ideas in Western sport psychology (e.g., the concept of self, the sources of anxiety in sport) and tackle them (embracing no-self and nonclinging or letting go) through a discussion of the alternative view of Buddhism with a focus on the interpersonal and intimate world of applied sport psychology service.

In some Western psychotherapy traditions, Buddhism has had a substantial influence (see Epstein, 1995, 1999, 2002, 2005; Kabat-Zinn, 1990, 1994, 2003, 2005), but in applied sport psychology there are few references to Buddhist concepts of self, mindfulness, what it is to act, or the roots of anxiety. There are noteworthy exceptions. Marks (2008) examined neural correlates of mindfulness in sport, and Maddux (1997) discussed health and happiness in sport from an Eastern philosophical perspective. The Inner Game series of books by Timothy Gallwey gets at some principles (e.g., self 1 and self 2) that pass close to Buddhist concepts. *Zen in the Art of Archery* (Herrigel, 1999) and *Zen in the Martial Arts* (Hyams, 1982), although not really sport psychology texts, did bring sport and Buddhism together. In the philosophy of sport literature, one finds several examples of discussions of Buddhism and sport (e.g., Abe, 1986; Becker, 1982; Wertz, 1977), but translating those lofty academic works into applied sport psychology practice is not an easy task. In the popular sport press, one can find many articles using the word *Zen* or the term *mindfulness*, but the academic literature in applied sport psychology offers little on these Buddhist topics. This state of affairs seems odd given that most applied sport psychology texts include at least one section about staying in present time, which is a core feature of mindfulness and Buddhist philosophy.

Mindfulness

Mindfulness is not really foreign or mystical, even for Western psychologies. For example, Freud's therapeutic method of free association is a type of mindful practice. Clients are asked to speak about whatever comes to mind (emotions, thoughts, images) in the moment with as little censoring as possible. One is also being mindful when absorbed in a riveting movie and closely following the unfolding story. And some, though not all, of the features of flow (Csikszentmihalyi, 1990) look like mindfulness. Kabat-Zinn (2003) offered the following observation:

> *Mindfulness, it should be noted, being about attention, is also of necessity universal. There is nothing particularly Buddhist about it. We are all mindful to one degree or another, moment by moment. It is an inherent human capacity. The contribution of the Buddhist tradition has been in part to emphasize simple and effective ways to cultivate and refine this capacity and bring it to all aspects of life.* (p. 146)

The practice of mindfulness—the moment-to-moment awareness of one's body, thoughts, emotions, and actions—has, in the past few decades, become all the rage in clinical and counseling psychology, and literally hundreds of articles address mindfulness in psychology, medicine, education, and business. The mindfulness bandwagon has also arrived in applied sport psychology or, rather, has been appropriated from Buddhist philosophy and practice. Kee and John Wang (2008) examined interconnections between mindfulness, mental skills, and flow. Gardner and Moore (2004) discussed theoretical underpinnings of mindfulness and performance enhancement, and, in their text *The Psychology of Enhancing Human Performance: The Mindfulness-Acceptance-Commitment Approach* (Gardner & Moore, 2007), they have made a significant contribution to bringing mindfulness into applied sport psychology practice.

One criticism of the mindfulness approach in applied sport psychology (and elsewhere) is that mindfulness is one part of the Eightfold Path in the fourth noble truth of Buddhism. When practitioners appropriate this path and take it out of context, then, its use (e.g., for performance enhancement) seems, at times, almost antithetical to its original purpose. Chögyam Trungpa (1973) described the Western inclination to use meditative practices (e.g., mindfulness, yoga, zazen) to increase personal power, self-esteem, or success or to compensate for feelings of existential emptiness as forms of what he called spiritual materialism (acquiring spiritual practices for material or ego-oriented gain). The goal of the Gardner and Moore (2007) text, as reflected in its title, is to enhance performance. Using mindfulness techniques to enhance performance, get more medals, receive more attention, or meet a compensatory need in response to feeling unloved or unworthy, then, seems to be a type of spiritual materialism that strays from the practice's original purpose. The purpose of mindfulness is to be mindful, and being mindful is one path to *sukha* (translated from Sanskrit and Pàli as happiness, ease, pleasure, or bliss) and the cessation of *dukkha* (suffering, pervasive unsatisfactoriness). A whole issue of the *Journal of Clinical Sport Psychology* (Gardner, 2009) was dedicated to mindfulness for performance enhancement. We do not think that such an approach optimally advances mindfulness in sport psychology; rather, it restricts its usefulness to a narrow species of performance-based spiritual materialism. But, we also believe that some mindfulness in applied sport psychology is better than none.

No-Self and Mindfulness

One central feature of Buddhist mindfulness is recognizing that there is only a continual rolling flow of thoughts, emotions, perceptions, and actions; there is no attached thinker, emoter, perceiver, or actor. However, this recognition of egolessness is often fleeting or absent because most of us believe there is an *I*, or ego, doing all our thinking and acting. We are attached to our (false) sense of self, and it is that attachment to self that often trips us up and gets in the way of *being*. This egoless state (in Pàli, *anatta,* meaning "no-self") may be helpful when one steps into a batting box in baseball, but it is also something we want to talk about, a bit later in this essay, for sport psychologists when they sit down with athletes in their offices or on the playing field.

Bruce Ogilvie, arguably the father of modern applied sport psychology, gave us a statement that we return to over and over again: "The extent to which you can lose your ego as a consultant in this field is going to determine the extent to which you are truly a contributor in the lives of the athletes you seek to serve" (quoted in Simons & Andersen, 1995, p. 467). One might argue that there are other criteria for defining successful treatment of athletes, such as whether a gold medal is won, but that approach veers so far away from the humanistic goals of psychology that we cannot give it much credence. From a Buddhist perspective, "to be is to be related," and that stance is central to what we mean when we talk about service. Compassionate service to others is the core of Buddhist practice, and it is that compassionate relatedness in the therapeutic relationship that fuels change. Buddhist themes of mindfulness are involved in problems having to do with ego and egolessness (i.e., self and no-self) in athletes and sport psychologists in service, and we refer to them often in this essay. Before discussing the concept of ego from a Buddhist perspective, we should probably start with some principles.

The Four Noble Truths

In this section, we focus on the first three noble truths; the fourth noble truth is the Eightfold Path to enlightenment and would take a whole chapter to cover adequately. We focus on one path, right-mindfulness, that underpins the others.

- **The first noble truth.** Many Western people may balk upon hearing the first noble truth of Buddhism. "Life means suffering" sounds like the language of victimization. One might respond, "But life is full of joy and happiness too; this view is way too pessimistic and negative." What the first noble truth addresses is often misinterpreted. Another version of the first noble truth is "all is suffering," a statement that many Westerners also find too global and pessimistic. The term used in Pàli is *dukkha,* and its translation into "suffering" has caused no end of misunderstandings. The term *dukkha* can mean a few different things, and its translation into the more accurate expressions of "pervasive unsatisfactoriness" or "disquietude" sets the first noble truth in a clearer light. Even in moments of joy there is a tinge of unsatisfactoriness because of the transience and impermanence of the experience. Great athletic achievements, gold medals, and such are often followed by feelings of regret ("Was it really worth it?") or a desire to cling to glory ("I wish I could have that feeling again"). The whole culture of sport could be seen as a culture of pervasive unsatisfactoriness. One is not training enough (i.e., training unsatisfactorily). One is not achieving enough. One must do more. You're not *citius, altius, fortius* enough!

For the beginning sport psychologist (see Stoltenberg, 1981), life may truly feel like suffering. Neophyte sport psychologists are often highly anxious. They worry about competence, anguish over doing the right thing, and feel vulnerable and naked in the face of supervisors' evaluation threats (real or imagined). They paint good pictures of their work with athletes to gain supervisor approval, then feel guilty. They feel like frauds and are anxious that they will be found out (see Andersen & Stevens, 2007). They translate supervisors' criticism into messages that tell them they are not good enough; they are not even satisfactory. And then they behave in ways that ensure their negative beliefs about themselves will be confirmed. They want or need to be competent (even exemplary) sport psychologists, but their needs mock their gear. Beginning sport psychologists are often in the hell realm of Buddhism (a state of being in which anxiety is dominant).

- **The second noble truth.** This truth addresses the origin of *dukkha*, or pervasive unsatisfactoriness. The second noble truth has been variously translated, and one common mistranslation is "the origin of suffering is desire," which is usually further explained as a "desire for permanence and needing attachment." Desire itself is not the culprit; a lack of desire would be apathy. The use of this word is another translation misrepresentation. The second noble truth is more subtle; it means that "the source of pervasive unsatisfactoriness is clinging." It is the clinging to impermanent objects, both internal and external, that brings about suffering. External objects include, for example, significant others, material possessions, fame, and gold medals. Academic sport psychologists may cling to tenure, prestigious publications, and status; applied sport psychologists, on the other hand, may cling to clients and teams. Students may cling to their supervisors, their grades, or their peers. Internal objects may be associated with one's pride, intelligence, self-esteem, ego, or, in the realm of sport, athletic identity (see Brewer, 1993). One may cling even to happiness, wanting momentary happiness to continue. Attachment is based on a fundamental misunderstanding of, and a desire for, permanence. The world is not a permanent place; things come into being, and things pass, all in ceaseless becoming and deterioration.

This noble truth about attachment and clinging is not so foreign to Western philosophical and literary traditions. When Heraclitus spoke 2,500 years or so ago (near the time of the Buddha) about not being able to step in the same river twice, he was talking about continual change. His element was fire, ceaseless becoming, transformation, and destruction. He stated that "nothing endures but change." Actually, you can't even step in the same river once, because the river and the stepper are both constantly changing. He and the Buddha would probably have gotten along well. Freud's (1916/1959) essay "On Transience" is probably one of the most Buddhist examples there is in literature of classic psychology on the impermanence of beauty, clinging, rejection of joy, and mourning.

The ego, or sense of I, is also not permanent; it is actually an illusion. There is no core; there is no I. There are only behaviors, emotions, and thoughts. As Epstein's (1995) book title suggests, there are only "thoughts without a thinker." But we are attached to this sense of ego, of self; we invest that self with gigantic meaning and significance, and we will defend it, even to the point of self-destruction. Athletes often construct false selves, known in the literature as athletic identity (see Brewer, 1993). Such identities are impermanent; they have use-by dates and ultimately collapse, sometimes catastrophically. When one no longer has an identity to cling to (e.g., when a career-ending injury collapses the vector of the athletic self), one may end up mired in the horror of emptiness, depression, and suicidal ideation.

This defended (and fragile) self is also the source of many sport psychology trainees' problems in supervision. They may not report some difficulties with clients because those issues will reflect poorly on their sense of self-competence and open them up to criticism. They may be supercompliant with supervisors to protect the ego from threat. They may report failures and frustrations that are congruent with poor self-images, confirming that they are incompetent (Andersen & Stevens, 2007). They may act in antagonistic ways for the unconscious purpose of eliciting caustic responses from their supervisors, responses that re-create abusive environments that are familiar to their own histories of being abused and are hence more comfortable (providing confirmation of their beliefs about themselves and the world). We cling even to negative self-images, because they are ours, and even though they are negative, we would be truly lost without them.

- **The third noble truth** states that the cessation of *dukkha* is attainable. In some translations and misrepresentations, this truth seems to say that "to be free of suffering, one must be free of desire and attachment." That sounds terribly schizoid, as if one is not connected. The opposite is actually the case. Our attachments, our quests for permanence, our needs to have things (people, ideas, egos) are what really keep us separate. When we let go of attachment, of ego, it is then we can truly be with ourselves and with others. Here is where Bruce Ogilvie's observation rings especially true. The cessation of *dukkha*, however, does not mean the end of painful experiences; rather, it transforms one's experience of them.

- **The fourth noble truth** involves the paths to the cessation of pervasive unsatisfactoriness. We address one of the Eightfold Paths (i.e., right mindfulness) later in the essay. Let's return now to the problems of the Western self.

Ego Development

The constitutions of most academic and athletic environments include a host of complex norms that one must meet to gain acceptance (and exceed to gain distinction): To gain tenure or entrance into doctoral programs, to secure a position on a team, or to please our mentors, our loved ones, or ourselves, we must manage our grade-point averages, our individual performances, and especially our issues and insecurities. We must play well with others yet be wary enough to avoid getting taken for a ride by politics and competitors. We often have the feeling of being pulled in many directions, and sometimes the Klaxon of our anxieties and doubts about the present and the future booms loudly.

Faced with encroaching demands, we are compelled to protect our fragile egos with an imposed, self-styled coherence or armor. This emotionally protective gear covers the parts of us felt to be undesirable or unintegrated, and, for stretches, it keeps the caustic elements at a safe distance. The success we experience in using our armor inflames an almost universal desire for permanent coherence. Winnicott (1971), a British psychoanalyst, referred to the arbitrary coherence we create to meet such demands as a "false self."

This false self, however facilitative, comes at a price. Sensing the incongruence between the coherence we present for survivability and the chaos and unintegration under this armor, we are left feeling inauthentic, fearing eventual exposure as frauds (Andersen & Stevens, 2007). This conflict is frequently exacerbated by a sense that to be helpful to others, to make a valuable contribution, we must already be perfect. As we internalize these standards for acceptance, we further identify with our false selves in the childlike hope that perhaps our inner conflict was somehow a mistake. We begin to fear being engulfed by difficult emotions, and we tighten our protective gear, especially our helmets and chest pads (i.e., head and heart), to restrict this range of emotional experience. Our determined but unsuccessful attempts leave us further estranged from others and ourselves.

Some supervisors and supervisees, some therapists and athletes, will be able to fortify these defenses until the temporal demands subside or mount enough energy to overcome them. Others may flee such environments altogether. For many, it is only a matter of time before a transition between developmental stages, or an unforeseen circumstance or event (internal or external), occurs that brings such everyday neurosis to crisis levels.

When we accept suffering, unsatisfactoriness, and difficult emotions as inevitable parts of our lives, we can begin to relax our rigid grip on our protective gear. No gear can protect us from the injurious conditions of life. We are going to be hurt. With this simple acknowledgment, we can begin to see the futility of all the energy we feed into our false selves. We begin to glimpse how our protective pads come to restrict our ability to breathe, to connect, to love, and to be still in the comfort that is realistically available. With the recognition of the first two noble truths, we can see a new kind of liberation accessible for our clients, for our graduate students, and for ourselves.

When parents or guardians provide a reassuring, unobtrusive presence in a child's environment, the child is free to explore, to wonder, to play, and to develop. Epstein (1995) described this way of parenting as "good enough" (as did Winnicott [1971] originally) because it precludes the need for a child to develop "false selves" to deal with parental difficulty. When parents or guardians are absent, physically or emotionally, or are overinvolved and overprotective, they disrupt the spontaneity and continuity of developmental experiences.

An emotionally or physically absent parent or guardian can void the sense of security and stability that is important to the child's internal development. Prematurely forced to cope with uncertain parents and left to their own devices, children often form "false selves" that arbitrarily protect such inner fragility. This false self, like that of the graduate student, the professor, or the athlete, becomes the basis for identity with all of its inherent trade-offs. Often, the void becomes internalized as a sense of emptiness and a fear, fundamentally, of nihilism or nonexistence. This more Western concept of emptiness is not to be confused with the emptiness described in Buddhist psychology, which disputes the reification of notions such as identity and emotion. The false self, or any self, is an illusion. It is empty.

Likewise, when the parent or guardian's needs supersede the child's needs, the child is forced to form a false self to meet these premature demands. The parental needs may be related to resolving their failed attempts in sport, soothing their irrational fears for the child's safety, or easing their insecurities by being the "perfect" parent with the "perfect" kids. False selves with these origins may take the form of "caretakers," who do not care for their own well-being (their job is to take care of their parents' emotional states), and "perfectionists," who strive to be deserving of love.

Being and Doing

Many beginning applied sport psychologists, and even seasoned ones, feel that they need to do something with their clients. They need to solve problems or fix something that is wrong. This need to do something is a cart-before-the-horse problem. We teach our applied sport psychology graduate students how to do things such as imagery and relaxation, but how much time do we spend in teaching them something about how to *be* with their athletes? We may talk to them about Rogerian characteristics (Rogers, 1957, 1961, 1992) of competent practitioners (e.g., empathetic, genuine, authentic, having unconditional positive regard), but how does one become empathic or authentic? We may teach techniques such as empathic reflection, mirroring, and active listening skills, but these tactics are still more doing than being.

Freud's (1912/1958) suggestions to practitioners on how to be with clients sound like they come from a Buddhist psychologist's handbook. In commenting on the psychoanalyst's stance in therapy, he wrote the following:

> *As we shall see, it rejects the use of any special expedient (even that of taking notes). It consists simply in not directing*

one's notice to anything in particular, and in maintaining the same "evenly suspended attention" (as I have called it) in the face of all that one hears. . . . The rule for the doctor may be expressed: "He should withhold all conscious influences from his capacity to attend, and give himself over completely to his 'unconscious memory.'" Or to put it purely in terms of technique: "He should simply listen, and not bother about whether he is keeping anything in mind." (pp. 111–112)

Freud is describing, in analytic terms, what it is to be a mindful practitioner. So why should a therapist or sport psychologist take a mindful stance, a stance of being, not necessarily doing, in practice? Part of the answer to that question lies in the need to form a therapeutic alliance with clients.

Mindfulness and the Therapeutic Alliance

Although mindfulness practices have been in mainstream clinical and counseling psychology for many years (e.g., Kabat-Zinn, 1990), most attention has been paid to helping clients become mindful. Recently, however, the mindfulness spotlight has been turned on the therapeutic alliance (e.g., Hick & Bien, 2008). We know that the quality of the therapeutic relationships between practitioners and clients usually accounts for more variance in outcomes than any specific interventions or models of treatment (Sexton & Whiston, 1994). In psychodynamic and object-relations therapies, the relationship is the vehicle through which change occurs. A few applied sport psychology authors and researchers (e.g., Andersen, 2007; Petitpas, Giges, & Danish, 1999) have drawn attention to the relationships and dynamics between sport psychologists and their clients, but there has been no extensive inquiry into this central aspect of service.

Carl Rogers (1957, 1961, 1992) is a source we continually go back to when we think about the position of the applied sport psychologist in service to others. Rogers' descriptors of ideal psychologists as genuine, authentic, open, empathic, nonjudgmental, and caring (even loving), and as having unconditional positive regard for clients, seem to point to personal and professional attributes that most of us would wish to cultivate or at least strive toward. All of these attributes help the practitioner and the client form a therapeutic alliance, or at least they increase the probability that a therapeutic relationship will develop, thus increasing the chances for positive change to occur. These attributes are ways of being, not doing. Being nonjudgmental, open to anything, empathic, and authentic are all descriptors of mindfulness. But let's take one of these qualities of being, empathy, and examine it more closely. Rogers (1992) described empathy this way:

> *To sense the client's private world as if it were your own, but without ever losing the "as if" quality—this is empathy, and this seems essential to therapy. To sense the client's anger, fear, or confusion as if it were your own, yet without your own anger, fear, or confusion getting bound up in it, is the condition we are endeavoring to describe.* (p. 832)

To empathize, to feel with clients, one needs to be open, nonjudgmental, and accepting of clients as who they are at this moment. The mindful stance of the therapist seems almost perfectly designed to promote empathy, and empathy seems to be a foundational state of being for the development of a therapeutic relationship. Its power lies in clients' perceptions that the stories they tell in therapy are understood, felt, and embraced with loving care no matter how scary, horrible, despairing, or shameful they are. To be heard and understood is a huge gift, and to feel that one is not alone is itself therapeutic. Positive relationships fuel change, and mindful therapists, with all their attributes, especially empathy, are well equipped to connect deeply with those in their care. In the two tales related in the following section, empathy, mindfulness, and the therapeutic alliance are the vehicles through which positive change occurs.

TWO TALES FROM OUR PRACTICE

Neither of us would call ourselves Buddhist, nor are we as accomplished at mindfulness or egolessness as we would like to be. We often find ourselves not being present in our encounters with clients and supervisees. Our stance of evenly suspended attention collapses over and over again. In these two tales we describe moments when we were able to stay mindful and drop our false selves and remain therapeutically present with a client and a supervisee.

Ivan: Anxiety and Mindfulness

I (Joe) worked with a junior elite 13-year-old golfer experiencing hellish competitive anxiety. Although he presented as a straightforward case of needing some tools to induce relaxation to counter his anxiety, a little exploration revealed his complaints to be the safe version of a more complicated situation and indicated that the usual relaxation interventions would likely prove futile in the larger picture. Ivan, whose parents were Russian immigrants, was particularly sensitive to criticism and would have anxiety attacks before and during competition. His mom was heavily involved in every aspect of his golfing career and frequently sat near the practice range as he worked with his coach.

I was having occasional panic attacks around the same time I worked with Ivan. Although my experience enabled me to recognize and identify with the subtle, and not so subtle, manifestations of Ivan's neurosis, I realized that our discussions of his competitive anxiety stoked the flames of my own panic disorder. My panic and Ivan's anxieties spoke to each other. When Ivan and I met and my anxieties flared, I maintained a mindful presence, allowing them to exist without needing to flee from Ivan, emotionally or physically. I did not prematurely try to save him and thereby save myself from my panic. I was able to use his idealizing transference to me (i.e., I seemed to be the fantasized wonderful parent he always wanted) to be the "good enough" (see Winnicott, 1971) psychologist, present but not overinvolved or overprotective. This therapeutic space, in which I held both my panic and Ivan's anxieties in evenly suspended attention and care, enabled Ivan to find the courage necessary to begin exploring his experience of his disruptive emotions. He discovered and reported a great sense of guilt that his parents were spending a disproportionate amount of money on his membership in the golf academy. I detected an unspoken assumption from his parents that he would more than make up for the family debt once he became hugely successful on the PGA Tour. Breathing techniques, though part of the practical intervention, would be unlikely to obviate such enormous pressure on a 13-year-old boy or change the perpetuating dynamics.

As we walked the fairways of Ivan's inner hell, one important feature of my role involved serving as a sort of emotional caddie, offering context and interpretation for this previously unplayed internal course and holding Ivan through the journey. Epstein (1995) described a number of common misconceptions we have about emotions, especially those difficult ones that are central to anxiety. One misconception is that emotions are like wild animals that must be controlled or tamed. They are reified, or perceived as concrete, and viewed as threats to our existence. These threats cause, for example, anxiety about experiencing anxiety or fear of experiencing phobia, which, of course, become self-fulfilling. The core of this terror, the fear of annihilation or being torn apart by wild animals, of being nothing or being devoid of reality, was a central feature of my own panic experiences.

A key function of my job in our collaborative alliance was to help Ivan face these supposed wild animals and see their ephemeral reality. By mindfully being with my anxiety and by being with his, I served as a mirror of this basic tenet of Buddhist psychology. With this new insight—this new, more flexible experience of being "Ivan" (and with some extensive, but less than optimal, work with his parents), he was then able to use the usual sport psychology cognitive-behavioral techniques (e.g., reinterpreting his precompetition anxiety as a sign of readiness and creating performance routines) to address his original complaint.

If my fear of being overwhelmed by panic had led to a discontinuity of my therapeutic presence, or to the prioritizing of my need to escape over Ivan's needs for immediate assistance, I would have repeated the patterns that led to his predicament, reinforcing his fears. The opportunity for liberation would have been missed, perhaps for both of us. Athletes, and people in general, often give therapy only one chance to succeed or fail. If Ivan had finally found someone with no personal stake in his career, whose only agenda was his well-being and happiness, and then even that person had failed to just *be* with him and mindfully hold his difficulties with loving care, the result could have been catastrophic. Alternatively, if I had been seduced into simply prescribing a set of relaxation exercises, they would likely have failed and further alienated Ivan in his hell, sending the horrifying and demonizing message, "You are beyond help."

Sean: Egolessness and Letting Go

I (Mark) have a story of supervision that speaks of suffering, clinging, and dropping egos in order to just be with one another. In supervision with my doctoral student, Sean, we had discussed his need to be the perfect athlete, the perfect sport psychologist, the perfect son. We had not delved into the origins of those needs (an issue for his personal psychotherapy), but we had discussed how those needs might influence his interactions with athletes and coaches in his role as a psychologist (an issue for his supervision).

I wanted to get across that perfection is impossible, that we are all damaged goods in some way, and that clinging to perfection only increases suffering. I decided to self-disclose, to drop my false self and show myself as damaged. My mother struggled with depression for much of her life. As her only son, I took it upon myself to try to fix her, to make her happy (my false caretaker self). One way I tried to accomplish this impossible task was to achieve. Another painfully obvious result of wanting to fix my mother is that I became a psychologist (fixing Mom [and myself] by proxy). By most standards, I am an overachiever—not exactly the perfectionism Sean has, but a closely related species. I used my achievements as gifts to my mom to treat her depression: "See, Mom, see what I have done; now please be happy." I clung to my achievements (still do, though maybe not so tightly now) in order to cling to my fantasies of fixing my mom. Of course they never worked, or they worked only briefly enough for me to be reinforced for accomplishing more, for desperately trying to fill her unfillable emptiness with my success. I wanted Sean to understand the damage, the clinging, and the unsatisfactoriness of his supervisor so that he might be kinder to himself and possibly let go of the false self of the perfect boy for a little while. During a supervision session with Sean, as he told his tales, I was mindful that I was experiencing waves of sadness that seemed to belong not only to me but also to Sean. I did not address my internal processes with Sean during the formal supervision hour, but later, when I was in a parking lot with Sean after supervision, I said, "Epstein described my life perfectly when he said, 'Or like the son of a depressed mother, trying to distract her with his accomplishments.' That would be me. That's my life and accomplishments in a nutshell." My main goal was to let down my defenses, drop the ego, and model openness and sadness and vulnerability. And Sean started to cry. I did not know that the roots of his perfectionism had similar ones to my overachieving.

My mindfulness of some shared sadness between us and my self-disclosure allowed Sean to drop his false perfect-boy self and become the confused hurt child who took on the task of trying to ensure his parents' happiness. A supervisor's modeling disclosure of his own clinging, and the unsatisfactoriness of his life, may free students to do the same and see their pain in a new and different light.

CONCLUSION

Mindfulness is not a fad in clinical and counseling psychology. It is part of universal human experience. Freud was mindful with his patients, and we imagine Carl Rogers was too. Many of us experience mindfulness on a more or less regular basis, although it is often fleeting. So why haven't mindfulness and its partner, no-self, made significant inroads in applied sport psychology? Gardner and Moore's (2007) text is an advancement in our field that we welcome, but it also seems to represent a narrow version of the original Buddhist practice and philosophy, and it contains aspects of spiritual materialism (as does the 2009 issue of the *Journal of Clinical Sport Psychology*, Gardner, 2009). Maybe a full embrace of mindfulness and no-self is too foreign for our self-oriented field. Maybe we are just too hung up on ourselves and can't let go. Athletic identity researchers and authors (e.g., Brewer, 1993) have shown us the intrapsychic pain (e.g., depression) that can accompany the collapse of a narrowly circumscribed (false) sense of self. And the solution is to construct a broadly circumscribed, a bigger and better, false self, and then to cling to that new and improved "me."

We don't want to put down research and practice that address the problems of narrow selves and that provide ways to become relatively free of imprisoning identities. The authors of essay 1 in this book, Carless and Douglas, have written in a previous journal article (2008) about how men with mental illnesses were able to restory their narratives about themselves through sport and exercise. The restorying probably helped reduce these men's *dukkha*, and maybe we should be happy with such outcomes and leave it at that. It seems that the men constructed new and healthier false selves than they had before. A Buddhist argument that they are still false selves would seem insensitive, even churlish. Carless and Douglas write about relational narratives and performance narratives and about how relational narratives appear to be less fraught with problems, more fluid, and more promoting of happiness than does the constricted performance narrative. And maybe the relational narrative, or the relational self, is good enough. Maybe we don't have to tackle and embrace the Buddha, but in the relational narrative we have a sense of his being there. As he would say, "To be is to be related."

IDEAS FOR REFLECTION AND DEBATE

1. Buddhism is probably misunderstood in the West on many levels. Did this essay help or hinder your understanding? Either way, how so?

2. Considering the major emphasis on the self in Western psychology, do you think Buddhist concepts have much to offer? If yes, how so? If not, why not?

3. How do you respond to the concept of "no-self"? Is it useful in practice? Is it too esoteric?

4. How might radical behaviorism and Buddhist philosophy be similar?

5. Freud believed that the therapist should take the stance of evenly suspended attention. The Buddha recommended something quite similar with the path of right mindfulness. How does your stance as a sport psychologist compare with the stances of the Buddha and Freud?

REFERENCES

Abe, S. (1986). Zen and sport. *Journal of the Philosophy of Sport, XIII,* 45–48.

Andersen, M.B. (2007). Collaborative relationships in injury rehabilitation: Two case examples. In D. Pargman (Ed.), *Psychological bases of sport injuries* (3rd ed., pp. 219–234). Morgantown, WV: Fitness Information Technology.

Andersen, M.B., & Stevens, L. (2007). On being a fraud. *Sport and Exercise Psychology Review, 3*(2), 43–46.

Becker, C.B. (1982). Philosophical perspectives on the martial arts in America. *Journal of the Philosophy of Sport, IX,* 19–29.

Brewer, B.W. (1993). Self-identity and specific vulnerability to depressed mood. *Journal of Personality, 61,* 343–364.

Carless, D., & Douglas, K. (2008). Narrative, identity and mental health: How men with serious mental illness re-story their lives through sport and exercise. *Psychology of Sport and Exercise, 9,* 576–594.

Csikszentmihalyi, M. (1990). *Flow: The psychology of optimal experience.* New York: HarperCollins.

Epstein, M. (1995). *Thoughts without a thinker: Psychotherapy from a Buddhist perspective.* New York: Basic Books.

Epstein, M. (1999). *Going to pieces without falling apart: A Buddhist perspective on wholeness.* New York: Broadway Books.

Epstein, M. (2002). *Going on being: Buddhism and the way of change.* New York: Broadway Books.

Epstein, M. (2005). *Open to desire, embracing a lust for life: Insights from Buddhism and psychotherapy.* New York: Gotham Books.

Freud, S. (1958). Recommendations to physicians practicing psychoanalysis. In J. Stachey (Ed. & Trans.), *The standard edition of the complete psychological works of Sigmund Freud* (Vol. 12, pp. 111–120). London: Hogarth. (Original work published 1912.)

Freud, S. (1959). On transience. In J. Stachey (Ed. & Trans.). *The standard edition of the complete psychological works of Sigmund Freud* (Vol. 14, pp. 305–306). London: Hogarth. (Original work published 1916.)

Gardner, F.E. (Ed.). (2009). Mindfulness- and acceptance-based approaches to sport performance and well-being [Special issue]. *Journal of Clinical Sport Psychology, 3*(4).

Gardner, F.E., & Moore, Z.E. (2004). A mindfulness-acceptance-commitment-based approach to athletic performance enhancement: Theoretical considerations. *Behavior Therapy, 35,* 707–723.

Gardner, F.E., & Moore, Z.E. (2007). *The psychology of enhancing human performance: The mindfulness-acceptance-commitment approach.* New York: Springer.

Herrigel, E. (with Suzuki, D. T.). (1999). *Zen in the art of archery* (R.F.C. Hull, Trans.). New York: Vintage Books. (Original work published 1948.)

Hick, S.F., & Bien, T. (Eds.). (2008). *Mindfulness and the therapeutic relationship.* New York: Guilford Press.

Hyams, J. (1982). *Zen in the martial arts.* New York: Bantam Books.

Kabat-Zinn, J. (1990). *Full catastrophe living: Using the wisdom of your body and mind to face stress, pain, and illness.* New York: Dell.

Kabat-Zinn, J. (1994). *Wherever you go, there you are. Mindfulness meditation in everyday life.* New York: Hyperion.

Kabat-Zinn, J. (2003). Mindfulness-based interventions in context: Past, present, and future. *Clinical Psychology: Science and Practice, 10,* 144–156.

Kabat-Zinn, J. (2005). *Coming to our senses: Healing ourselves and the world through mindfulness.* New York: Hyperion.

Kee, Y.H., & John Wang, C.K. (2008). Relationships between mindfulness, flow dispositions and mental skills adoption: A cluster analytic approach. *Psychology of Sport and Exercise, 9,* 393–411.

Kopp, S.B. (1974). *If you meet the Buddha on the road, kill him: The pilgrimage of psychotherapy patients.* New York: Bantam Books.

Maddux, J.E. (1997). Habit, health, and happiness. *Journal of Sport & Exercise Psychology, 19,* 331–346.

Marks, D.R. (2008). The Buddha's extra scoop: Neural correlates of mindfulness and clinical sport psychology. *Journal of Clinical Sport Psychology, 2,* 216–241.

Petitpas, A.J., Giges, B., & Danish, S. (1999). The sport psychologist-athlete relationship: Implications for training. *The Sport Psychologist, 13,* 344–357.

Rogers, C.R. (1957). Training individuals to engage in the therapeutic process. In C.R. Strouther (Ed.), *Psychology and mental health* (pp. 76–92). Washington, DC: American Psychological Association.

Rogers, C.R. (1961). *On becoming a person.* Boston: Houghton Mifflin.

Rogers, C.R. (1992). The necessary and sufficient conditions of therapeutic personality change. *Journal of Consulting and Clinical Psychology, 60,* 827–832.

Sexton, T.L., & Whiston, S.C. (1994). The status of the counseling relationship: An empirical review, theoretical implications, and research directions. *The Counseling Psychologist, 22,* 6–78.

Simons, J.P., & Andersen, M.B. (1995). The development of consulting practice in applied sport psychology: Some personal perspectives. *The Sport Psychologist, 9,* 449–468.

Stoltenberg, C. (1981). Approaching supervision from a developmental perspective: The counselor complexity model. *Journal of Counseling Psychology, 28,* 59–65.

Trungpa, C. (1973). *Cutting through spiritual materialism.* Berkeley, CA: Shambala.

Wertz, S.K. (1977). Zen, yoga, and sports: Eastern philosophy for Western athletes. *Journal of the Philosophy of Sport, IV,* 68–82.

Winnicott, D.W. (1971). *Playing and reality.* London: Routledge.

TAMING THE WILD WEST:

Training and Supervision in Applied Sport Psychology

David Tod
Aberystwyth University, United Kingdom

David Lavallee
Aberystwyth University, United Kingdom

Drawing on the literature and their experiences as educators and practitioners, the two Davids reflect on ways in which current training and supervision practices might be insufficient for preparing students for applied sport psychology careers. They begin by asking if a focus on performance enhancement, underpinned by a psychological skills training (PST) approach, is leading to a large number of trained professionals relative to the number of jobs available. The Davids then ask if there is an overemphasis on a PST model when evidence suggests that exposure to a variety of approaches may better prepare students for the range of issues that clients present. In addition, they identify an underemphasis on process and relationship issues that also affect service delivery. The Davids then review evidence about whether the quality and quantity of supervision in the field are adequate for helping practitioners develop as professionals and meet their clients' needs. They also ask if the focus on research in universities creates environments that hinder educators' attempts to assist students' development. In conclusion, they suggest that much can be gained when applied sport psychology training and supervision are brought under the providence of mainstream psychology departments and professional bodies.

INTRODUCTION

The term *spaghetti Western* is a nickname for any of a string of movies produced in Italian studios in the 1960s and 1970s. They were set in the Wild West of North America at a time when law and order were minimal and cowboys roamed the land. In spaghetti Westerns, cowboys lived how they wished, often as loners, and frequently took the law into their own hands to resolve their issues. Over the past 35 years, there has been tremendous growth in applied sport psychology (Williams & Straub, 2010), and perhaps the spaghetti Western and the Wild West provide useful metaphors for describing how in parts of the sport psychology frontier some individuals have acted like cowboys (in positive and not so positive ways), either by choice or through the natural consequences of what may have been patchwork quilts of training and supervision.

The new frontier of applied sport psychology began to open up in earnest during the late 1970s and early 1980s as athletes and coaches sought help in their quests for performance enhancement, and a growing number of practitioners marketed themselves. Law and order were in short supply, and, as Andersen and Tod (in press) documented, there was little agreement regarding suitable codes of practice or boundaries within which practitioners might operate or the titles by which they could refer to themselves. There was also little agreement regarding the suitable types of training, supervision, and licensing (certification, accreditation, registration) models to ensure that practitioners were safe, ethical, and effective (Andersen & Tod). In some places, the environment was similar to that of the Old West's Dodge City: unruly and chaotic. In the absence of suitable training and licensing models, some consultants operated independently and were self-taught (Simons & Andersen, 1995). Many of these practitioners developed the knowledge and skills to be safe and ethical and have provided athlete-clients with high-quality services. A few unscrupulous (or, more likely, unreflective) individuals, however, have left trails of alienation behind them, giving some people the impression that sport psychologists are frauds selling snake oil. Even today, many services advertised on the Internet make suspect claims of success and offer assessment tools that are even more suspect. Also during this period, many sport psychology practitioners borrowed interventions from the cognitive-behavioral therapy approaches, from which the psychological skills training (PST) model has evolved.

As sport psychology continued to grow and spread across the world (Lidor, Morris, Bardaxoglu, & Becker, 2001), law and order were established in some areas through the development of training programs and certification (registration, licensure) schemes (Morris, Alfermann, Lintunen, & Hall, 2003). As these programs (graduate university degrees) and schemes (e.g., United States Olympic Committee Registry of Sport Psychology Providers) became recognized and accepted, cowboys found fewer opportunities to live outside the law. Just as remnants of the Wild West remain in the American mountains and deserts, however, some territories of the sport psychology frontier are far from domesticated or tamed. Even now, some cowboys in the field have not obtained status as certified (accredited, licensed) consultants (Morris et al., 2003), and it is likely that this will always be the case, because clients choose psychology practitioners based on who they believe will help them with their issues—not primarily on consultants' training and qualifications. Some of these practitioners will probably not enroll in established applied sport psychology training programs, expose themselves to critical and reflective supervision, or apply for licensure. At the same time, it is not obligatory to complete an applied sport psychologist training program or achieve licensure to deliver effective service. Some cowboys, like many lay helpers, may be able to help athletes adequately with a range of issues and needs. In addition, undertaking applied sport psychologist training and supervision does not necessarily mean that a qualified practitioner is able to help with the breadth of issues that athletes present. Sometimes qualified practitioners may be unable to assist clients because they have not retained the knowledge or skills addressed in graduate school, perhaps because their own needs and issues hindered their learning (Andersen, Van Raalte, & Brewer, 2000). In other cases, qualified practitioners may be unable to help clients because the training programs in which they enrolled did not prepare them for addressing certain issues.

In this chapter, we reflect on ways in which some current training and supervision practices in the field might be insufficient for equipping future practitioners. Specifically, we consider issues associated with curriculums, supervision, and educator training. In doing so, we draw on the published literature and reflect on our experiences as sport psychology practitioners and educators. We acknowledge that for some readers we may not provide satisfactory answers to the issues we raise. Given the scope of this book, however, perhaps our thoughts will stimulate debate and assist educators and supervisors in reflecting on their own beliefs and practices.

THE CURRENT STATE OF APPLIED SPORT PSYCHOLOGY PRACTICE

In determining suitable training and supervision practices in applied sport psychology, we must identify the careers for which trainees are ostensibly prepared. Students usually want to work with athletes and often (legitimately) ask about the amount of sport psychology work that is available, but only a limited amount of data is readily available to document recent graduates' employment patterns. The few such investigations conducted have produced data that are limited primarily to Australia and the United States (Aldridge, Andersen, Stanton, & Shen, 1997; Andersen, Williams, Aldridge, & Taylor, 1997; Waite & Pettit, 1993; Williams & Scherzer, 2003). Much of the research is dated, and the employment landscape may have changed since the data were collected. With these caveats in mind, U.S. data from these graduate tracking studies indicate that the majority of doctoral students find jobs teaching in higher education. Most master's degree graduates continue on to further education or become physical education teachers and coaches (Williams & Scherzer, 2003). Only a minority of graduates make a full-time living by consulting with athletes. Also, in the last 10 to 15 years, membership has not grown much in one of the largest sport psychology professional organizations, the Association for Applied Sport Psychology (AASP; Andersen, 2009). AASP has had between 1,000 and 1,200 members for the last 15 years, and usually about half of those members are students. Thus the field seems relatively stagnant as compared with other sport professions that started out at about the same time; the National Strength and Conditioning Association, for example, started in the late 1970s and now has more than 30,000 members worldwide. So where have all the potential sport psychology practitioners gone?

Traditionally, postgraduate sport psychology education was based in kinesiology, exercise science, and physical education departments and focused on research theses, scientific investigation skills, and some practical experience in working with athletes (Andersen & Tod, in press; Zaichkowsky, 2006). In more recent years, applied sport psychology training programs have evolved and focused on developing practitioner-related skills and knowledge, as documented in the *Directory of Graduate Programs in Applied Sport Psychology* (Burke, Sachs, Fry, & Schweighardt, 2008). Many of these programs have continued to be based in kinesiology departments, and given that a PST model pervades the research and practice literature it is likely that this approach still dominates applied sport psychology teaching in many places. As a consequence of the PST model, some applied sport psychology training programs may be preparing students for a limited number of employment possibilities. There are not many jobs in which the individual's core role is to teach athletes skills such as imagery, self-talk, goal setting, concentration, and relaxation for the purpose of performance enhancement. Other psychology-related jobs, such as athletic counselor and athlete career advisor, involve applying a broader range of skills to a greater variety of issues (Lavallee & Andersen, 2000).

It is also possible that future employment opportunities have not been taken into account when developing training programs. In our experience over the last 15 years, universities appear to be applying more pressure to increase student intake and develop popular courses to ensure financial viability. Some administrators or program leaders have argued that it is students' responsibility to find employment after completing their degrees and that university staff are not accountable to anyone if trainees cannot find suitable jobs. Some sport psychology professionals (such as those in Australia and Belgium), however, appear to have considered trainees' employment prospects. For example, one reason that the Australian sport psychology community came under the umbrella of the Australian Psychological Society was to help ensure that graduates who earn master's and professional doctorate degrees with an emphasis on sport and exercise psychology could obtain state registration (and now, national registration) as psychologists first and thus be eligible for a wider range of jobs (Morris, 1995).

Although there may not be many full-time jobs that involve traditional sport psychology work, according to Hanrahan and Andersen (2010), when we consider the number of helping-profession practitioners who assist athletes as all or part of their workload, we find that a large amount of psychology work is occurring in sport settings. The professionals mentioned by Hanrahan and Andersen include psychologists, psychiatrists, counselors, psychotherapists, hypnotherapists, and social workers. In terms of the services being used by athletes, Andersen (2009) reported the following:

The Australian (Rules) Football League Players' Association (AFLPA) about 4 years ago hired a graduate of a professional doctoral sport psychology program to direct and coordinate psychological services to current and former players and their families. The service is strictly confidential. Even coaches do not know who is receiving care. The approach is the health, welfare and happiness of footballers. The director contracts a raft of psychologists around Australia to provide service. Business is booming, and the director is constantly looking for more psychologists to help meet the AFLPA's needs. What percentage of the service is performance enhancement related? It may not be quite 0 percent, but it isn't more than 3 percent. (p. 14)

Andersen's observation is supported by findings from two longitudinal studies in which researchers followed a cohort of practitioners for 6 years since they began their postgraduate training (Tod, Andersen, & Marchant, 2009, 2011). Of the seven participants interviewed after 6 years, two were involved in sport full time, two did not work with athletes, and the remaining three helped sport and exercise participants on a part-time basis. In addition, the participants who did work with athletes reported that less than 20 percent of their service with this population focused on performance enhancement. The figure of 20 percent was inflated by one individual, and for the other folks the percentages were under 10 percent.

From a pragmatic perspective, students wishing to consult with athletes might consider obtaining qualifications that allow them to become psychologists, counselors, or social workers so that they are able to find jobs and work with a broader base of clients to supplement income generated from athletes, coaches, and teams. Such qualifications are more likely to be delivered in psychology than in kinesiology departments. This discussion echoes Feltz's (1987) earlier advice that for those people interested in service delivery for athletes, an education predominantly in psychology would be most suitable, whereas those folks wishing to do research and assume academic positions would be better advised to follow an exercise science path.

OVEREMPHASIS ON THE PST APPROACH

Recently, I (David T.) attended a national workshop run by an experienced consultant for the purpose of professional development. The practitioner began the workshop by saying that he did not use theory to guide his service delivery. He believed that theory and research were of no help. During and after the workshop, I talked with participants about their views on theory, and, though many of the individuals subscribed to a PST model, it was clear that they had limited understanding of the cognitive-behavioral approaches underpinning their service delivery practices (e.g., Ellis' rational-emotive behavior therapy perspective; Ellis & Dryden, 2007). Perhaps it is a reflection of the current training models in the United Kingdom (and possibly elsewhere) that individuals can become qualified practitioners and work with athletes without needing to understand, comprehend, or be otherwise knowledgeable about the theories on which their modes of operation are based. Students are able to pass applied sport psychology training programs and complete supervision requirements without needing to delve into the original works of the master cognitive-behavioral practitioners and theorists. In our experience, trainees may say their theoretical orientation is cognitive-behavioral, but often they are unable to elucidate the principles advocated by the theorists because they have not read or been exposed to them.

Speculating more broadly, sport psychology training in many programs might offer limited theoretical basis for suitable service delivery. This limited education seems particularly noticeable in students who are completing research-based degrees in the United Kingdom, Australia, and New Zealand. Students may have read some of the important sport psychology works associated with service delivery practice, training, and supervision—such as those by Hill (2001); Poczwardowski, Sherman, and colleagues (Poczwardowski, Sherman, & Henschen, 1998; Poczwardowski, Sherman, & Ravizza, 2004); and Andersen (2000a, 2005c)—but these writings are, or should be, just the beginning for trainees. One result of such limited reading is that trainees may develop uninformed and uncritical allegiances to the models they learn. For example, trainees might state that they are humanistically oriented because they try to establish rapport with clients and consider them holistically. Or they might say they are psychodynamically oriented because they ask athletes about their family relationships. Often, however, beyond such broad statements, trainees are unable to describe the details of the various schools of thought. It quickly becomes apparent they have not read the original works of masters such as Freud, Erikson, Rogers, Beck, and Yalom. Reading (and discussing with knowledgeable mentors) the classic references of the master theorists allows trainees to recognize where secondary sources often misrepresent the original documents (for some humorous examples, see Handelsman & Palladino, 1999).

In addition, although cognitive-behavioral theory can provide a solid base to underpin trainees' attempts to assist clients, exposure to other approaches adds to students' service delivery armamentaria. In two recent studies, neophyte practitioners whose professional development was followed across a 6-year period discussed how drawing on more than one approach to service delivery gave them flexibility in helping athletes (Tod et al., 2009). Although the cognitive-behavioral model can provide practitioners with the skills to help a range of clients with a number of issues, there is a risk in having only one hammer because practitioners may then be inclined to see only nails. A well-trained practitioner can wield a hammer, a saw, and a plumb line.

UNDEREMPHASIS ON PROCESS-ORIENTED ISSUES

According to the Sy Oliver song, it's not what you do, it's the way that you do it; that's what gets results. These lyrics suggest another view of the ways in which applied sport psychology training programs may inadequately prepare trainees for careers as consultants. Research has provided evidence that effective practitioners do more than teach athletes a range of psychological skills for performance; they are also skilled at developing and managing professional working relationships (Andersen, 2006; Anderson, Miles, Robinson, & Mahoney, 2004; Tod & Andersen, 2005). Such research is paralleled by counseling and clinical psychology investigations revealing that the main active ingredients in psychotherapy are not necessarily the specific interventions and tools associated with the various schools of thought. Instead, research suggests that common factors in most therapies, such as the working relationship, may account for a substantial amount of variance in client outcomes (Wampold, 2001).

In other words, it does not matter so much which counseling model practitioners use (e.g., CBT, psychodynamic, existential). One consistent factor in treatment outcome that is common to most therapy models is the quality of the working alliance formed with the client (Sexton & Whiston, 1994). Close, caring relationships with clients usually help them get better at what they do (in their lives or in their sports; see Andersen, 2005a). Some applied sport psychology models of training (e.g., those with primarily a PST approach), however, often emphasize the specific factors (e.g., interventions) at the expense of the common factors (e.g., relationships).

As one example, transference and countertransference are relationship processes that occur during service delivery yet have not been mentioned a great deal in the sport psychology literature beyond a small number of authors (e.g., Andersen, 2000b, 2004; Henschen, 1991; Strean & Strean, 1998; Yambor & Connelly, 1991) and may well get only superficial attention in educational programs underpinned by a PST model. Transference occurs when clients react to practitioners in ways that reflect past real or fantasized relationships with significant others (Andersen, 2004); for example, athletes may treat their practitioners like the parental figures they wish they had had when they were teenagers. Countertransference occurs when practitioners react to athletes in similar ways; for example, Tod (2007a) discussed how his desire to be the mentor he had never had as an athlete may have influenced the help that he gave a rugby league player. Transference and countertransference may help or hinder service delivery either with or without practitioners' understanding or awareness. The first data-based survey on countertransference in sport psychology appeared recently in the literature (Winstone, & Gervis, 2006), and with increased attention educators and supervisors may realize that teaching trainees to recognize and manage transference and countertransference helps their charges to develop skills that both deepen and broaden the service delivery process.

Erotic transference is another relationship topic that, beyond the writings of Stevens and Andersen (Andersen, 2005b; Stevens & Andersen, 2007a, 2007b), has received only limited attention in sport psychology literature. It is likely that erotic transference is seldom discussed or addressed in sport psychology training. It would seem probable, however, that practitioners who engage in any reasonable amount of applied work will come across situations in which one or both of the individuals involved begins, at least, to have erotic fantasies. For example, in a study on consultants' experiences in using self-talk, one interviewee discussed how the help she gave a client had been compromised because she had been attracted to, and had tried to impress, the athlete (Tod, Hardy, Niven, & Lavallee, 2008). This individual had not been taught how to recognize and deal with erotic countertransference. Unless practitioners are trained and prepared to deal with such situations, it is possible for erotic transference and countertransference to interfere with service delivery, compromise positive outcomes, leave people feeling guilty and betrayed, and possibly result in practitioners' transgressing boundaries and facing disciplinary actions from professional boards (as happened in Australia with a sport psychologist in 2004).

Yet another topic that has not received extensive attention in the literature is that of individuals' motives for working as consultants (Andersen et al., 2000; Tod et al., 2009), and it is likely that supervisors and educators seldom ask trainees to examine their own motives. Although applied psychology is, by and large, a generative profession, it would seem unrealistic to expect practitioners to be altruistic, and most would need some personal, material, psychological, or other gains to continue offering services. Trainees' motives are likely to influence their client interactions in both helpful and unhelpful ways (Tod et al., 2009). For example, I (David T.) was speaking with a colleague about a consultant who became angry when the national team with whom he was working failed to qualify for an international competition. When asked about his reaction, he replied that he had always wanted to represent his country in the sport, and it annoyed him when talented athletes did not try as hard as he had tried to succeed. If not reflected on and worked through, such a reaction may strain and disrupt working alliances and prevent athletes from seeking assistance from this practitioner. Applied sport psychologists are humans who have desires and motives. It would seem salubrious if supervisors and educators were to ask trainees to reflect on their motives and then provide assistance to ensure that students can manage their own longings and emotional reactions during service delivery.

In addition to supervision, which is discussed next, personal psychotherapy is a place where trainees can learn about how relationship processes and their own motives influence service delivery. Many counseling and clinical psychology training programs encourage, or even require, their students to undertake personal psychotherapy, and a number of professionals have made a similar recommendation for sport psychology trainees (Andersen et al., 2000; Petitpas, Giges, & Danish, 1999; Tod, 2007b). Evidence that sport psychology trainees benefit from undergoing psychotherapy emerged from two studies focused on professional development (Tod, Andersen et al., 2009; Tod, Marchant, & Andersen, 2007). Trainees' self-explorations in therapy helped them learn more about themselves and how their needs, histories, and inclinations might influence their relationships with others and their service delivery behaviors. Trainees also stated that seeing a therapist in action provided them with another model from which they learned how to help athletes. The number of sport psychology training programs that require or encourage students to undertake personal therapy is unknown, but it is likely to be small because most programs are housed in exercise science departments, not psychology or counseling departments (Andersen et al., 2000). We would recommend that sport psychology educators consider providing opportunities for trainees to gain academic credit for their own personal counseling or psychotherapy.

Although little research documents the frequency with which process-oriented topics are included in training, historically these subjects in applied sport psychology have not been commonly taught outside of programs in psychology and counseling departments. Supervised work experience is one point in training where students can deal with process-oriented and relationship issues. Research (e.g., Watson, Zizzi, Etzel, & Lubker, 2004) into current supervision practices in the field, however, suggests that trainees are often unlikely to gain enough opportunities to get experience in many of the process-oriented and relationship issues they will face as practitioners.

SUPERVISION DURING TRAINING

Graduates and staff members of master's and professional doctorate degree programs indicated that supervised client experience was a central component in the development of service delivery competence (Tod et al., 2007). During an apprenticeship, individuals are engaged in supervised work experience from the beginning of their training, in addition to spending time in the classroom. Supervised work experience is an ideal place for trainees to learn the art and science of applied sport psychology, and it helps protect both athletes and trainees. For example, athletes know that experienced practitioners are overseeing the trainees, and neophyte consultants can feel comforted that they have the guidance and support of interested professional elders (Van Raalte & Andersen, 2000). It is unlikely that many applied sport psychology professionals would disagree that supervised work experience contributes to practitioners' growth. Although supervision practices in applied sport psychology are not well documented, the available research seems to provide evidence that both the quantity and quality of supervision might be questionable in the training of many students.

The amount of supervised experience that trainees receive appears to vary depending on the country and institutions in which they are trained. In Australia, for example, students enrolled in master's of applied psychology programs (with an emphasis on sport and exercise) complete 1,000 hours of supervised experience, and individuals undertaking professional doctorates complete 1,500 hours (Tod et al., 2007). In the absence of a master's or professional doctorate degree, Australian trainees normally need 2 years of full-time supervised work (beyond their 4 years of psychology education) to obtain registration. In the United States, the Association for Applied Sport Psychology (AASP) certification guidelines require 400 hours, including at least 100 hours of direct contact with clients (which amounts to 2.5 weeks of full-time work). These numbers seem minimal when compared with what is required of service providers in other industries. In the United States, for example, athletic trainers complete 1,500 hours, and clinical and counseling psychologists undertake 3,000 to 4,000 hours of supervised practice (Van Raalte & Andersen, 2000). The California Board of Barbering and Cosmetology requires 3,200 hours (www.barbercosmo. ca.gov/laws_regs/regulations.shtml).

In a study, applied sport psychology graduates discussed variation in the quality of supervision they received as part of their training (Tod et al., 2007). Participants shared a perception that their counseling and clinical psychology supervisors had contributed more than their sport psychology supervisors had to their development. We may find these views understandable when comparing the counseling and clinical supervisors with their sport psychology counterparts. The counseling and clinical supervisors were often practicing psychologists who worked in the same establishments as the trainees, and these supervisors would have been familiar with the typical issues arising in the client populations. In contrast, the sport psychology supervisors were often academics and may have lacked extensive applied sport psychology experience, been unfamiliar with the issues that students were dealing with, or been unable to provide immediate feedback.

In some professional organizations that regulate licensure (accreditation, certification, registration) schemes, the characteristics of suitable supervisors do not appear to have been given sufficient consideration. Suitable supervisors, according to some bodies, are deemed to be those individuals who have been accredited or certified (or the equivalent). Such a criterion might be considered similar to the "good athletes make good coaches" argument. Good athletes may become superb coaches, but they often need additional training and preparation. Similarly, although effective applied sport psychology practitioners will most likely have a broad range of knowledge, skills, and experiences to draw on when supervising trainees, they may need additional training to learn the optimal ways in which to help the next generation. Barney, Andersen, and Riggs (1996) addressed the issue of teaching individuals the knowledge and skills that are needed for becoming helpful supervisors. Like many other works on supervision, their article appears to have been largely ignored by the sport psychology community (at the time of this writing, it has been cited only five times in 14 years, according to the ISI Web of Knowledge database, available at http://wokinfo.com). Barney et al. described a model in which advanced trainees take coursework in supervision and in supervising beginning trainees while also receiving supervision of their supervision (i.e., metasupervision) from peers and professional elders. The model was probably ahead of its time in light of the limited amount of regular supervision that occurs in applied sport psychology (see Watson et al., 2004). Nevertheless, given the observation that some graduates may be unhappy with the quality of the supervision they receive (Andersen, Van Raalte, & Brewer, 1994; Tod et al., 2007), the issue of how to prepare individuals to become effective supervisors may need to be revisited.

SUPERVISION AFTER TRAINING

In recognition that practitioners need opportunities to update their skills and expand their repertoires, professional development programs have arisen in a number of applied sport psychology organizations. Supervision, however, is not generally a central requirement for continued registration or for membership in professional organizations. Instead, individuals normally demonstrate their continued professional development via activities such as staying up to date with the literature, publishing, and attending and presenting at workshops or conferences. Practicing psychotherapists, however, have indicated that continuous supervision (as well as experience with clients and personal psychotherapy) contributes more to their professional development than do reading, publishing, and presenting (Orlinsky, Botermans, Rønnestad, & The SPR Collaborative Research Network, 2001). Despite the finding that practitioners benefit from supervision, research suggests that applied sport psychologists do not typically seek supervisors after graduation (Watson et al., 2004). Given the low number of supervised experience hours needed to satisfy applied sport psychologist training and certification criteria, especially when compared with those required of other mental health care providers, practitioners may come across situations that they are ill equipped to handle. The lack of supervision during these early years of practice may result in stunted growth as a consultant, ineffective service delivery, and a feeling among clients that sport psychology is unhelpful.

In this section, we have painted a somewhat bleak picture of the state of supervision in the field, suggested that it does not take place often enough, and questioned the quality of some of the guidance that is given. There is evidence, however, that high-quality supervision can contribute much to the professional growth of applied sport psychology practitioners (Tod et al., 2009). In some countries, such as the United Kingdom, steps are being taken to address the training of supervisors. Thus, the landscape is perhaps not entirely a desert, and much has been achieved since supervision first appeared in the literature (the earliest discussion seems to be Carr, Murphy, & McCann's 1992 AAASP [now AASP] conference presentation). It has not been easy, however, to establish supervision as a legitimate topic for debate and discussion. Andersen, a leading authority on supervision in applied sport psychology, had his first supervision journal manuscript rejected in 1992 because the editor believed that the topic had no relevance for the field (Andersen, personal communication, May 28, 2008). Supervision is now getting attention beyond the writings of Andersen, Van Raalte, and colleagues (e.g., Petitpas, Brewer, Rivera, & Van Raalte, 1994; Poczwardowski et al., 1998; Watson et al., 2004, Winston & Gervis, 2006). We hope supervision continues to be recognized as a central component in the training of future practitioners and in helping established consultants remain effective, ethical, and safe.

DISCONNECTED STAFF

The observation that trainees considered counseling and clinical psychology supervisors to have been more helpful than their sporting counterparts may reflect a deeper issue in neophyte practitioner training. Typically, academics trained in sport psychology find themselves in university teaching or research positions on the basis of having PhDs, not necessarily because of their applied experiences. Also, in many institutions, promotion is earned through winning research grants and producing publications. Many academics engage in limited, if any, applied practice (Etzel, Watson, & Zizzi, 2004; Petitpas et al., 1994). In addition, the pressure to win funding, publish, and develop research programs may mean that professionals are experts in a narrow range of topics and do not have time to keep abreast of the other developments in the field. Their limited experience in service delivery and their narrow focus may have implications for training. For example, classes may not be based on the most up-to-date knowledge about what is effective in the field, and theory and practice may be insufficiently integrated. In addition, academics may not be able to respond adequately to trainees' questions and needs. The training and background of many lecturers may be one contributing factor to the perceived chasm between research and practice, insofar as they are unable to help students develop the skills to use science to underpin service delivery. Another possible contributing factor to the gap is the perception, held by many trainees and practitioners, that the majority of research is irrelevant for service delivery (Tod et al., 2007). Some researchers also question the relevance of much research published in sport psychology journals. For example, Andersen and colleagues (Andersen, McCullagh, & Wilson, 2007; Speed & Andersen, 2000) have criticized the usefulness of studies in which researchers have not reported and interpreted effect sizes and have used arbitrary metrics that are not calibrated against real-world behaviors. When poor research has been used in training and supervision, trainees may develop a faulty sport psychology knowledge base that hinders the quality of their service delivery.

Evidence shows that interpersonal interaction between trainees and academic staff members influences students' development (for better or for worse) as practitioners (Tod et al., 2009; Tod et al., 2007). The concept of a working alliance applies to education as well as to service delivery. Close, caring working alliances between students and professional elders will usually help trainees develop as practitioners. If university staff do not have time to stay current in their knowledge about service delivery, gain applied experience, and adequately engage students on personal levels, then perhaps universities could develop partnerships with practitioners in the field. For example, training could be split so that academics continue to offer expertise in theory and research while practitioners who operate in the real and messy world also contribute to supervision.

As a result of their training and the need to focus on developing successful research programs, many academics may be passing on the service delivery limitations and overemphasis on PST approaches that they were taught as graduate students. One misconception involves the false categorization of individuals as either educational or clinical sport psychologists. The educational–clinical separation can be traced back to the United States Olympic Committee's (1983) tripartite clinical, educational, and research sport psychologist taxonomy that was introduced to identify individuals adequately trained to help U.S. Olympic athletes, and such a division is still infused in the literature today (Andersen & Tod, in press). The classification of folks as either educational or clinical consultants seems based, at least in part, on a misunderstanding of psychological service delivery. A survey of many applied sport psychology books suggests that educational sport psychology practitioners generally operate from a PST model grounded in cognitive-behavioral approaches to therapy (Vealey, 1988). A comparison of applied sport psychology with cognitive-behavioral textbooks indicates many similarities, such as the types of interventions advocated by authors. Founders of cognitive-behavioral approaches to psychotherapy such as Aaron Beck and Albert Ellis could not be called educational psychologists. Beck was a psychiatrist and Ellis a clinical psychologist. Regardless of whether the objective is to help a weightlifter manage prelift anxieties or to help him or her resolve relationship difficulties with a spouse, the practitioner is still engaged in psychological service delivery that has counseling or clinical qualities.

The educational and clinical separation is also part of another misconception about service delivery in that some practitioners argue that they focus on sporting rather than personal issues. Performance is, however, a personal issue; indeed, it cannot be otherwise (Tod & Andersen, 2010). To state that sporting issues are not personal ignores a great deal of sport psychology research on topics such as career transition, injury rehabilitation, and exercise dependence (Kolt, 2000; Lavallee & Wylleman, 2000; Smith & Hale, 2004). For example, some athletes are highly invested in their sports, and their self-identities are threatened if they are unable to play or perform as well as they might expect (Lavallee, Grove, Gordon, & Ford, 1998). Other athletes are less invested in sport participation and will not be as troubled if they do not perform to expectations. Practitioners professing to focus on sport-related rather than personal issues may limit the athletes they help to those folks who are less invested in their sports (the "worried well") and may miss out on assisting athletes who have a great deal to lose (the worried obsessed) if their sporting participation does not match expectations.

By reinforcing narrow models of service delivery (e.g., PST approaches), academic staff may be limiting students' abilities to help with the variety of issues for which clients seek assistance. Educational practitioners who focus on sport-related problems may be restricted to teaching goal setting, imagery, self-talk, and relaxation to athletes. This type of knowledge, however, can often be obtained from a well-informed coach, a commercial sport psychology video recording (e.g., Virtual Brands), or a well-written book. Well-trained and effective applied sport psychologists provide a broader perspective and take into account the theoretical, human, and relationship factors associated with behavior change. Herein lies the rub: If individuals say they do more than just teach athletes mental skills, then by implication they acknowledge that they are not just educators but are closer to being counselors or psychologists in the more traditional sense of the profession.

CONCLUSION

In years past, Silva and colleagues (Silva, Conroy, & Zizzi, 1999; Silva, Metzler, & Lerner, 2007) have called for the accreditation of graduate applied sport psychology programs to help demonstrate academic credibility and build public confidence in training and practice. Others, such as Andersen and Tod (in press) and Hale and Danish (1999), have argued that program accreditation may be counterproductive because there are so few full-time practitioners. Program accreditation schemes are, however, already in place around the world for other applied fields of psychology, and there are good reasons for sport psychology communities around the globe to amalgamate with mainstream psychology organizations and tap into the existing individual registration and program accreditation schemes. First, regardless of background, applied sport psychology practitioners are engaged in the process of psychological service delivery. Applied sport psychology work may have strong parallels to that undertaken by educational, occupational, and counseling psychologists, and it seems prudent to draw on the systems and processes of training and supervision that have been developed across the entire field of psychology over the last 100 years. Second, it appears that the full-time work available in performance enhancement is insufficient to support the number of graduates being produced, and in Australia and other places around the globe individuals can participate in training programs that allow them to satisfy mainstream psychologist registration (certification, licensure) requirements.

Over the past 35 years, parts of the applied sport psychology Wild West have become increasingly domesticated as professional organizations have developed and grown as certification schemes have been implemented and as training programs have been offered. Now, applied sport psychology practitioners are finding work in a range of settings,

such as sports medicine facilities, obesity clinics, and cardiac rehabilitation programs. As this Wild West becomes further domesticated,
traditional applied sport psychology training, which is focused on a
PST model, may become increasingly inadequate in preparing trainees for their careers. Although exemplary training programs for sport
psychologists can be found around the world, it is likely many institutions are inadequately preparing trainees in some of the areas outlined
in this essay. Possible solutions include broadening the theoretical
knowledge base of training, increasing the number of hours and the
quality of supervision that trainees receive, encouraging students to
undertake personal psychotherapy, and amalgamating with mainstream
psychology organizations around the globe. Unless professionals in the
discipline address these important issues and come to a consensus
about how to train future practitioners, some increasingly isolated
parts of the Wild West may remain untamed and eventually become
deserts.

IDEAS FOR REFLECTION AND DEBATE

1. Are the authors being unfair? How did you respond to their representations of applied sport psychology training and supervision?

2. How can cowboys help inform (or hinder) practice?

3. The authors question the use of the PST approach as the dominant
   model in practitioner training. Where do you stand in regard to its
   place in the training of applied sport psychologists?

4. In terms of membership in professional associations such as AASP
   and the International Society of Sport Psychology, the field of sport
   psychology hasn't grown much in the past 15 years. In comparison
   with other sport professions that grew up at about the same time,
   our field looks like a stagnant backwater of service. What do you
   believe is the problem?

5. What do you think it will take for sport psychology to become as
   accepted and used as other allied sport professions (e.g., exercise
   physiology)?

REFERENCES

Aldridge, T., Andersen, M., Stanton, B., & Shen, C. (1997). Past and future training for careers in sport psychology. *Australian Journal of Career Development, 6*(2), 26–31.

Andersen, M.B. (Ed.). (2000a). *Doing sport psychology.* Champaign, IL: Human Kinetics.

Andersen, M.B. (2000b). Beginnings: Intakes and the initiation of relationships. In M.B. Andersen (Ed.), *Doing sport psychology* (pp. 3–16). Champaign, IL: Human Kinetics.

Andersen, M.B. (2004). Transference and countertransference. In G.S. Kolt & M.B. Andersen (Eds.), *Psychology in the physical and manual therapies* (pp. 71–80). Edinburgh, Scotland: Churchill Livingstone.

Andersen, M.B. (2005a). Coming full circle: From practice to research. In M.B. Andersen (Ed.), *Sport psychology in practice* (pp. 287–298). Champaign, IL: Human Kinetics.

Andersen, M.B. (2005b). Touching taboos: Sex and the sport psychologist. In M.B. Andersen (Ed.), *Sport psychology in practice* (pp. 171–191). Champaign, IL: Human Kinetics.

Andersen, M.B. (Ed.). (2005c). *Sport psychology in practice.* Champaign, IL: Human Kinetics.

Andersen, M.B. (2006). It's all about sport performance . . . and something else. In J. Dosil (Ed.), *The sport psychologist's handbook: A guide for sport-specific performance enhancement* (pp. 687–698). Chichester, England: Wiley.

Andersen, M. (2009). Performance enhancement as a bad start and a dead end: A parenthetical comment on Mellalieu and Lane. *The Sport and Exercise Scientist,* (20), 12–14.

Andersen, M.B., McCullagh, P., & Wilson, G.J. (2007). But what do the numbers really tell us?: Arbitrary metrics and effect size reporting in sport psychology research. *Journal of Sport & Exercise Psychology, 29,* 664–672.

Andersen, M.B., & Tod, D. (in press). On becoming a sport psychologist: Professional pathways and territories in the field. In T. Morris & P. Terry (Eds.), *Sport and exercise psychology: The cutting edge.* Morgantown, WV: Fitness Information Technology.

Andersen, M.B., Van Raalte, J.L., & Brewer, B.W. (1994). Assessing the skills of sport psychology supervisors. *The Sport Psychologist, 8,* 238–247.

Andersen, M.B., Van Raalte, J.L., & Brewer, B.W. (2000). When sport psychology consultants and graduate students are impaired: Ethical and legal issues in training and supervision. *Journal of Applied Sport Psychology, 12,* 134–150.

Andersen, M.B., Williams, J.M., Aldridge, T., & Taylor, J. (1997). Tracking the training and careers of graduates of advanced degree programs in sport psychology, 1989 to 1994. *The Sport Psychologist, 11,* 326–344.

Anderson, A., Miles, A., Robinson, P., & Mahoney, C. (2004). Evaluating the athlete's perception of the sport psychologist's effectiveness: What should we be assessing? *Psychology of Sport and Exercise, 5,* 255–277.

Barney, S.T., Andersen, M.B., & Riggs, C.A. (1996). Supervision in sport psychology: Some recommendations for practicum training. *Journal of Applied Sport Psychology, 8,* 200–217.

Burke, K.L., Sachs, M.L., Fry, S.J., & Schweighardt, S.L. (2008). *Directory of graduate programs in applied sport psychology* (9th ed.). Morgantown, WV: Fitness Information Technology.

Carr, C.M., Murphy, S.M., & McCann, S. (1992, October). *Supervision issues in clinical sport psychology.* Workshop presented at the annual conference of the Association for the Advancement of Applied Sport Psychology, Colorado Springs, CO.

Ellis, A., & Dryden, W. (2007). *The practice of rational emotive behavior therapy* (2nd ed.). New York: Springer.

Etzel, E.F., Watson, J.C., II., & Zizzi, S. (2004). A Web-based survey of AAASP members' ethical beliefs and behaviors in the new millennium. *Journal of Applied Sport Psychology, 16,* 236–250.

Feltz, D.L. (1987). The future of graduate education in sport and exercise science: A sport psychology perspective. *Quest, 39,* 217–223.

Hale, B.D., & Danish, S.J. (1999). Putting the accreditation cart before the AAASP horse: A reply to Silva, Conroy and Zizzi. *Journal of Applied Sport Psychology, 11,* 321–328.

Handelsman, M.M., & Palladino, J.J. (1999). Classic studies revisited *Eye on Psi Chi, 3*(2). www.psichi.org/pubs/articles/article_119.aspx.

Hanrahan, S.J., & Andersen, M.B. (2010). *Routledge handbook of applied sport psychology: A comprehensive guide for students and practitioners.* London: Routledge.

Henschen, K. (1991). Critical issues involving male consultants and female athletes. *The Sport Psychologist, 5,* 313–321.

Hill, K.L. (2001). *Frameworks for sport psychologists: Enhancing sport performance.* Champaign, IL: Human Kinetics.

Kolt, G.S. (2000). Doing sport psychology with injured athletes. In M.B. Andersen (Ed.), *Doing sport psychology* (pp. 223–236). Champaign, IL: Human Kinetics.

Lavallee, D., & Andersen, M.B. (2000). Leaving sport: Easing career transitions. In M.B. Andersen (Ed.), *Doing sport psychology* (pp. 249–260). Champaign, IL: Human Kinetics.

Lavallee, D., Grove, J.R., Gordon, S., & Ford, I.W. (1998). The experience of loss in sport. In J.H. Harvey (Ed.), *Perspectives on loss: A sourcebook* (pp. 241–252). Philadelphia: Brunner/Mazel.

Lavallee, D., & Wylleman, P. (Eds.). (2000). *Career transitions in sport: International perspectives.* Morgantown, WV: Fitness Information Technology.

Lidor, R., Morris, T., Bardaxoglu, N., & Becker, B., Jr. (Eds.). (2001). *The world sport psychology sourcebook* (3rd ed.). Morgantown, WV: Fitness Information Technology.

Morris, T. (1995). Sport psychology in Australia: A profession established. *Australian Psychologist, 30,* 128–134.

Morris, T., Alfermann, D., Lintunen, T., & Hall, H. (2003). Training and selection of sport psychologists: An international review. *International Journal of Sport and Exercise Psychology, 1,* 139–154.

Orlinsky, D.E., Botermans, J.-F., Rønnestad, M.H., & The SPR Collaborative Research Network. (2001). Towards an empirically grounded model of psychotherapy training: Four thousand therapists rate influences on their development. *Australian Psychologist, 36,* 139–148.

Petitpas, A.J., Brewer, B.W., Rivera, P.M., & Van Raalte, J.L. (1994). Ethical beliefs and behaviors in applied sport psychology: The AAASP ethics survey. *Journal of Applied Sport Psychology, 6,* 135–151.

Petitpas, A.J., Giges, B., & Danish, S.J. (1999). The sport psychologist-athlete relationship: Implications for training. *The Sport Psychologist, 13,* 344–357.

Poczwardowski, A., Sherman, C.P., & Henschen, K.P. (1998). A sport psychology service delivery heuristic: Building on theory and practice. *The Sport Psychologist, 12,* 191–207.

Poczwardowski, A., Sherman, C.P., & Ravizza, K. (2004). Professional philosophy in the sport psychology service delivery: Building on theory and practice. *The Sport Psychologist, 18,* 445–463.

Sexton, T.L., & Whiston, S.C. (1994). The status of the counseling relationship: An empirical review, theoretical implications, and research directions. *The Counseling Psychologist, 22,* 6–78.

Silva, J.M., III., Conroy, D.E., & Zizzi, S.J. (1999). Critical issues confronting the advancement of applied sport psychology. *Journal of Applied Sport Psychology, 11,* 298–320.

Silva, J.M., III., Metzler, J.N., & Lerner, B. (2007). *Training professionals in the practice of sport psychology.* Morgantown, WV: Fitness Information Technology.

Simons, J.P., & Andersen, M.B. (1995). The development of consulting practice in applied sport psychology: Some personal perspectives. *The Sport Psychologist, 9,* 449–468.

Smith, D., & Hale, B. (2004). Validity and factor structure of the Bodybuilding Dependence Scale. *British Journal of Sports Medicine, 38,* 177–181.

Speed, H.D., & Andersen, M.B. (2000). What exercise and sport scientists don't understand. *Journal of Science and Medicine in Sport, 3,* 84–92.

Stevens, L.M., & Andersen, M.B. (2007a). Transference and countertransference in sport psychology service delivery: Part I. A review of erotic attraction. *Journal of Applied Sport Psychology, 19,* 253–269.

Stevens, L.M., & Andersen, M.B. (2007b). Transference and countertransference in sport psychology service delivery: Part II. Two case studies on the erotic. *Journal of Applied Sport Psychology, 19,* 270–287.

Strean, W.B., & Strean, H.S. (1998). Applying psychodynamic concepts to sport psychology practice. *The Sport Psychologist, 12,* 208–222.

Tod, D. (2007a). Reflections on collaborating with a professional rugby league player. *Sport & Exercise Psychology Review, 3*(1), 4–10.

Tod, D. (2007b). The long and winding road: Professional development in sport psychology. *The Sport Psychologist, 21*, 94–108.

Tod, D., & Andersen, M. (2005). Success in sport psych: Effective sport psychologists. In S. Murphy (Ed.), *The sport psych handbook* (pp. 305–314). Champaign, IL: Human Kinetics.

Tod, D., & Andersen, M.B. (2010). When to refer athletes for counseling or psychotherapy. In J.M. Williams (Ed.), *Applied sport psychology: Personal growth to peak performance* (6th ed., pp. 443–462). Boston: McGraw-Hill.

Tod, D., Andersen, M.B., & Marchant, D.B. (2009). A longitudinal examination of neophyte applied sport psychologists' development. *Journal of Applied Sport Psychology, 21*(Suppl. 1), S1–S16.

Tod, D., Andersen, M.B., & Marchant, D.B. (2011). Six years up: Applied sport psychologists surviving (and thriving) after graduation. *Journal of Applied Sport Psychology, 23*, 93–109.

Tod, D., Hardy, J., Niven, A., & Lavallee, D. (2008, October). *Helping athletes talk the walk: Consultants' experiences in using self-talk with athletes.* Paper presented at the Nordic Conference on Health, Participation and Effects of Sport and Exercise, Halmstad, Sweden.

Tod, D., Marchant, D., & Andersen, M.B. (2007). Learning experiences contributing to service-delivery competence. *The Sport Psychologist, 21*, 317–334.

United States Olympic Committee. (1983). US Olympic Committee establishes guidelines for sport psychology services. *Journal of Sport Psychology, 5*, 4–7.

Van Raalte, J.L., & Andersen, M.B. (2000). Supervision I: From models to doing. In M.B. Andersen (Ed.), *Doing sport psychology* (pp. 153–165). Champaign, IL: Human Kinetics.

Vealey, R.S. (1988). Future directions in psychological skills training. *The Sport Psychologist, 2*, 318–336.

Waite, B.T., & Pettit, M.E. (1993). Work experiences of graduates from doctoral programs in sport psychology. *Journal of Applied Sport Psychology, 5*, 234–250.

Wampold, B.E. (2001). *The great psychotherapy debate: Models, methods, and findings.* Mahwah, NJ: Erlbaum.

Watson, J.C., II., Zizzi, S.J., Etzel, E.F., & Lubker, J.R. (2004). Applied sport psychology supervision: A survey of students and professionals. *The Sport Psychologist, 18*, 415–429.

Williams, J.M., & Scherzer, C.B. (2003). Tracking the training and careers of graduates of advanced degree programs in sport psychology, 1994 to 1999. *Journal of Applied Sport Psychology, 15*, 335–353.

Williams, J.M., & Straub, W.F. (2010). Sport psychology: Past, present, future. In J.M. Williams (Ed.), *Applied sport psychology: Personal growth to peak performance* (6th ed., pp. 1–17). Boston: McGraw-Hill.

Winstone, W., & Gervis, M. (2006). Countertransference and the self-aware sport psychologist: Attitudes and patterns of professional practice. *The Sport Psychologist, 20,* 495–511.

Yambor, J., & Connelly, D. (1991). Issues confronting female sport psychology consultants working with male student-athletes. *The Sport Psychologist, 5,* 304–312.

Zaichkowsky, L.D. (2006). Industry challenges facing sport psychology. *Athletic Insight, 8*(3). www.athleticinsight.com/Vol8Iss3/IndustryChallenges.htm.

EPIPHANIES AND LEARNING:

A Rejection of Performance-Based Myopia

David Gilbourne
University of Wales Institute, Cardiff, United Kingdom

David Priestley
Private practice, London, United Kingdom

In this essay, David Gilbourne draws from a series of career moments that have steered his allegiances away from applied sport psychology and toward applied qualitative research. These moments are presented as epiphanies that have affected his critical thought processes and moved him to consider the academic backdrop of applied sport psychology in the UK as one that is limited both by the cold abstraction of preestablished theory and by researchers' limited engagement with emotional and untidy matters. The second author, David Priestley, a freelance consultant in sport, contributes to the text through a series of vignettes (set in a different font) in which he muses over what applied sport psychology practice has come to mean to him. The two narrative threads connect and reconnect as the story unfolds.

INTRODUCTION

I received an e-mail from David Priestley earlier this year. There is nothing unusual in this. David often e-mails or phones, usually to talk about or share thoughts on applied practice issues, and I am always in trouble for not phoning or e-mailing in return. This is our dance.

David issues a rebuke ("I'm still waiting for you to call me"), and I say sorry, blaming workload or the fatigue of middle age for my poor social skills. On this particular day, however, I sensed an underlying motive to his e-mail. His message was simple enough: "Just look at these slides." It turned out that David had attended a training course that included a presentation. He sent me the first and last slides used by the presenter, and to me they represented something depressing, sinister, and oddly plausible. In fact, the message was shocking to me. The general point was that you should ensure that you are working with people who will win rather than with those who are struggling to match the pace—the "debris," as the slides described them. As a piece of sporting debris myself, I read and reread the message, eyes wide, mouth agape.

My own professional soccer career was short lived; I failed while others succeeded. Some would say, "So what?" Others might say, "Get over it." I suppose those sentiments house a degree of pragmatic realism, but at the age of 54 my own failure still resonates within me and with my father. In fact, I believe that my own failure is a defining moment in both our lives, a burden we have carried and tried to work through ever since. Did I move on? Well, yes I did. Did I forget? Well, no.

After I returned David's e-mail and asked how the presentation was received, he explained that nobody had questioned or challenged the presenter. David observed that only a few people had queried (in the relative safety of coffee and biscuits) the sentiments presented in the slides. Given my own sporting and applied history, I was fascinated both personally and professionally by the notion that those who lead the field of applied sport psychology and associated support professions would openly contemplate a strategic position in which they encourage practitioners (often young, eager practitioners) to turn away from those athletes, those *people,* who demonstrate performance failure in order to turn toward those who look like winners. There are many dangers here—some ethical, others just human (or maybe that amounts to the same thing).

I clicked Reply and started typing furiously. The underlying message, one based on the thinking presented here, was that such strategies must be challenged. In the remainder of this essay, I outline, illustrate, and reflect on my case for challenge; in doing so, I present elements of David Priestley's applied wisdom.

QUALITATIVE METHODOLOGY AND APPLIED THINKING: THE RATIONALE FOR MY CHALLENGE

According to Smith (2009), all researchers, be they quantitative or qualitative, are storytellers. This assertion would, I suspect, be greeted with greater enthusiasm by an autoethnographer than a statistician, yet all researchers seek to communicate, and all have a story to tell. Because Smith's article appeared in a dedicated qualitative journal, it's likely that his sentiments were warmly greeted by reviewers and read with anticipation and regard by editors. Away from this newly established haven for the hitherto unspoken, applied sport psychology in the United Kingdom has not sought any bond with those disciplines that are readily associated with storytelling. I am thinking here of disciplines such as English literature, cultural studies, anthropology, creative writing, and drama. I suspect that such approaches are not entertained for the simple reason that they may not house the potential to garner respect—at least not the kind of respect and kudos that are afforded to science.

In my view, applied sport psychology in the United Kingdom has always demonstrated a peculiar eagerness to tether expertise and applied status to the natural science landscape, and this tendency has clear limitations. I do not question science at a fundamental level, for it seems logical to say that there is good science and less good science (a bit like there is good and less good Shakespeare). If pushed, I would say that it is the overwhelming *dominance* of science, and the postpositivist hangover that stems from it, that I could never quite stomach.

Once I decided that the present essay would, in some way, offer a challenge to the sentiments of leaving debris alone (for others to worry over), I began to wonder how we (those in the applied sport psychology profession) had stumbled to a point where expressions of applied priority could be voiced in such a seemingly callous way. My mind wandered around a little. I began to think increasingly about the times when David and I had talked about applied work (his, mainly). I recalled that however our conversations began, we always seemed to end up at the same point—discussing the value of unconditional support, of listening, of watching, of caring practice. David and I both know that many who reside in the sport sciences would consider these notions to be either soft or atheoretical, or both; furthermore, since applied sport psychologists are very proud of their theory and often set out to make people tough, we also understand that in challenging these notions we are unlikely to be overwhelmed by letters of support.

As I planned this essay, I decided to emphasize the themes of listening (really listening) and being unconditional. I attempted to thread these themes around my increasing rejection of the primacy of psychosocial theory. In a stylistic decision, I opted to explain my thinking through the medium of autoethnographic short stories and, later, through critical analysis of them. I hope that these stories will reach out to you, the reader, in a way that helps you somehow understand (and maybe appreciate) my point of view.

Sometimes I think that the epistemological doubts over the value of story and the rejection of autoethnography, life history, and biography have encouraged generations of applied researchers to turn away from the messiness of people's lives and toward the tidiness of theories that talk about coping and achieving. In doing so, we may have missed the facts that even winners can be troubled and that most of those who set out to win actually fall short. Maybe our regimen, so tidy and winner oriented, allows the proposition of turning away from *the majority* and turning toward *the few* to appear quite normal, unremarkable even. Yet, for David and me, such sentiments invite a response.

SOME STORYTELLING

The stories I use here stretch back over my own applied experiences in professional sport and consider some of the dilemmas that I associate with practicing from the theory-led perspective of psychological skills training. David's short vignettes (in italics) relate to his applied work in professional sport and are positioned around my stories. In combination, our thoughts coalesce around the notion of working with people in an open way that allows anyone to be listened to and allows conversations to embrace topics other than sport. My applied conversations with David have taken place almost entirely outside the structure imposed by academia. As you read his words, imagine us talking over the phone, via e-mail, occasionally in coffee shops, or, reluctantly (because neither of us would want to be there), at conferences. In this first excerpt, David talks about his own sense of place as a sport psychologist who works with professional athletes.

It was like I was not allowed to be any other way but performance focused. In fact, at times, it was almost as if, as support staff, we were being encouraged to adopt the same procedure of a player in battle and so being "tough" in our own manner (was meant) to show that we were highly committed and competent professionals. . . . [B]ut I felt that there was more to me, and certainly more to my work with players and coaches, than any absolute, or, dare I say, obsessive focus on winning.

Doing Theory-Bound Action Research

I think in the past I was a pretty typical applied qualitative researcher in that I was guided primarily by theory and in that I ran around trying to extract evidence for the theory in the wider world of sport. In effect, I tried to turn something that is essentially abstract (theory) into a reality, to transform it into a form of lived truth by eliciting and interpreting what athletes had to say through the lens of various constructs, perspectives, models, or frameworks—essentially, a deductive process.

When I was working on my own PhD in the early 1990s, my heavy involvement with sport psychology at the applied and teaching levels was reflected in my research. During the course of my PhD study, I followed an action research design, which meant that I was very interested in how practitioners (in this case, physiotherapists) went about their work and so sport injury was a core focus.

Action research, in my view, is all about tempo and engagement, and in my own work I tried to facilitate reflective cycles during which practitioners would think about their own practice (with injured athletes) and through this try to find ways of improving or changing the work they did. I would supplement this activity by undertaking interviews with injured players and feeding back to the physiotherapists the athletes' perceptions of being injured and their perceptions of the support they received. If that sounds a bit untidy, then that's about right. Action research is, in my experience at any rate, an unpredictable way to get around a research question; it can be both great fun and madly frustrating.

During one of my action research days (at a sport injury rehabilitation center), I went with the physiotherapist to help with an outdoor training session in which three rehabilitating players participated. One was a lower-league player 12 months post-ACL surgical repair, one was a mid-league player 2 months past the partial removal of a cartilage, and the other was 2 months past a minor shaving on the cartilage.

The players did a range of exercises (e.g., short sprints, two-foot jumps over low hurdles, zigzag runs). Throughout, the physiotherapist constantly asked about their knees. How did they feel? He congratulated all the players regularly on their effort, and they had indeed worked very hard.

After the session was over, I was helping the physiotherapist collect things, and he said of the 12-month-ACL-postop player, "That is the best I have seen him work since he has been here." I later caught up with that same player; he was sitting alone outside the changing room area. I asked how he felt the session had gone, and he replied, "You must have thought I looked a right donkey. . . . I was . . . useless . . . leggy . . . slow."

I had not really expected this response, and I quickly accessed my scholarly records (based on papers, essays, and books that I had read). This internal Google search, as it were, led me to conclude that the player had evaluated all activities interpersonally. Yes, of course, that was it—the disgruntled player had constantly compared himself with the other players. It fit so neatly. Yet, the player's thinking did seem irrational. All the other players hailed from higher leagues and were working with less-problematic injuries (and with recovery almost complete). Later in the day, I talked to the physiotherapist about the way I saw the situation. I talked to him about the tenets of achievement goal theory and emphasized the interlinked themes of ego involvement and low self-efficacy. I felt good, in control, informed. I had engaged the practitioner with the authority bestowed on me by professional knowledge.

Later that week, the injured player had traveled a short distance to watch his team play away at a local club. His team won. I saw him the next day and asked how he found the game. He said nothing for a few seconds, then, without looking at me, he told a short story. "One of the home team players had the ball on the halfway line. . . . [H]e hit this fantastic diagonal ball . . . great strike. . . . [T]he guy playing in my position . . . in my . . . shirt . . . he just like spun and tracked the ball. [H]e really . . . shifted. . . . [H]e got there on the half-volley and crashed the ball and the center forward off the pitch. [B]rilliant." Then he stopped talking, looked at me, paused for a second, and said, "I'll never be able to do that now."

Again, I heard the signature of achievement goal theory—ego involvement, to be more precise—and later I heard myself telling the same physiotherapist my thoughts, impressing again with knowledge deductively extracted from the player's narrative. The player retired 2 weeks later. The physiotherapists could not really find any problems with the knee; in their minds, it seemed to have recovered. The player kept asking for more time, but eventually time ran out.

In my past life as a sport psychologist, I have used that story in lectures many times; I have linked it *always* with the various components of achievement goal theory and proposed the neat and dangerous linkage between ego involvement and low efficacy. It's a great example—or is it?

I have since come to feel that I failed to make a diagnostic leap and wonder about my eagerness to emphasize the deductively clean osmosis between a short exposure to narrative and theory of whatever shape or form. A year or so later, while training to be a counselor, I sat, rather bored, at the back of the class. The course tutor punched out another PowerPoint slide, which listed five or six descriptors of depression. In a second, my boredom changed to panic; I felt my heart beating in my chest. My mind raced back to the sport injury research and to that same player. Every one of the descriptors of depression fit him perfectly. I was devastated and felt physically sick. Achievement goal theory has little (if anything) to say about depression. My mind scrambled back to my action research days. I wondered if the player reached out to me on those days—days when all I could see was theory and my PhD. Yet I had been so sure footed, so theoretically informed. In fact, my depiction of that event received acclaim in the PhD viva voce and formed part of a peer review paper in 1998. There we are!

If he was indeed reaching out, it went over my head, and he was wasting his angst. I was far too secure to be troubled by other possibilities—too focused on what theory afforded me. I suppose there is little wrong with the theories as such; my angst is more over the way I allowed myself to see and hear and feel *only* what these theories might guide me to hear and see and feel. I bought into the truth they appeared to offer.

As for the player, well, he retired in 1998. I wonder how he is now. Who could have helped? Who failed to listen? He was, I suppose, a piece of debris; as such, he was useful to me as a form of data. I was not guilty of turning away from him, but I was guilty of not seeing his pain.

David has a few applied views on this:

In my opinion it is neither "soft" nor "fluffy" nor easy to listen to someone sharing their innermost difficulties. In fact, when someone feels able to bare their soul and be completely vulnerable in my company, I actually believe it to be an incredibly privileged experience. Those (sport psychologists) obsessed with performance will never even get close to touching this kind of information. . . . When you are told you need to be tough, why show that you are vulnerable?

The Applied Arm of My Crisis

Around the time that I was finishing my PhD, I was doing some applied sport psychology work in professional soccer. This was my zone—a place, a culture, in which I felt at home. Once, when working with a team in danger of being relegated to a lower league, I had sensed the pressure building, game by game, loss by loss. After another limp-away defeat, the manager and I were walking off the pitch when he asked my advice about what he should do.

I suggested that he listen to the players and allow them to offer some kind of view about the game. Maybe, I suggested, we might get an explanation of sorts. For my part, I had been particularly disappointed with the center forward; he was the captain of the team but for several games he had not (in my view) really contributed to the team effort. On this particular day, I felt that the player had again been ineffective. We all returned to the changing rooms, a silent space. No one spoke, and no one moved. One player, whose grandmother had died on the previous Thursday and who had begged the manager to be released for this game, sobbed in the corner; it was a pitiful place.

The center forward (the one I had doubts about) was the first to speak. He said that it was hopeless for him. Every time he jumped for the ball, the ref blew up for arms (he was using his arms to get leverage); it was, he said, "a waste of time trying to play." I had heard similar comments from this player before, and those who enjoy the twists and turns of attribution theory may have suspected an external ascription there. I picked up on just that. Using theory to guide my thinking, I asked if there was anything else he could have done—anything he had control over. He glared back at me. I kept going and, now acting as a theoretical bully, asked if he could not have run more, chased players down more. His glare intensified, but I felt sure of myself. I was, after all, following attribution-based logic and so felt secure theoretically. The look on his face suggested I was not so safe physically. Later, I explained my line of thinking to the manager. I hear a narrative; I deploy a theory. I was also angry that I had seen the bereaved player run hard and then sit sobbing in a disheveled heap, whereas I had seen the center forward do nothing and then offer an excuse. So yes, I abused him with theory and used theory to hit him hard—and in front of his teammates. Looking back, I think I was cowardly.

Later that week, I walked into the physiotherapist's room (it functioned as a shortcut to the changing areas). I had not expected anyone else to be present, but there was. A doctor was in attendance with the physiotherapist and the center forward. As best as I could understand, he was having cortisone injections. Later, the physiotherapist took me to one side and told me that the player's hips had gone and that he was in real financial trouble and needed a new contract; finally, he said that I should tell no one. I went outside, sat in the empty stands, and stared out across the pitch—more debris, more information missed. The player never spoke to me again.

Time for some Priestley wisdom:

It seemed to me that being unconditional in my attitude toward supporting and listening to players and coaches . . . had the effect of drawing out some (but by no means all) players. . . . Being unconditional seemed almost to have a magnetic quality . . . ; in this regard, experiencing inner disparity between emotions, ambitions, and reality often seemed the most difficult of matters for players to come to terms with. . . . I found that by being unconditional (empathic and nonjudgmental), it not only encouraged them to speak honestly and feel freely about their game, but, crucially, also encouraged them to talk about any aspects of their life that they found difficult.

If, first and foremost, working with people in the way just described can be seen as a moment-to-moment thing, then it follows that no one can ever know what the next moment will bring. This view of practice embraces uncertainty, and what follows in practice might also be seen in opaque terms. In addition, David and I have often talked about the importance of seeing people, not players or athletes; in that regard, David has always seemed genuinely interested in those people who just happen to play sport. We have also talked many times about treating people with a true sense of equity. David does not seem particularly vulnerable to big names and those who carry star status; he is not influenced unduly by who is on the team. This makes no difference in the way he greets them and shakes their hand, the time he gives them, or the way he sits and listens.

I get a sense from many players and coaches that they have rarely come across anyone without a vested interest in them. Players would often react to my acceptance of their frailty in a way that suggested to me that it shocked them. It somehow seemed surprising to players that I could accept and not show disdain for the fact that they were scared or unmotivated. It was as if players couldn't quite imagine that someone might genuinely care about how they felt inside. (Many times) I could have positioned myself alongside a young or older player in a way that suggested I was inputting and making a difference. Instead, I often chose to distance myself from those talents (at least at those moments—never clapping on balconies when they performed well or giving big high fives following victories). Instead, I knew that such moments were my cue to silently leave. I might add, however, that I never disappeared from view at an individual's or team's side when they were struggling or losing. Instead, I tried to let them know I was there if they needed me.

From Crisis to Action

All in all, the various theoretical blips (and there are many more stories I could relate) began to alter my thinking and the direction my career would take. In response to these experiences, I began to alter my view of what I needed to know. I had found theories wanting. I found that the performance agenda narrowed my lens; it made me focus on a limited number of possibilities and explanations. I understood both theory and the applied agenda well enough, but, when I started to understand the complexity of people's lives, both seemed inadequate.

So I made some decisions. I needed to know more about context. I was starting to detach from a certain way of doing sport psychology and move toward a way of working that is illustrated here by David's thoughts just quoted—about accepting athletes for the people they are. Around the same time, I also became interested in more expansive ways of interpreting the world and in emotive forms of writing, such as life history, autoethnography, and fiction.

I now think that information about, or illustration of, applied context is a critical area for expansion and development within applied sport psychology. In my student and lecturing days, I could not readily draw on texts that explored practice in this way. I was (and still am today) convinced that texts exploring context offer students another insight into a landscape in which they might one day seek to work.

This writing journey (one that has highlighted depth, context, and the critical day-to-day) has brought with it a need for me to engage with emotion. In the past, I lectured about emotion but was never required to engage with it. Now, driven by a different approach to writing, I come face to face with the emotions of self and of others. To be candid, in my increasing interest and exploration of context (and the people who inhabit it), I had not expected to come across *emotion;* it was a revelation to me. Maybe that was foolish. Maybe I should have understood beforehand that looking at matters in more depth, in more detail, would unveil the emotional side of experience. I suddenly saw and heard and felt and wrote emotionally. This hit me hard. What had I been doing for the past 15 years? Had I really been seeing theory first and people second? In my own defense, I told myself that I had done what I needed to do, what I had been *expected* to do (by the powerful ones such as editors and examiners). So, in my early days, I had tried to write as concisely as I could, as acceptably as I could, in APA style and form, but in doing this (in my compliance), I had written coldly.

There was no turning back. In this new landscape, I began to see people—players, coaches—and their lives in a completely different way. I began to write about what I had started to see and appreciate differently.

Challenging the Status Quo

The game has become a bad-tempered affair. Steve and I sit six rows back from the touchline. Steve just talks away. I half-listen. Then a nasty tackle slams in. Both sets of coaches react. A halfhearted fight breaks out on the pitch. The referee pulls out a red card. Steve leans forward. I say, "That's a bit harsh." Steve ignores me and mutters, "Get to him." I feel rebuked. Then I follow his gaze. He's looking at the player, the one who's been sent off (he's 15, maybe 16). The player is standing, head bowed, hands on hips; he seems confused, exposed, suspended in an unfamiliar red-card world. The crowd hurls abuse at the referee, and the noise gets to a distracting pitch. Steve's agitated now. His voice carries urgency: "Somebody get to him!" I look on in despair as the boy breaks down. Under public and peer gaze, he sobs and stumbles past both sets of coaches and eventually (thankfully) he walks down the tunnel. His day ends in tears. I look across at Steve and sense that he has walked every step with the boy; he holds his head in his hands. "Someone should have got to him; he's just a kid" (Gilbourne & Richardson 2006, p. 333).

"He has walked every step with the boy." I recall writing that line as if it were yesterday. It was an important moment for me. I think that one line led me to understand and accept that I was suddenly in an emotional place. Now, I feel strongly that engaging with people emotionally has implications for the way in which research is conducted and written. The texts that I was brought up with never went near emotion; they started and ended with theory—cold theory. They explained who the subjects were (in the methods section), but I never recall meeting them in the text or getting to know them in any way at all. Indeed, many contemporary qualitative texts still manage to suggest a distance between the subject and the author (and thus the reader). It is almost as if a researcher seeks to arrive at a place where he or she can (reasonably) apply a theory; then, having gotten to that point, it seems that the subject or participant has somehow fulfilled a purpose, and so a form of icy, deductive surgery has been completed, and graduation ensues.

THE VALUE OF STORIES

If people are to work in a world that is emotionally charged, then how are we to prepare them if not by providing some means of moving them, of making them reflect on their own emotions? With this question in mind, I either have written or told stories for several years, but I think I have made some mistakes along the way. For example, I have been privileged to share and tell stories about bereavement in elite sport and about career-ending injury, and although audiences have listened in a polite enough way, one question I have faced repeatedly could be paraphrased as "Are these not extreme cases?"

I think, in my eagerness to promote a new language or genre, I also risked setting up a bogeyman, for although the stories were engaging and moving, they were that way in part because they were so unusual—and, yes, possibly extreme. Here was my mistake: allowing listeners to think that the stories I read were interesting enough but that their uniqueness meant they had nothing to do with the listeners. I feel now that by focusing on the extreme, I let people off the hook, and by *people* I mean those who work and research and practice in sport. I had engaged people with powerful tales but had singularly failed to get across the *everyday* traumas and battles that many people face. By conveying the extreme, I had allowed listeners to think, *Maybe there are always those who somehow fall by the wayside* [perhaps we are back to the notion of debris], *but that's nothing to do with me.* In short, had I done those who owned the stories—and those I had sought to influence—a disservice?

CONCLUSION

I began this essay with reference to a disconcerting view of failing athletes as debris, and, as I suggested earlier, I have written this piece (and others) through the lens of my own failure, both in sport and in scholarly terms. Maybe these experiences have, in combination, led me to consider applied sport psychologists as people who should and could and sometimes do offer critical support to *all* athletes, regardless of their current win–loss record. David Priestley's brief narratives offer an illustration of this mind-set in action; they also show that it is possible to work in a caring way within an elite setting and to help all who commit to the elite agenda rather than just a chosen few. This view is not meant to suggest that, in showing interest, a sport psychologist can somehow turn would-be losers into winners; the message here is not talking to that agenda. I have sought to avoid talk of sport psychology as a performance profession dominated by winning outcomes and similar kinds of objectives; rather, I have tried to replace that metanarrative with an alternative one that is based on working with all people. This view rejects any notion that a sport psychologist would work (or seek to work) solely with winners; in this alternative approach, they would happily work with those who are winning but also (and just as happily) work with those who are struggling, failing, or exiting—that is, with the debris, as some might see it.

If I revisit my own case, way back in time, and deploy all the power of hindsight now available to me, I suspect that if David Priestley had been around my soccer team, working in the same way he does now, I would still have failed. However, if someone like David had shown an interest in me, if someone had displayed a caring tone at critical moments, if someone had shown (by these actions) that I mattered, then, although my career would not have changed direction greatly (I doubt that I could have stopped my decline or resurrected my form and fitness), such genuine interest and sincere care might have made the defining crises in my own life far less damaging.

Many years later, after my own applied journey has taught me that isolated theories cannot possibly unpack the complexities of someone's life, I have come to feel that restrictive methodologies focused on the narrow confines of a particular theory constrict or reduce the attention of researchers so that they interpret events solely through the lens of applied sport psychology texts and the theories that inform them. As a profession, surely we have suffered from this applied and research-based myopia for long enough.

To my way of thinking, qualitative methodology offers one way forward. Embedded approaches to research such as action research and ethnographic inquiry allow open-minded longitudinal engagement and also encourage researchers to embrace new, fresh writing practices. In combination, these methodology and writing developments encourage researchers to fully appreciate and report on lives as they are lived. Dissemination of embedded qualitative research is often conveyed through the writing of stories, and these developments offer readers new approaches to help them better understand the applied sport psychology landscape. My own engagement with qualitative methodology and the writing that stems from it have taught me that the people we study are complex. They have fears, worries, weaknesses, and needs; they are vulnerable, just like other people. In fact, they are *just people*. For all our huffing and puffing and theorizing, we have assembled and disseminated little knowledge of the people we study. Of their stories and their lives, we know virtually nothing; of the contexts in which they live, we remain largely ignorant. David Priestley's contributions have shown us that through the applied practitioner (the one who is respected by the hardest-faced professional or the one who catches the eye of a wise administrator) a different way of *being* a sport psychologist might be appreciated.

IDEAS FOR REFLECTION AND DEBATE

1. As the issues of applying theory to practice are revisited in this essay, then it is possible to revisit questions at the end of essay 12 in this book and answer them in relation to the present essay.

2. Consider the notion of working with "winners" rather than with "debris." How do your own practice and your aspirations for your future practice fit into your consideration?

3. Reflect on the ways that qualitative research methods might explore issues of success and failure in sport. Discuss the benefits for applied sport psychology in understanding failure as well as success.

REFERENCES

Gilbourne, D., & Richardson, D. (2006). Tales from the field: Personal reflections on the provision of psychological support in professional soccer. *Psychology of Sport and Exercise, 7,* 325–337.

Smith, J. (2009). Judging research quality: From certainty to contingency. *Qualitative Research in Sport and Exercise, 1,* 91–100.

PART III

ISSUES IN SPORT PSYCHOLOGY PRACTICE

In this final section of the book, the authors grapple with both the sport-specific and the general sociocultural contexts in which applied sport psychologists may find themselves. These explorations come in different forms (e.g., autoethnographic representations, formal academic critique), but all deal with how, why, where, and when sport psychologists insert themselves, function, and maintain themselves in complex sociocultural milieus.

Essay 15 deals with some challenging issues. Some Christians speak of "being in the world, but not of the world" as a way of existing in the world but of also being separate from the world's temptations and sins. Many applied sport psychologists may find themselves in this type of tension, wanting to be immersed in sport but separate from the questionable (and sometimes dangerous) cultural ideals and practices of sport, "to be on the team but not of the team." There are advantages and drawbacks of this stance that involve questions of professional distance versus professional intimacy, ethical interventions versus standing by and watching abusive practices, and, in an Eriksonian sense, identity versus role confusion. The authors of essays 14 and 16, respectively, examine issues of transition and power and do so by considering everyday examples and using illustrations of day-to-day issues. Traditional critique and autoethnographic storytelling are deployed as the authors explore the importance of looking at commonplace events in different ways. All three essays in this final section question the status quo in applied, theoretical, and epistemological terms. These authors challenge and invite us to confront broader social issues through sport psychology practice.

MAKING YOUR WAY IN THE GAME:

Boundary Situations in England's Professional Football World

Mark Nesti
Liverpool John Moores University, United Kingdom

Martin Littlewood
Liverpool John Moores University, United Kingdom

In this essay, Mark and Martin focus on research and applied interventions that influence sport career transitions. They present a series of creative nonfiction vignettes based on the applied experiences of the authors in elite professional football (called *soccer* in the United States), and they engage an associated theme of existential psychology in order to highlight issues such as personal authenticity, anxiety, and isolation. The authors also consider constant selection and deselection pressures, intense public and media scrutiny, disparate financial reward structures, staff role insecurities, irregular feedback strategies, and an intensely results-focused environment. Other cultural factors that affect players include the predominant communication styles of staff and the football milieu. By presenting the narratives of players in ways that capture the realities of their uncomfortable journeys, the authors enable insight into the challenges of applied practice.

INTRODUCTION

In this essay, we challenge prevailing theoretical and research assumptions about career transitions in professional sport, and we focus specifically on professional football. We argue that the literature has not acknowledged or adequately described the daily experiences of players but has opted instead to focus primarily on career termination issues. We feel that it is timely to expand the landscape of transition and narratives of players experiencing career transitions, or, as we prefer to suggest, boundary situations. By presenting these ideas in narrative form, we hope to capture the reality of their uncomfortable journeys as encountered on a daily basis. Our writing draws specifically from our experiences of delivering applied sport psychology support in English Premier League professional football that amounts to more than 8 years of engagement.

The world of professional football has been, and continues to be, subject to intense media focus. Much of this interest is devoted to professional football clubs in England's top professional division. These clubs have been described as insular, and their everyday working practices are rarely open to the public eye (Magee, 2002; Parker, 1998). Tomlinson (1993) described football clubs as

> *jealously guarded worlds. Like governments, clubs are interested in good publicity or no publicity at all. They are, therefore, quite suspicious of social researchers and of press and broadcasting journalists, whose interests lie in anything other than the straight report or the novelty item.* (p. 152)

THE FOOTBALL ENVIRONMENT

Parker (1995) suggested that the lack of empirical research into the experiences of players in professional football is due to the closed environment that has been created by those living and working in the sport. That said, Hunter Davies' (1972) work provided one of the earliest insights into life in professional football. Davies spent a year during the 1971–72 playing season inside the Tottenham Hotspur Football Club with the aim of exploring the realities of the occupation. He reported that, despite some cases of financial affluence among players even in the 1970s, there were also widespread experiences of insecurity, loneliness, and rejection—an issue discussed more recently by Potrac, Jones, and Armour (2002) and Littlewood (2005). Parker's (1995, 1996a, 1996b, 2000, 2001) research complements Davies' earlier work and offers further insights into the culture and context of professional football. Parker conducted a sociological case study analysis of youth traineeship in English professional football in an attempt to discover the features of the construction of masculinity. Using an ethnographic research design, Parker identified the professional football environment as a key location for the demonstration and reinforcement of traditional working-class masculine values. He suggested that the identities of the youth trainees were shaped and constructed in unison with a series of official and unofficial institutional norms, values, and assumptions. For example, Parker made reference to the players' experiences and perceptions of the menial chores that they had to engage in, the coaching style and communication strategies of the youth team coach, the authoritarian club culture, and the role of education. All of these facets shaped the youth trainees' lives inside the professional football club. Reflecting on his fieldwork, Parker (1995) remarked, "As my experience at Colby Town proved, football apprenticeship is not about feelings or personal dignity. It's about opinions, authoritarian attitudes, and domination. About discipline, tradition, superiority, and respect for professional reputation" (p. 123).

Bourke's (2002) work on the motives and career planning of young Irish players also offers a glimpse into the lives of individuals who enter the football industry. Bourke noted that working in, and coping with, a foreign culture can lead to what is termed culture shock, a psychological phenomenon that may lead to feelings of fear, helplessness, irritability, and disorientation. She emphasized the importance of both pre- and postawareness training for players making the migration to another country to enhance their knowledge about situations and experiences they may face. This approach is aligned with the sport psychology literature on the management of career transitions in professional sport (Lavallee & Wylleman, 2000). Bourke found that players thought little about the reality of club life. A number of players did observe, however, that they would have done things differently, since the reality of living and working in new surroundings provided many challenges. The prominent difficulties that players reported upon entering their respective training schemes included the absence of family and close friends as well as difficulty in coping with and adjusting to their first time living away from home. Although the players (generally) agreed that the decision to pursue a professional career was a satisfying one, some negative issues arose, such as not getting along with the manager and feeling pressure to perform.

TRANSITION AND IDENTITY

Lavallee and Wylleman (2000) and Bourke (2002) allude indirectly to the notions of transition and identity, along with a number of career points that players need to negotiate. The literature on transitions in sport has largely focused on retirement and career termination (Wylleman, Lavallee, & Alfermann, 1999), and this focus has undoubtedly helped sport psychologists understand how athletes experience this stage of their sport lives. Some research has examined how athletes attempt to deal with the negative factors associated with the end of playing (Werthener & Orlick, 1986), especially when it comes unexpectedly (Taylor & Ogilvie, 1998) or is due to injury (Kleiber & Brock, 1992). Despite this work, which has helped generate further useful studies and assist the activities of sport psychologists, a number of important issues appear to be in need of further research attention.

Researchers have tended to view transition and career termination as negative and unappealing factors in sport. This view is easy to accept in the case of career-ending injuries. The literature seems to have overlooked, however, the fact that for some fulfilled athletes retirement from playing may be viewed positively and even welcomed. Studies outside of sport indicate that retirement may be a cause for celebration and may be eagerly anticipated as an opportunity to pursue other tasks and take on new identities.

Transition research has focused primarily on retirement or career termination. Lavallee and Wylleman (2000) noted that there had been over 226 studies on this topic since 1950. Nevertheless, until the work by Pummell, Harwood, and Lavallee (2008), little had been done to investigate the experiences of within-career transitions. In addition—and apart from Petitpas, Brewer, and Van Raalte (1996)—few have written about this phenomenon from an applied practice perspective. This seems surprising in light of definitions of transition suggesting that, for most athletes, competitive sport in particular is about constant change on a daily or weekly basis. Schlossberg (1981), for example, described transition in terms of changes in thoughts and behaviors that take place in reaction to some event or its absence. When applied to sport, this basic yet elegant definition suggests that such moments are central to the lives of many competitive athletes. These changes are especially likely for people operating in highly challenging, volatile, and pressured environments such as elite and professional sport. Other definitions of transition are almost indistinguishable from accounts of learning. For example, existential phenomenological approaches to the psychology of learning describe genuine learning as involving a relatively permanent and personally felt shift in meaning and knowledge. This and other definitions of learning and transition highlight the similarities between the terms. In developmental psychology, it is common to read about social readjustment, midlife crisis, consciousness transformation, and identity crisis. Again, this body of work is strong on theory and covers transitions from childhood to later life. The adoption of such perspectives in sport psychology might have resulted in a greater interest in transitions across all stages of athletes' lives.

Despite Lavallee and Wylleman's (2000) attempts to inject some theoretical substance into the research in this area, most of the empirical studies investigating sport transitions have been largely atheoretical. Lavallee, Nesti, Borkeles, Cockerill, and Edge (2000) claimed that "the theoretical models of social gerontology, thanatology, and transition that have been applied to athletic career termination have been instrumental in stimulating research on a number of career transition issues" (p. 112). Though Lavallee has clearly been influenced by these models and theory in his work, the same cannot be said for most other studies. In some ways, it may be easy to understand why this has occurred. Thanatological models focus on death, dying, and stages of death. Although it can be argued that, for some athletes, career termination may feel like a kind of death, others find the analogy strained.

A more important criticism, however, focuses on social gerontology and thanatological theories as based on cognitive and social learning approaches, whereas sport transition models appear to be essentially atheoretical. As a result, studies in sport often adopt a descriptive and superficial account of stages of transition, lacking any depth or grounding in psychological theory. Sport psychology researchers delving into transitions have rarely considered the work of Erikson (1968), who was one of the first and most influential psychologists to write about stages of development, crisis, and identity. We view it as an oversight to ignore someone whose life's work was devoted to engaging with people and writing about their roles, identity formation, and human development. This oversight might be explained through reference to the disciplines associated with cognitive and behavioral approaches. The education and training of many sport psychologists may also have been limited by an apparent reluctance to embrace established theories in domains such as education, psychotherapy, and counseling.

We suggest that a richer, more complete, and more helpful approach to understanding transitions in sport would be to draw on the original theory of personality provided by Erikson (1968), especially the description of eight stages of human development. This dynamic account is also attractive because each stage involves a crisis, which Erikson describes as a turning point. As far as sport is concerned, these crises contain both positive and negative elements. This approach would seem to offer a useful and realistic account of transition in sport, where moving on to the next phase, level, or stage, though desired and welcomed by the athlete, is rarely easy or fully completed. Two other factors are important as well. Most of sport is driven by transition—both up and down! Changes happen in the lives of all athletes daily, weekly, and across their careers. Again, the current literature has tended to focus on retirement because it represents a clear example of a major and (usually) irreversible change. For some professional and elite-level athletes, however, major transitions are encountered repeatedly throughout their sporting lives. These changes are sometimes initially perceived negatively and even seen as serious threats to success and progress. At the same time, such challenges can also lead to improvement and further achievement. This feature, wherein uncomfortable and difficult moments are associated with (an eventual) positive movement toward new roles and tasks, appears not to have been considered in the research to date. There may be two reasons. First, there is an absence in the sport psychology literature of studies acknowledging that competitive and performance sport always involves some amount of suffering, sacrifice, and hardship. Such experiences may bring positive benefits to the athlete in terms of developing mental toughness, existential courage, and personality (Nesti, 2007). A second reason that the negative experiences of athletes in transition have gone mainly unacknowledged may involve the lack of a suitable theoretical perspective. Thus we turn to existential psychology, which, in contrast to humanistic theory, accepts that negative experiences, uncomfortable emotions, and anxiety can be psychologically beneficial, especially when these feelings accompany a task that has been chosen by the individuals themselves.

EXISTENTIAL PSYCHOLOGY

Following earlier work by Fahlberg, Fahlberg, and Gates (1992) and Dale (1996) in sport and exercise psychology, Lavallee et al. (2000) have advocated that existential phenomenological psychology could provide a much-needed additional theoretical approach to understanding anxiety and transitions in sport. In contrast to the dominant perspective during the past 30 years, the existential account of anxiety emphasizes that this emotion can be positive despite the fact it feels anything but! As Corlett (1996) pointed out, sport psychologists have invariably seen anxiety as a problem and as something to be managed away or diminished. The exception is where researchers (e.g., Jones, 1995) have discussed the notion of facilitative anxiety, but this type of anxiety still rests on a theoretical approach that views anxiety as a negative construct. Existential psychologists argue that anxiety is often something found alongside growth, change, and transition and therefore should be faced up to and accepted. Proponents also claim that the core self of a person is strengthened by confronting and moving through anxiety, which make him or her readier to accept these moments in the future (Nesti, 2004). It has been suggested by Spinelli (1994) that the strongly positive view of anxiety taken by existential therapists sets it apart from other approaches in psychotherapy.

An existential approach also has much to say about the development of new personal meaning through learning and change. Commenting on the roots of humanistic psychology, Maslow (1968) suggested that when the much older approach of European existential psychology arrived in North America in the 1950s, psychologists there translated meaning into the term "identity." Accepting the discomfort of normal anxiety associated with the experience of transition can, according to Maslow and existential psychologists, help develop authenticity, a process whereby an individual develops greater self-knowledge and a more clarified sense of self as identity develops through learning and change.

EXISTENTIAL PSYCHOLOGY AND TRANSITION IN SPORT

Our (the authors') applied practice is presently based on the delivery of sport psychology support at three Premiership football clubs. It is our belief that the experience of transition is ever present. The environment of professional sport tends to accelerate processes of change and places severe pressure on athletes in the form of performance demands, media management or intrusion, contract negotiations, and new roles and positions. These and other factors must be dealt with constructively if the athlete wishes to make the transition to a higher level. In this regard, Salter (1997) suggested that sport psychologists could be described as "purveyors of immortality" (p. 253). He argued further that a sport psychologist's task, especially with professional athletes, is to help keep them at the top for as long as possible. We do this in part by helping them meet the demands of the frequently encountered experience of transition and keep progressing for as long as possible. Salter has acknowledged an ethical dimension in that it is essential that the athletes themselves want to make the choice to stay at the top despite the difficulties it may bring in their sports and broader lives. Transitions also involve movement downward, and this reversal can be a frequent experience in the lives of top professional football players. The first-team Premiership football players we have worked with have revealed that dealing with transition successfully is essential to survival in such a demanding sport.

From the perspective of existential psychology, the term *boundary situations* is preferred to the word *transition* because it conveys the understanding that change can often be quite traumatic and personal and involve new levels of self-awareness. Existential psychologists argue that boundary situations (i.e., critical moments encountered during an episode of change; Yalom, 1999) are likely to be accompanied by feelings of normal anxiety. Normal existential anxiety refers to anxiety that is almost ever present in one form or another and is not disproportionate to the perceived threat. The challenges faced at boundary situations may relate directly to sport performance or be more indirect and involve broader life concerns. Ultimately, existential anxiety is anxiety about existence. Nesti (2007) has pointed out that it is possible to view this anxiety as addressing nonbeing (i.e., death) in symbolic terms in sport. He claims that for some professional football players, leaving the sport can be viewed as a form of social death because it involves what for some feels like the obliteration of their identity and existence.

The narrative account that follows highlights how these experiences can be encountered in the lives of professional football players. Smith and Sparkes (2009) suggested that adopting a narrative perspective has the potential to make a positive contribution to psychological research into sport and exercise. They define narrative as

> . . . *a complex genre that routinely contains a point and characters along with a plot connecting events that unfold sequentially over time and in space to provide an overarch-*

ing explanation or consequence. It is a constructed form or template which people rely on to tell stories. (p. 2)

The approach adopted in the narrative conforms to the principles associated with a confessional tale (Sparkes, 2002). The writing explicitly locates the author in the text as the first person and reveals what happened in the practitioner's experience. It illuminates the first author's world in a creative nonfiction approach and guides the reader through the narrative by attempting to outline the effect that the experience had on the practitioner.

A NARRATIVE: TRUSTING YOURSELF IN CRITICAL MOMENTS

As I drove into the training ground that morning, my mind began to wander toward the fallout that might come from some of the issues we had been facing during the past month or so. Not for the first time, it dawned on me that so few things seemed permanent in this environment. Yet, as a sport psychologist drawing on existential ideas about authenticity and facing up to challenges, my work centered on encouraging players to stay true to themselves and embrace moments of change in their lives. These thoughts led me to consider whether it was really possible for players to maintain such an outlook in such a fast-paced and, at times, cynical environment.

As I got out of the car, I noticed one of the first-team squad players lifting his training bag from the trunk of his new Range Rover. I had known Simon for 3 years. He had joined our club after a successful early career at a top club. I moved across the parking lot to intercept him as he walked toward the main entrance. He saw me coming and gave a slightly embarrassed look in my direction. I remember thinking I had seen this kind of look many times before, especially after the type of conversation we had been having in the previous weeks. After exchanging the usual greetings, I went straight into where we had last left off. "Have you taken some time to think hard about the things that we have been discussing together over the last few weeks?" He glanced at me with a mixture of surprise and relief. I remembered that often players would need to speak to you very soon after confidential one-to-one meetings in which they had been open about themselves and their wishes. As we got through the front door and into the reception area, we carried on into one of the small meeting rooms. "It's really hard to get the energy to face up to this situation that I'm in," Simon said. "I felt that I had already done enough in the early part of the season to show what I could do for the team, especially playing those five games on the bounce out of my normal position. I can't talk to anyone about this because I don't know what to say apart from sounding really negative, and no one likes to listen to that stuff for too long. I've read a few times the notes you sent me on our conversations, and I know what I should do next, which is really to keep my focus on this next few weeks and months and to keep doing my job better each day. It's really knackering at times, especially when the gaffer doesn't seem to notice."

Simon looked out of the window to where the fitness staff were methodically putting out cones and stakes for the morning's session. It was one of those moments where I wanted to say things that would help Simon, to suggest strategies and even solutions, but I knew that would not be what he wanted or needed. True to the existential psychology principles on which I base some of my approach, I challenged him to consider what he found so difficult about his current situation. Simon explained that he knew that difficult and uncomfortable moments were almost ever present in his life in football and that he could avoid them only by lowering his aspirations and being satisfied with being just a squad player. Eventually his language and tone of voice began to change as he started to tell me about how well respected he had been as a player with other managers and the fact that, beneath it all, he only really fully valued his own opinion of himself. "Is that so wrong?" he asked to no one in particular. I looked straight at him, and the glance said all that needed to be said. Simon knew that ultimately the most important person to wrestle with during the inescapable moments of change encountered in the game was himself. This had taken us 25 minutes to get to—such a long time for what looked like so little. Simon grabbed his bag and made toward the door before turning to shake my hand. "That was great, mate," he said. "We need to do this again sometime soon."

I sat there for some time after he left, reflecting on what had just taken place. It confirmed again how important it was that I was able to work fully confidentially with the first-team players and be someone they would trust since I was in and around the club 3 or 4 days a week. In terms of psychological theory, it seemed to me that yet again this was an example of the experience of existential anxiety that is associated with identity change, growth, and transition. As with many of the Premiership players I've worked with, this dialogue seemed to suggest that the resources to meet the challenge of change already reside, for the most part, in the earlier journeys that these individuals have made in their personal and professional lives.

Later that day, I attended the first-team staff meeting, at which we discussed selection for Saturday's game and how different players were responding to being part of such a competitive squad. When the conversation turned to Simon, several of the key staff and the manager sang his praises in relation to how motivated, driven, and focused he seemed to be no matter what challenges they threw at him. I felt a mixture of emotions ranging from anxiety to excitement and even pride upon hearing that Simon would start in the 11 on Saturday. After we left the meeting, I remember thinking how wonderful it must be on these occasions to be the one who tells the player that they are in the side.

Before the end of the day, I popped in to see the manager for the usual 15 to 20 minutes to check his thinking on where players were psychologically and to go through my list of other tasks to do in the week ahead. He asked me, as he always did, how certain players were doing and whether they were on the train or had decided to stay on the platform. Again, as usual, my feedback was geared toward protecting the confidentiality of my work with the players, which was something the manager fully accepted and understood. When we got to Simon, he told me how impressed he had been with his attitude in adapting and changing to the new situation he had found himself in: "Putting him in the team for such an important game on Saturday is my way of rewarding him and telling others that this is the response I'm always looking for." The manager then spoke at length about how we could create a more supportive environment for the young professional players so that they could develop the character to step away from the comfort zone of the youth academy and forge new identities as first-team players. As we sat there talking about how ultimately only the player himself could make this choice, I found myself thinking about the many I had worked with who had become tired of this process of constant and difficult change. Some of these players had left the game early, whereas others had fallen well short of fulfilling their potential, despite often being some of the most able performers physically and technically.

On the drive home that night, I received a call from one of the younger players, who arranged to see me early in the next week to help with confidence. At first, I was taken aback because this individual was considered to be among the most confident and outgoing of all the young players and was viewed as a potential leader. As we finished our conversation, his final words pointed yet again to how what is visible to others is not always the reality of individual lives: "I don't think I can keep up this level of acting much longer. It's beginning to show, and I am taking it out on those closest to me, like my girlfriend and family at home. The club and coaches think I'm well sorted, but really I am stumbling from day to day and wish there was an easier way to go past this stage of my life and career in the game."

Clearly, such a challenge is common in professional team sport, where squads often comprise two or even three times the number of players who are selected for first-team duty and young professionals face constant boundary situations. The senior Premiership player in this example was wrestling with a boundary situation involving a new role and position on the team rather than the one he had expected. This moment of real existential significance involves anxiety about moving into a new challenge and frustration at recognizing that even for an established team player, boundary situations are still part of professional life. The existential literature and humanistic approaches (Gilbourne & Richardson, 2006) would add here that these situations are also personal issues, because for many professional athletes what they do in sport is inseparable from who they are as people. This holistic perspective maintains that in such situations it is rather futile and unhelpful to ask the player to approach the boundary situation in a detached, systematic, and dispassionate way. Again, the existential psychology view warns the sport psychologist away from attempting to alleviate the suffering and distress that the athlete is feeling, because, unlike most humanistic perspectives according to Spinelli (1994), existential psychology is more prepared to accept that confronting issues and making choices often bring anxiety and pain. If one avoids choosing, or is given answers or solutions to the sport psychologist, the uncomfortable feelings may be removed, and the result, according to Buber (1923/1970), is that the individual eventually develops "a stunted person centre" (pp. 178–179). This diminished self, in turn, is less able to stand up to the anxiety associated with choosing in the face of boundary situations, and so the downward cycle continues.

This dialogue suggests that professional athletes can experience competitive anxiety alongside the normal anxiety described in existential psychology (May, 1977). In pointing out that the roots of modern anxiety lie in the destruction of community, May discussed how individualism "became competitive in nature" and addressed "the consequences of this competitive individualism for interpersonal isolation and anxiety" (p. 177). As May has pointed out, this type of anxiety can be more discomforting and painful than fear and competitive anxiety because competitive anxiety is clearly related to specific future events that are easy to identify, whereas existential normal anxiety results from what Kierkegaard (1844/1944) called "the possibility of freedom." May claimed that this occurs when "recalling that every person has the opportunity and need to move ahead in his development. Such possibilities, like roads ahead which cannot be known since you have not yet traversed and experienced them, involve anxiety" (p. 38). According to May, this normal anxiety results from increased self-awareness and self-knowledge. In other words, as individuals become more aware of their responsibilities to choose various courses of action, they correspondingly feel some level of inner conflict over their expanded freedom to choose. This approach to a boundary situation agrees with Lindsay, Breckon, Thomas, and Maynard (2007) in that within the existential encounter the psychologist has allowed "these often uncomfortable and anxiety producing moments to run their course" (Nesti, 2004, p. 113). Through use of presence, spontaneity, and empathy during the encounter, the sport psychologist has drawn on an important central tenet of existential psychology, which is "not about making . . . client[s] feel comfortable, but . . . helping them to face up to the anxiety associated with thinking for themselves and making choices" (Nesti, 2004, p. 113).

When professional athletes talk about their careers, personal identities, and the boundary situations they come up against, the language they use and the thoughts they express are deeply personal and real rather than detached or theoretical. From the phenomenological existential perspective, we need to remain with the real Lebenswelt, or "lived world," of the person we are working with in order to "help the session to remain focused on the most important and personally significant aspects of the athlete's sporting life" (Nesti, 2004, p. 112). This approach demands that boundary situations be dealt with seriously, cautiously, and respectfully, especially for professional athletes, given the centrality of their sport lives to their personal meanings or identities. Goal setting and most other mental skills interventions would be of little use here, because we are not dealing with an easy-to-address symptom but with real lives of people and with the existential crises they face when stages of their lives are under threat.

CONCLUSION

We accept that researchers and practitioners may recognize some of the issues articulated here yet also have their own different understandings of the environments of professional football. We hope that this chapter encourages others to document their own understandings of the complex nature of development and progression in high-level professional football. We feel that the messages contained in this chapter have implications for the training of sport psychologists, as well as important methodological and research implications that we would suggest have emerged from our applied experiences and our view of the existing literature. For example, we see a greater need for researchers to embrace phenomenological methods and alternative forms of representation in order to capture the lived experiences of football players at different stages of their careers. We also see an opportunity to broaden the foundation on which research is based through the use of other established theoretical approaches. The main theoretical approach considered in this chapter has been that of existential psychology. However, as we have suggested earlier, the work of Erikson (1968) could provide another perspective on transition in sport. We hope that more researchers will consider how his work could enhance our understanding of identity and transition for young players in professional football, especially since much of Erikson's work focused on stages of identity and young people.

IDEAS FOR REFLECTION AND DEBATE

1. Consider the applied implications of viewing transition in terms of day-to-day events rather than as a longer-term process.

2. By viewing daily events through an existential lens, Mark and Martin promote a particular theoretical or philosophical agenda. Reflect on the degree to which existentialism and associated constructs feature in your own curricular or scholarly history and draw some conclusions about the strengths and weaknesses of your own training.

3. What applied skills would you see as being associated with an existential approach to practice? Do you have them? Would you like to have them? Where could you get them?

REFERENCES

Bourke, A. (2002). The road to fame and fortune: Insights on the career paths of young Irish professional footballers in England. *Journal of Youth Studies, 5*, 375–389.

Buber, M. (1970). I and thou (W. Kaufmann, Trans.). New York: Scribner. (Original work published 1923.)

Corlett, J. (1996). Sophistry, Socrates, and sport psychology. *The Sport Psychologist, 10*, 84–94.

Dale, G.A. (1996). Existential phenomenology: Emphasizing the experience of the athlete in sport psychology research. *The Sport Psychologist, 10*, 307–321.

Davies, H. (1972). *The glory game.* Edinburgh, Scotland: Mainstream.

Erikson, E.H. (1968). Identity, youth, and crisis. New York: Norton.

Fahlberg, L.L., Fahlberg, L.A., & Gates, K.W. (1992). Exercise and existence: Exercise behavior from an existential-phenomenological perspective. *The Sport Psychologist, 6*, 172–191.

Gilbourne, D., & Richardson, D. (2006). Tales from the field: Personal reflections on the provision of psychological support in professional soccer. *Psychology of Sport and Exercise, 7*, 325–337.

Jones, G. (1995). More than a game: Research developments and issues in competitive anxiety in sport. *British Journal of Psychology, 86*, 449–478.

Kierkegaard, S. (1944). The concept of dread (S. Lowrie, Trans.). Princeton: Princeton University Press. (Original work published 1844.)

Kleiber, D.A., & Brock, S.C. (1992). The effect of career-ending injuries on the subsequent well-being of elite college athletes. *Sociology of Sport Journal, 9*, 70–75.

Lavallee, D., Nesti, M., Borkeles, E., Cockerill, I., & Edge, A. (2000). Approaches to counseling athletes in transition. In D. Lavallee & P. Wylleman (Eds.), *Career transitions in sport: International perspectives* (pp. 111–130). Morgantown, WV: Fitness Information Technology.

Lavallee, D., & Wylleman, P. (Eds.). (2000). *Career transitions in sport: International perspectives.* Morgantown, WV: Fitness Information Technology.

Lindsay, P., Breckon, J.D., Thomas, D., & Maynard, I. (2007). In pursuit of congruence: A personal reflection on methods and philosophy in applied practice. *The Sport Psychologist, 21*, 335–352.

Littlewood, M. (2005). The impact of foreign player acquisition on the development and progression of young players in elite level English professional football. Unpublished doctoral dissertation, Liverpool John Moores University, England.

Magee, J. (2002). Shifting balances of power in the new football economy. In J. Sugden (Ed.), *Power games: A critical sociology of sport* (pp. 216–239). London: Routledge.

Maslow, A.H. (1968). *Toward a psychology of being*. New York: Van Nostrand Reinhold.

May, R. (1977). *The meaning of anxiety*. New York: Ronald Press.

Nesti, M. (2004). *Existential psychology and sport: Theory and application*. London: Routledge.

Nesti, M. (2007). Suffering, sacrifice, sport psychology and the spirit. In J. Parry, S. Robinson, N. Watson, & M. Nesti (Eds.), *Sport and spirituality* (pp. 119–134), London: Routledge

Parker, A. (1995). Great expectations: Grimness or glamour? The football apprentice in the 1990s. *The Sports Historian, 15,* 107–126.

Parker, A. (1996a). Professional football club culture: Goffman, asylums and occupational socialisation. *Scottish Centre Research Papers in Sport, Leisure and Society, 1,* 123–130.

Parker, A. (1996b). Chasing the Big Time: Football apprenticeship in the 1990s. Unpublished doctoral dissertation, University of Warwick, Coventry, England.

Parker, A. (1998). Staying on-side on the inside: Problems and dilemmas in ethnography. *Sociology Review, 7,* 10–13.

Parker, A. (2000). Training for "glory," schooling for "failure"?: English professional football, traineeship and educational provision. *Journal of Education and Work, 13,* 61–76.

Parker, A. (2001). Soccer, servitude and sub-cultural identity: Football traineeship and masculine construction. *Soccer and Society, 2,* 59–80.

Petitpas, A.J., Brewer, B.W., & Van Raalte, J.L. (1996). Transitions of the student-athlete: Theoretical, empirical, and practical perspectives. In E.F. Etzel, A.P. Ferrante, & J.W. Pinkey (Eds.), *Counseling college student-athletes: Issues and interventions* (2nd ed., pp.137–156). Morgantown, WV: Fitness Information Technology.

Potrac, P., Jones, R., & Armour, K. (2002). "It's all about getting respect": The coaching behaviours of an expert soccer coach. *Sport, Education and Society, 7,* 183–202.

Pummell, B., Harwood, C., & Lavallee, D. (2008). Jumping to the next level: A qualitative examination of within-career transitions in adolescent event riders. *Psychology of Sport and Exercise, 9,* 427–447.

Salter, D. (1997). Measure, analyse and stagnate: Towards a radical psychology of sport. In R.J. Butler (Ed.), *Sports psychology in performance* (pp. 248–260). Oxford, England: Reed.

Schlossberg, N.K. (1981). A model for analyzing human adaptation to transition. *The Counseling Psychologist, 9,* 2–18.

Smith, B., & Sparkes, A.C. (2009). Narrative inquiry in sport and exercise psychology: What can it mean and why might we do it? *Psychology of Sport and Exercise, 10,* 1–11.

Sparkes, A.C. (2002). *Telling tales in sport and physical activity: A qualitative journey*. Champaign, IL: Human Kinetics.

Spinelli, E. (1994). *Demystifying therapy.* London: Constable.

Taylor, J., & Ogilvie, B.C. (1998). Career transition among elite athletes: Is there life after sports? In J.M. Williams (Ed.), *Applied sport psychology: Personal growth to peak performance* (3rd ed., pp. 429–444). Mountain View, CA: Mayfield.

Tomlinson, A. (1993). Tuck up tight, lads: Structures of control within football culture. In A. Tomlinson (Ed.), *Explorations in football culture* (pp. 149–174). City, Country: Leisure Studies Associations.

Werthner, P., & Orlick, T. (1986). Retirement experiences of successful Olympic athletes. *International Journal of Sport Psychology, 17,* 337–363.

Wylleman, P., Lavallee, D., & Alfermann, D. (Eds.). (1999). *Career transitions in competitive sports.* Biel, Switzerland: FEPSAC.

Yalom, I. (1999). *Momma and the meaning of life: Tales of psychotherapy.* London: Piatkus.

ESSAY 15

SAFEGUARDING CHILD ATHLETES FROM ABUSE IN ELITE SPORT SYSTEMS:

The Role of the Sport Psychologist

Trisha Leahy

Hong Kong Sports Institute

Trisha's powerful and challenging essay argues that psychological safety can be lacking in a sporting environment marked by abusive, threatening, or humiliating coaching styles. She argues that this problem not only significantly increases the immediate stress on athletes but also has been associated with long-term psychological harm. Physical safety can also be compromised when extreme physical activities are used as punishment for errors or for failure to perform or when training regimens are not developmentally appropriate. In addition, sexual abuse of young athletes is a documented reality in many countries and has been associated with long-term post-traumatic symptomatology. Trisha overviews some of the research and practice in this area and discusses the implications with a view to empowering and enabling sport psychologists to be effective gatekeepers protecting young athletes from harm and to be valuable advocates for child and youth protection policies within sport systems. She argues that, as a key person in the athlete's entourage, the sport psychologist is often the first point of contact for athletes in distress, and thus needs to be aware of the potential for these forms of harm as well as the relevant social policy and procedures for reporting and referring.

INTRODUCTION

Organized competitive sport forms a social institution in many countries that addresses specific provisions in articles 29 and 31 of the United Nations (2002) Convention on the Rights of the Child. The main directives of these articles hold that (a) every child has the right to play and (b) children's talents and mental and physical abilities should be developed to their fullest potential. High-performance sport systems, often funded by governments, have become more prevalent in recent years as countries compete to develop athletic giftedness and perform successfully on the world stage of elite sport. It is now recognized in high-performance sport systems that individual success at the elite level is a function of the complex interplay of multiple factors. Apart from individual talent and expert coaching to facilitate that talent, the development of athletic giftedness to its fullest potential requires a comprehensive support infrastructure to minimize risk and maximize results.

In this chapter, I highlight the role and function of sport psychology personnel from within a biopsychosocial framework, particularly with reference to the role of gatekeepers, in promoting a best-practice sport environment that facilitates the development of athletic giftedness within a safe, ethical delivery system. I focus on sexual abuse and the role of the sport psychologist as a core member of the elite athlete's entourage in intervening and advocating for systemic child and youth protection measures within the sport system.

ISSUES OF SAFEGUARDING

Sport is a permitted social institution and requires thoughtful stewardship if it is to fulfill its social responsibility. Sport industries, however, like other organizations, represent complex social systems in which structural and relational characteristics are inherently value laden. To be a successful professional coach, one needs to produce winning teams; to be a successful professional sport, a given sport needs to attract fans, provide entertainment value, and deliver value for money for its sponsors. To attract and retain young gifted athletes, sports at all levels need to provide developmentally suitable and safe training environments. In such a climate of competing interests, how do we ensure that socially responsible and ethical directions are consistently taken and that the rights of young athletes are not being violated?

During the past few years, the occurrence of sexual harassment and abuse in sport has been systematically documented by researchers in a number of countries in Europe, Australia, Canada, and the United States (e.g., Brackenridge, Bishop, Moussalli, & Tapp, 2008; Fasting, Brackenridge, Miller, & Sabo, 2008; Kirby, Demers, & Parent, 2008; Leahy, Pretty, & Tenenbaum, 2002, 2008; Vanden Auweele et al., 2008). Research documenting this abuse and other forms of violence against young athletes in sport has led to a more critical analysis of the sporting environment itself as a sociocultural system and of its effect on young people. Both human rights frameworks and the scientific biopsychosocial paradigm are being brought to bear in the development of preventive policy and practice (Leahy, 2008). At the highest level of elite sport, the International Olympic Committee (IOC) has recently issued a consensus statement regarding sexual harassment and abuse in sport. The IOC has stated that its aim is to improve the health and protection of all athletes by promoting effective preventive policy and to increase awareness of these problems among athletes' support personnel. The IOC specifically recognizes all the rights of athletes, including the right to enjoy a safe and supportive sport environment. It is in such conditions that athletes are most likely to flourish and optimize their sporting potential (IOC Medical Commission, 2007). UNICEF (2011) has now taken up the issue under its mandate, defined by the Convention on the Rights of the Child, of preventing violence against children, which it defines as those under the age of 18.

THE BIOPSYCHOSOCIAL MODEL

In behavioral medicine and the social sciences, the term *biopsychosocial* is used to refer to the interaction between biological, psychological, and social factors, which are inextricably linked in the overall development of any individual. In the elite sport sector, whose objective is to develop high-performance athletes, and specifically in the servicing infrastructure, which facilitates such development, the biopsychosocial paradigm is particularly informative. Many of our international elite sport support systems are underpinned by this biopsychosocial framework with centralized, integrated support systems that target all aspects of each athlete's medical, physiological, psychological, social support, and welfare needs.

A multidisciplinary approach is the logical corollary to the biopsychosocial paradigm, which assumes that athletes rarely, if ever, exhibit unidimensional problems. Effective solutions, therefore, are almost always the result of multidisciplinary, integrated, science-based interventions. Additionally, office- or laboratory-based servicing is increasingly not the norm for the delivery of scientific support services in elite sport. Thus scientific support staff members, including sport psychologists, need to be highly mobile, traveling with athletes to local and overseas venues for training and competition.

In the biopsychosocial model, scientific support personnel, including sport psychologists, are key frontline members of the elite athlete's entourage, tasked with providing scientific training methodologies to support coaching, training, and performance. In general, there is now a sound scientific base and well-established practice guidelines for monitoring individual health and performance parameters. Systemic health and performance parameters, however, have been less visible in our performance-related research and applied interventions. Systemic parameters are an important component of the biopsychosocial framework, requiring our attention if we are to effectively use the framework as our operating model for high-performance service delivery. The increasing recognition that social institutions, including sport, should provide systemic risk-reduction strategies has stimulated policy initiatives in a number of countries, including the United Kingdom (Child Protection in Sport Unit, 2006) and Australia (Australian Sports Commission, 2007), that focus on safeguarding athletes (Brackenridge et al., 2008).

As part of the multidisciplinary biopsychosocial support system, the sport psychologist is in a key position to monitor the maintenance of a psychologically, physically, and sexually safe system in which athletes can achieve their potential. Sport psychologists, because of their close involvement with the team, are often the first point of contact for athletes in distress, and therefore need to be aware of the potential for various forms of harm and the relevant social policy and procedures for reporting and referring. Using a sport injury analogy, sport psychologists, as members of the multidisciplinary scientific support team, can effectively use their position, in the athlete's entourage to contribute to the prevention of systemic injuries; to advocate for appropriate child and youth protection policies within the sport system; and to develop a culture of dignity, respect, and safety in sport (IOC Medical Commission, 2007). This positioning raises questions about the role and preparedness of sport psychologists to be able to function effectively as gatekeepers to ensure systemic safety for all athletes.

Before sport psychologists (as members of the biopsychosocial support team) can step up to the role of gatekeeper, effectively acting to protect the rights of young people in sport, we must first insist on our own rights to be educated and provided with clear ethical guidelines and core competencies embedded in a support system that empowers us to act on behalf of young athletes at risk. Violence against children in all its forms (physical, psychological, sexual) is a social problem, and, like other sectors of the community, the sport sector cannot prevent serial offenders from gaining entry into the system. What we can perhaps achieve is to increase deterrence by empowering all adults in the system, starting with ourselves as sport psychologists, with the specific knowledge and resources required to understand and to act to protect athletes.

SEXUAL ABUSE IN SPORT

Research into sexual abuse in sport began with both prevalence studies (Kirby, Greaves, & Hankivsky, 2000; Leahy et al., 2002) and qualitative investigations into the processes and experiences of sexually abused athletes (Brackenridge, 1997; Cense & Brackenridge, 2001; Leahy, Pretty, & Tenenbaum, 2003; Toftegaard-Nielsen, 2001). Depending on the definitions and methodologies used, the prevalence rates suggested by research reports range from 2 percent (Tomlinson & Yorganci, 1997) to 22 percent (Kirby et al., 2000). One study with an Australian sample employed a more precise, legally based definition of sexual abuse (Leahy et al., 2002). In that study, sexual abuse was considered to be any sexual activity between an adult and a child (under 18 years old), regardless of whether deception was involved or the child understood the sexual nature of the activity or not. This definition included sexual contact accomplished by force or by the threat of force regardless of the age of the victim or perpetrator. Sexual abuse included noncontact (e.g., exhibitionism, involving a child in sexually explicit conversation, engaging a child in pornographic photography), contact (sexual touching, masturbation), and penetrative (oral, vaginal, anal) acts. Results indicated that of 370 elite (national) and club (regional) athletes surveyed, 31 percent of female athletes and 21 percent of male athletes reported having experienced sexual abuse before the age of 18. Environment-specific sexual abuse rates were particularly high: 41 percent of the sexually abused female athletes and 29 percent of the sexually abused male athletes indicated that the abuse was perpetrated by sport personnel. The sport-related abuse was largely perpetrated by those in positions of authority or trust in relation to the athletes—primarily coaches and less frequently support staff and other athletes. The vast majority (more than 96 percent) of perpetrators were men.

Long-Term Effects

Prevalence studies suggest that sexual abuse and its psychological sequelae are areas of significant practice application for sport psychologists working with athletes. Yet empirical evidence about the psychological sequelae associated with sexual abuse in athlete populations and the implications for specific interventions are areas of research that have been conspicuously absent in the sport psychology literature. In the clinical psychology and psychiatric research base, investigators and clinicians have begun to apply a trauma framework to understand the impact of sexual abuse. Central to this evolving theoretical framework are the concepts of post-traumatic stress and dissociation as key responses to traumatizing events. There is now substantial evidence that survivors of sexual abuse may be particularly at risk for developing post-traumatic and dissociative symptomatology (Becker-Lausen, Sanders, & Chinsky, 1995; Briere & Runtz, 1990; Johnson, Pike, & Chard, 2001; Mulder, Beautrais, Joyce, & Fergusson, 1998).

Core post-traumatic symptoms of reexperiencing, avoidance, and hyperarousal have been frequently identified in sexual abuse populations (e.g., Carlson, Armstrong, Loewenstein, & Roth, 1998; Johnson et al., 2001). Symptoms related to reexperiencing and hyperarousal can include intrusive thoughts, physiological arousal, reactivity to trauma cues, and hypervigilance (American Psychiatric Association, DSM-IV-TR, 2000). Avoidant symptoms can include avoidance of thoughts, feelings, places, or people associated with the trauma. Dissociation is understood as "a disruption in the usually integrated functions of consciousness" (DSM-IV-TR, 2000, p. 477). Dissociative symptomatology (e.g., amnesia, derealization, depersonalization) involves a splitting between the observing self and the experiencing self. During a traumatic experience, dissociation provides protective detachment from overwhelming affect and pain, but it can result in severe disruption in the usually integrated functions of consciousness, memory, identity, and perception of the environment (van der Kolk, Pelcovitz, Roth, Mandel, McFarlane, & Herman, 1996).

The majority of people who manifest core post-traumatic symptoms also appear to develop complex sets of other interrelated or secondary symptoms (Carlson, 1997). These symptoms can include depression, impairment of self-esteem, and a disruption of important developmental processes leading to affect and impulse dysregulation and deformations of relatedness and identity (Briere, 1997; Courtois, 1999; Herman, 1997).

One published report to date has specifically investigated, from a trauma framework, the long-term effects of childhood sexual abuse on athletes (Leahy et al., 2008). Using a contextualized perspective taking into account childhood physical and psychological abuse experiences and adult trauma experiences, the study of 90 athletes (45 men and 45 women) suggested that childhood sexual, physical, and psychological abuse was strongly correlated and that the primary unique correlate of long-term traumatic sequelae was reported psychological abuse. Some researchers have argued that even though individual forms of child abuse are unlikely to be experienced unidimensionally (e.g., Higgins & McCabe, 2000a, 2000b), both sexual and physical abuse may be understood as inherently psychological forms of abuse (Hart, Binggeli, & Brassard, 1998). It may be, therefore, that the harm lies in the embedded psychological abuse of the sexual abuse experience (Hart, Brassard, & Karlson, 1996; Jellen, McCarroll, & Thayer, 2001; Sanders & Becker-Lausen, 1995). This variable may be particularly salient in the environment of competitive sport, as research has documented apparently normalized coaching and instructional practices and team initiation rituals that constitute psychologically abusive practices (Brackenridge, Rivers, Gough, & Llewellyn, 2006; Kirby & Wintrup, 2002; Leahy, 2001). It may also specifically relate to the particular strategies that appear to be used by perpetrators in athletes' environments.

Perpetrator Methodology

Leahy, Pretty, and Tenenbaum (2004) published data indicating the correlation of specific perpetrator methodologies with long-term traumatic outcomes in a sample of 20 athletes. A thematic analysis of data from semistructured interviews with these athletes was conducted. The group was purposefully selected to balance male and female participants with similar sexual abuse experiences, half of whom scored within the clinical range of traumatic sequelae in clinical assessments. Results revealed two general dimensions of perpetrator methodology apparently designed to engender feelings of complete powerlessness in the sexually abused athlete and, conversely, to present the perpetrator as omnipotent. The perpetrators' methodology seemed to be characterized—as was particularly obvious in cases where the abuse was prolonged and repeated—by the need to impose his version of reality on the athlete and to isolate the athlete within that reality. The perpetrator successfully maintained that reality by controlling the psychological environment. In addition to controlling the athlete's outer life, the perpetrator controlled his or her inner life through direct emotional manipulation and psychological abuse.

From the psychological literature, we know that the repeated imposition of a powerful perpetrator's world view, and the lack (due to isolating and silencing strategies) of alternative reference points, can entrap the victim within the perpetrator's viewpoint (Herman, 1997). This manipulation can be seen in the following statement from a male athlete who was abused by his coach: "At the time . . . I suppose I did wonder how he could get an erection in front of me, but . . . I didn't really think that he was getting off on it, because it was always presented as education, and that sort of thing" (Leahy et al., 2004, p. 533).

The athletes' reports in the study described a sport environment pervaded by an unpredictable and volatile emotional cycle of reward and punishment. In the closed context of a competitive sport team, this cyclical repetition of fear and reprieve and punishment and reward can result in a feeling of extreme dependence on the (perceived) omnipotent perpetrator (Herman, 1997). As one female athlete who was sexually abused by her coach said, "To us at that time, his word was like gospel." From the psychology literature, we understand this state as a traumatized attachment to the perpetrator. Under these conditions, disclosure simply does not happen. Silencing is an integral—not separate—part of the experience, and these aspects of the perpetrator's methodology target the individual's emotional life as a method of keeping that person in a state of confusion, fear, and entrapment. This method is illustrated in the following statements by three athletes who were sexually abused by their coaches.

The Bystander Effect

In a further examination of athletes' experiences of sexual abuse, Leahy et al. (2003) reported the prevalence of the bystander effect, which appeared to compound long-term psychological harm for sexually abused athletes. The bystander effect refers to the situation where the victim perceived that others who knew about (or suspected) the sexual abuse did nothing about it. One female athlete, sexually abused by her coach (who was simultaneously abusing others on the team), provided this distressing account of the bystander effect (Leahy, 2010):

*They saw things that were wrong, and they didn't do any-
thing about it. . . . [T]his is very bad, not only the fact that
I fell out of a sport that should have protected me. . . . I lost
so much. I lost my relationship with my family. . . . I could
have saved a few years of my life.* (p. 316)

Athletes' experiences of the bystander effect make clear the distress-
amplifying impact of abandoning the victim to isolation and silence
(Leahy et al., 2003). The apparent lack of systemically sanctioned
accountability in relation to the power of the coach-perpetrator
appeared to influence other adults in the competitive sport environment. These others included coaching staff members and other support
staff and volunteers who were not as senior in the competitive sport
hierarchy as the perpetrator. This situation was especially notable in
the elite sport context: "We were so elite and no one ever questioned
what we were doing" (Leahy, 2010, p. 327). Nonintervention by other
adults in a young person's environment is likely to be interpreted
as meaning that those adults are also powerless in relation to the
perpetrator.

Confusion

"It was more emotional, everything he did. . . . [H]e'd put me down; he'd
really put me down as an athlete and then build me up with his affection, and then it got really confusing, and I didn't know the difference, if
he was a coach or somebody who was just playing with my emotions."
(female athlete)

Fear (and Confusion)

"I didn't feel like I could tell . . . 'cause not only would I lose my sport, but
I was scared of what would happen. I think, you know, I wasn't thinking
that logically. . . . [A]t the time I was just so confused. I was just really
confused." (female athlete)

Entrapment

"So what do you do when you trusted this person, and you've got all
this at your feet, like your sport and a whole bunch of new friends, so
what are you going to do? It's just your word against his . . . and you don't
know, maybe it happens to everybody. Maybe this is the way it goes."
(male athlete)

For children, disclosure may be preempted if the child believes or is aware that other adults know about the abuse (Palmer, Brown, Rae-Grant, & Loughlin, 1999). If observing adults take no action, children may assume that the behaviors are socially acceptable or, in the case of older children, that perpetrators' messages that they are omnipotent are really true and that the athletes really are trapped.

IMPLICATIONS FOR SPORT PSYCHOLOGY PRACTICE

There is a clear need for more research on sexual and other forms of violence against children in sport in order to substantiate the scientific database and improve on the methodological limitations of the research to date. Nevertheless, implications for sport psychology practice involve individual assessment and intervention as well as, more generally, training and supervision programs for sport psychologists. Such programs should teach the necessary competencies and awareness to recognize and engage with sociocultural vulnerabilities in sport systems that facilitate, rather than inhibit, abusive behaviors. Therefore, implications for psychology practice may be understood as operating at individual and systemic levels.

Individual Issues

From previous research and documented clinical experience, we can assume that sport psychologists will come into contact with a significant percentage of athletes who are survivors of childhood sexual abuse, whether the abuse was perpetrated within or outside of sport. Assessment and treatment of athlete survivors of childhood sexual abuse warrant a contextualized trauma-based framework. Particularly important is the assessment of reported psychological abuse, because such mistreatment may indicate that other forms of abuse have occurred. The implication is that training programs for sport psychologists need to include comprehensive education in the assessment and treatment of childhood abuse and traumagenic symptomatology. Given that 20 to 30 percent of male and female athletes, respectively, report experiencing sexual abuse before the age of 18, sport psychologists are highly likely to be working with this population. Yet two of the largest certifying and accrediting bodies in sport psychology—the British Association of Sport and Exercise Sciences and the Association for Applied Sport Psychology—do not specify anything about training in sexual, physical, or psychological abuse in their guidelines for certification or accreditation. Are we, as a profession, maintaining a dissociative avoidance of the reality of abuse in the lives of athletes?

Data suggesting the association of childhood psychological abuse with long-term post-traumatic and dissociative symptomatology also highlights the importance of maintaining a psychologically safe and consistent therapeutic environment when working with athletes who have experienced childhood abuse. Therapy is a trust-based relationship that requires not only authentic engagement but also vigilance in maintaining a healing dynamic within the therapeutic environment (Leahy et al., 2003).

Sport psychologists often begin working with athletes on performance enhancement, which is a relatively safe area to explore. As the psychologist and the athlete get to know each other and become invested in the psychological work, they begin to develop rapport, trust, and a sound working alliance. Over time, if the athlete repeatedly experiences that it is safe to talk about anything, the working alliance becomes a beneficial therapeutic relationship with positive and healthy transference and countertransference wherein issues related to fear, shame, and feeling trapped can begin to be addressed. Many sport psychologists have the experience of starting out with a performance-enhancement focus, but after a month, or two, or three, the athlete builds up enough trust in the relationship to reveal a story about an eating disorder, an abusive alcoholic parent, self-harm, or sexual abuse. The quality of the therapeutic relationship allows the athlete to put into words that which previously seemed to be unspeakable. Maintaining this quality requires close attention to the relational dynamics with vulnerable athletes. The risk is high that even minor countertransferential errors may be experienced as harmful replications of psychological abuse patterns. Sport psychologists working with such athletes should ensure that they have access to ongoing supervision in order to maintain the quality of the therapeutic interactions and environments.

Systemic Issues

Effective abuse-related therapy must address the sociocultural context of the survivor's distress (Briere, 1992). Sport psychologists working with athletes who are survivors of childhood abuse also need to be aware of the sociocultural context of organized competitive sport, which in some countries has been criticized as normalizing psychologically abusive coaching practices (Brackenridge, 2001; Leahy, 2001; Leahy et al., 2004). This aspect of the athlete survivor's life, which may be unique to competitive sport, may add a layer of complexity and a further challenge to recovery and healing from abuse experiences. Sport psychologists working with athlete survivors need to be particularly vigilant in providing a therapeutic environment that challenges rather than facilitates harmful sociocultural norms. Psychological interventions targeted only at enhancing an individual athlete's coping skills without addressing the broader systemic problem can compound harm and exactly replicate perpetrator strategies of locating the problem within the victim.

It is particularly evident from research reports across a number of countries that certain aspects of the culture of competitive sport provide an environment that facilitates, rather than inhibits, sexually abusive strategies used by people in positions of authority and trust (Brackenridge, 1997; Kirby et al., 2000; Leahy et al., 2004; Toftegaard-Nielsen, 2001). One of the more urgent implications arising from this area of research is the need to eliminate apparently accepted psychologically abusive coaching styles. Psychological abuse has been uniquely implicated in long-term negative traumatic outcomes (Leahy et al., 2008). It also effectively masks sexual offender behaviors that rely on psychological abuse and emotional manipulation as primary strategies (Leahy et al., 2004; Toftegaard-Nielsen, 2001).

To overcome the bystander effect, comprehensive and ongoing sexual abuse awareness education is imperative for all those involved in organized sport, including athletes, parents, and all associated support personnel. Particularly, it is the responsibility of adults in the system to ensure children's safety. This responsibility should not be relegated to the children themselves. We need to understand that silencing is an integral—not separate—part of the sexual abuse experience. Nondisclosure is the norm. Every person in an athlete's entourage has a right to be informed and specifically empowered to act to safeguard the athlete's welfare through clear guidelines and procedures. The sport psychologist is in a key position to be at the vanguard of this level of intervention. Failure to engage effectively with this core component of the biopsychosocial model carries the risk of positioning the sport psychologist as a complicit bystander.

CONCLUSION

This chapter has provided a summary of recent research dealing primarily with child sexual abuse in sport. Some of the research points to particular systemic vulnerabilities in sport that may facilitate rather than deter some forms of violence against children. Some sport cultures appear to exhibit features of rigid hierarchical power structures that have been found to be associated with the bystander effect, in which observing adults feel unable to intervene in high-risk or suspicious circumstances. The chapter also reported the apparent normalization of psychologically abusive training environments.

We all recognize and understand the influential role of sport in the physical, psychological, and social development of individuals and communities. We acknowledge its importance to public health (Chan, 2006). The United Nations has begun to view sport not only as a vehicle for promoting self-esteem, leadership skills, and community spirit but also as a potential bridge across ethnic and communal divides (United Nations, 2002). If we are to achieve these aims, we need to engage in a more thoughtful stewardship of sport as a social institution that can help us confront broader social issues (Chan, 2006). Some of these social issues also occur within sport, including violence against children. It is only if we maximize the resources of multidisciplinary teams and empower each individual within them through appropriate and ethical competency training that the scientific, medical, and welfare support system will be able to provide an environment that promotes the health, welfare, and performance of athletes across the entire spectrum of the biopsychosocial model.

IDEAS FOR REFLECTION AND DEBATE

1. When have you been a bystander? What were the circumstances? Why did you choose not to act?

2. How have you acted for cultural or institutional change in sport?

3. If you have not acted for cultural or institutional change in sport, why not?

4. What arguments (if any) would you mount against what Leahy is saying in this essay?

5. Arguably, sport psychologists can help athletes change for the better through one-on-one treatment, but what are some of the problems

that occur when sport psychologists see most of an athlete's problems as housed within that athlete?

REFERENCES

American Psychiatric Association. (2000). *Diagnostic and statistical manual of mental disorders* (4th ed., text rev.). Washington, DC: Author.

Australian Sports Commission. (2007). Child protection. www.ausport.gov.au/supporting/ethics/child_protection.

Becker-Lausen, E., Sanders, B., & Chinsky, J.M. (1995). The mediation of abusive childhood experiences: Depression, dissociation, and negative life outcomes. *American Journal of Orthopsychiatry, 65,* 560–573.

Brackenridge, C. (1997). "He owned me basically . . .": Women's experience of sexual abuse in sport. *International Review for the Sociology of Sport, 32,* 115–130.

Brackenridge, C.H. (2001). *Spoilsports: Understanding and preventing sexual exploitation in sport.* London: Routledge.

Brackenridge, C.H., Bishop, D., Moussalli, S., & Tapp, J. (2008). The characteristics of sexual abuse in sport: A multidimensional scaling analysis of events described in media reports. *International Journal of Sport and Exercise Psychology, 4,* 385–406.

Brackenridge, C.H., Rivers, I., Gough, B., & Llewellyn, K. (2006). Driving down participation: Homophobic bullying as a deterrent to doing sport. In C. Atkinson (Ed.), *Sport and gender identities: Masculinities, femininities and sexualities.* (pp. 120–136). London: Routledge.

Briere, J. (1992). *Child abuse trauma: Theory and treatment of the lasting effects.* Newbury Park, CA: Sage.

Briere, J. (1997). *Psychological assessment of adult posttraumatic states.* Washington, DC: American Psychological Association.

Briere, J., & Runtz, M. (1990). Differential adult symptomatology associated with three types of child abuse histories. *Child Abuse and Neglect, 14,* 357–364.

Carlson, E.B. (1997). *Trauma assessments: A clinician's guide.* New York: Guilford Press.

Carlson, E.B., Armstrong, J., Loewenstein, R., & Roth, D. (1998). Relationships between traumatic experiences and symptoms of posttraumatic stress, dissociation, and amnesia. In J.D. Bremner & C.R. Marmar (Eds.), *Trauma, memory, and dissociation* (pp. 205–228). Washington, DC: American Psychiatric Press.

Cense, M., & Brackenridge, C.H. (2001). Temporal and developmental risk factors for sexual harassment and abuse in sport. *European Physical Education Review, 1,* 61–79.

Chan, K.M., (2006). FIMS Leadership: Prof Kai-Ming Chan—Hong Kong. In K.M. Chan & W.R. Frontera (Eds.), *Sports Medicine* (pp. 26–31). Hong Kong: FIMS.

Child Protection in Sport Unit. (2006). *Strategy for safeguarding young people in sport, 2006–2012.* Leicester: Sport England/Child Protection in Sport Unit.

Courtois, C. (1999). *Recollections of sexual abuse: Treatment principles and guidelines.* New York: Norton.

Fasting, K., Brackenridge, C.H., Miller, K.E., & Sabo, D. (2008). Participation in college sports and protection from sexual victimization. *International Journal of Sport and Exercise Psychology, 4,* 427–441.

Hart, S., Binggeli, N.J., & Brassard, M.R. (1998). Evidence for the effects of psychological abuse. *Journal of Emotional Abuse, 1,* 27–58.

Hart, S., Brassard, M., & Karlson, H. (1996). Psychological abuse. In J. Briere, L. Berliner, J. Bulkley, C. Jenny, & T. Reid (Eds.), *The APSAC handbook on child abuse* (pp. 72–89). Newbury Park, CA: Sage.

Herman, J.L. (1997). *Trauma and recovery: From domestic abuse to political terror* (2nd ed.). New York: Basic Books.

Higgins, D.J., & McCabe, M.P. (2000a). Multi-type abuse and the long-term adjustment of adults. *Child Abuse Review, 9,* 6–18.

Higgins, D.J., & McCabe, M.P. (2000b). Relationships between different types of abuse during childhood and adjustment in adulthood. *Child Abuse, 5,* 261–272.

IOC Medical Commission. (2007). *Consensus statement: Sexual harassment and abuse in sport.* http://multimedia.olympic.org/pdf/en_report_1125.pdf.

Jellen, L.K., McCarroll, J.E., & Thayer, L.E. (2001). Child psychological abuse: A 2-year study of U.S. Army cases. *Child Abuse and Neglect, 25,* 623–639.

Johnson, D.M., Pike, J.L., & Chard, K.M. (2001). Factors predicting PTSD, depression, and dissociative severity in female treatment-seeking childhood sexual abuse survivors. *Child Abuse and Neglect, 25,* 179–198.

Kirby, S., Demers, G., & Parent, S. (2008). Vulnerability/prevention: Considering the needs of disabled and gay athletes in the context of sexual harassment and abuse. *International Journal of Sport and Exercise Psychology, 4,* 407–426.

Kirby, S., Greaves, L., & Hankivsky, O. (2000). *The dome of silence: Sexual harassment and abuse in sport.* Halifax, NS: Fernwood.

Kirby, S., & Wintrup, G. (2002). Running the gauntlet: An examination of initiation/hazing and sexual abuse in sport. *The Journal of Sexual Aggression, 8,* 49–68.

Leahy, T. (2001). Preventing the sexual abuse of young people in Australian sport. *The Sport Educator, 13,* 28–31.

Leahy, T. (2008). Understanding and preventing sexual harassment and abuse in sport: Implications for the sport psychology profession [Editor's note]. *International Journal of Sport and Exercise Psychology, 4,* 351–353.

Leahy, T. (2010). Sexual abuse in sport: Implications for the sports psychology profession. In T. V. Ryba, R. J. Shinke, & G. Tenenbaum (Eds.), *The cultural turn in sport psychology* (pp. 315-334). Morgantown, WV: Fitness Information Technology.

Leahy, T., Pretty, G., & Tenenbaum, G. (2002). Prevalence of sexual abuse in organised competitive sport in Australia. *Journal of Sexual Aggression, 8,* 16–35.

Leahy, T., Pretty, G., & Tenenbaum, G. (2003). Childhood sexual abuse narratives in clinically and non-clinically distressed adult survivors. *Professional Psychology: Research and Practice, 34,* 657–665.

Leahy, T., Pretty, G., & Tenenbaum, G. (2004). Perpetrator methodology as a predictor of traumatic symptomatology in adult survivors of childhood sexual abuse. *Journal of Interpersonal Violence, 19,* 521–540.

Leahy, T., Pretty, G., & Tenenbaum, G. (2008). A contextualised investigation of traumatic correlates of childhood sexual abuse in Australian athletes. *International Journal of Sport and Exercise Psychology, 4,* 366–384.

Mulder, R.T., Beautrais, A.L., Joyce, P.R., & Fergusson, D.M. (1998). Relationship between dissociation, childhood sexual abuse, childhood physical abuse, and mental illness in a general population sample. *American Journal of Psychiatry, 155,* 806–811.

Palmer, S.E., Brown, R.A., Rae-Grant, N.I., & Loughlin, M.J. (1999). Responding to children's disclosure of familial abuse: What survivors tell us. *Child Welfare, 78,* 259–283.

Sanders, B., & Becker-Lausen, E. (1995). The measurement of psychological abuse: Early data on the Child Abuse and Trauma Scale. *Child Abuse and Neglect, 19,* 315–323.

Toftegaard-Nielsen, J. (2001). The forbidden zone: Intimacy, sexual relations and misconduct in the relationship between coaches and athletes. *International Review for the Sociology of Sport, 36,* 165–183.

Tomlinson, A., & Yorganci, I. (1997). Male coach/female athlete relations: Gender and power relations in competitive sport. *Journal of Sport and Social Issues, 2,* 134–155.

UNICEF. (2011). Convention on the rights of the child. www.unicef.org/crc.

United Nations. (2002, February 11). Right to play belongs to everyone, Secretary-General tells Olympic Aid forum [Press release]. www.un.org/News/Press/docs/2002/sgsm8119.doc.htm.

Vanden Auweele, Y., Opdenacker, J., Vertommen, T., Boen, F., Van Niekerk, L., De Martelar, K., et al. (2008). Unwanted sexual experiences in sport: Perceptions and reported prevalence among Flemish female student athletes. *International Journal of Sport and Exercise Psychology, 4,* 354–365.

van der Kolk, B.A., Pelcovitz, D., Roth, S., Mandel, F., McFarlane, A.C., & Herman, J.L. (1996). Dissociation, somatization, and affect: The complexity of adaptation to trauma. *American Journal of Psychiatry, 153,* 83–93.

NEGOTIATING EXPECTATIONS IN FOOTBALL'S COMPLEX SOCIAL CULTURE

Robyn L. Jones
University of Wales Institute, Cardiff, United Kingdom

Kieran Kingston
University of Wales Institute, Cardiff, United Kingdom

Carly Stewart
University of Wales Institute, Cardiff, United Kingdom

Robyn, Kieran, and Carly offer a complex and creative essay that develops the case for the applied use of autoethnographic narrative by framing a wider debate of practice around personalized accounts of lived experiences. The authors explore the process and culture of coaching in professional football (called *soccer* in the United States). Robyn's story emphasizes the context of professional football and asks how sport psychologists can help coaches better engage and deal with the demands they face. In the storied account, the authors consider a number of actors (players, other coaches, and a chairman) and emphasize a multilayered perspective on the pressures faced in a football environment. The authors consider how psychologists might work alongside coaches who regularly face issues of manipulation and morality in their daily practice.

INTRODUCTION

Our aims for this chapter are threefold. First, we develop the claim that engaging with creative coaching scenarios is a legitimate and stimulating means of interrogating sport coaching (e.g., Jones, 2009). Second, through the presentation of a personalized story, we highlight the contested, micropolitical nature of coaching, particularly in relation to the moral and manipulative dilemmas that coaches face in their everyday practice. Third, by addressing the given scenario, we provide an example of how sport psychologists might help coaches better navigate these sometimes-turbulent waters in moving toward desired ends.

After making the case for personalized problematic scenarios as a bona fide means of engaging with sport coaching, we relate a storied account of coaching practice in football from numerous perspectives—that is, from the viewpoint of players, assistant coach, and chairman. These individual tales are bound together and placed within the wider story of the principal actor: the head coach. Presenting a story from such diverse locations provides an illustration of the enduring multiple pressures that impinge on coaches from various directions. We then discuss potential strategies for dealing with some of the dynamic relational issues from an applied sport psychology standpoint. We do so first from a multitheoretical perspective, which is later placed within the confines of complexity or chaos theory. We then offer the concept of orchestration (Jones & Wallace, 2005, 2006) as a proactive strategy for taking better account of and then navigating the intricate, multifarious, and dynamic sport setting. Finally, our reflective conclusion draws together main points.

WRITING AND ENGAGING WITH CREATIVE COACHING SCENARIOS

Research into sport coaching has increasingly come to acknowledge the activity's social and dynamic essence (e.g., Jones, 2007). This approach reflects a recognition of coaching as a nuanced, personal endeavor that is shot through with issues of power and acquiescence. A particular aspect of this developing body of work has portrayed coaching as a social performance in which both coach and athletes are compliant (Cushion & Jones, 2006). An interesting finding is that practitioners see coaching as enactment aimed at managing the impressions of others (e.g., Jones, Armour, & Potrac, 2004). Such performances allow room to consciously play with behavior in order to present the desired image of the self; in other words, the impression is managed (Goffman, 1959). This work has problematized understanding of the micropolitical workings of coaching by portraying coaches as both moral and, to various degrees, Machiavellian actors. Indeed, with so many differing agendas at stake in cultural power relationships, the pedagogical context cannot help but be a contested and negotiated one (Purdy, Potrac, & Jones, 2008). This is not to portray coaches as unprincipled, devious, or conniving, but rather as earnest social beings reflecting on their interactive strategies to achieve appropriate relationships for the greater good (Jones et al., 2004). The performance given is not far removed from the roles played in everyday life. It is what Goffman (1959) referred to as the often seamless merger between the self as performer and self as character.

As previously argued, one current problem facing coaches and the sport psychologists who work with them relates to representation and access (Jones, 2009). The current rationality-dominant discourse has provided limited expression about the complexity inherent in coaching; as a result, practitioners cannot find the language to adequately convey what they know. Put another way, the embodied experience of the coach sometimes exceeds the narrative resources that are available, which has often resulted in an attempt to justify feelings, actions, and situations through superficially learned "sport science" speak. The belief that coaching knowledge has to be "cleanly" articulated in order to count marginalizes "those emotional, ethical and ambiguous aspects of it that defy such unproblematic treatment and interpretation" (Jones, 2009, p. 378).

If coaching is performative, in that it relates to a performance, then our texts must be equally evocative in order to capture the complexity involved in such behavior. Performance in this context is defined as an interpretive event involving actors, purposes, and interactions embedded in the ebb and flow of cultural life (Denzin, 2003). Indeed, literature has argued strongly that the theoretical tenets of performativity are in direct synch with more creatively written fashioned narratives (e.g. Denzin, 2003; Spry, 2001). This is because such tales, involving personalized accounts of lived experience, have the power to "seduce us into new ways of seeing the world" (Fasching, 1992, p. 94), thus forcing us to examine how we represent ourselves and live out "those representations within everyday life" (Striff, 2003, p. 1).

Following such a lead, some scholars have begun to engage with coaching from an autoethnographic perspective (e.g., Denison, 2007; Jones, 2006; Purdy et al., 2008). We similarly believe that accounts of coaching that draw on nontraditional genres such as creative nonfiction (Sparkes, 2002) or informed fiction (Gilbourne & Llewellyn, 2007) can assist in further exploring and deciphering coaching by helping us unmask the activity's many indeterminate faces—as impression, construction, intervention, and sociopolitical act (Denzin, 2003). For Gilbourne and Llewellyn (2007), informed fiction sits between creative nonfiction and "pure" fiction. Drawing from several sources (e.g., personal life experience, qualitative data from interviews, chance observations, overhead asides), these compositions are essentially informed but portrayed in a fictional manner in that names, places, and contexts are reinvented to house the story line and emphasize the message. In containing a plot that involves various characters, informed fiction can also deal well with the collective nature of coaching, wherein multiple stakeholders, actors, and careers intersect and combine, thus illuminating issues that currently lie largely undisturbed in coaching's muddy depths. The need to undertake such exploratory work is expressed by Mark Andersen and Harriet Speed in essay 6 in this book, where they call for practitioners and clients to look in places where they may find answers, no matter how dark or difficult to access those places may be. This kind of search, and the resultant writing it enables, allows creative engagement with novel situations by encouraging "reflective conversations" (Schön, 1987) between context, experience, and theory: that is, such work exists in the form of "stories seeking [or demanding] consideration" (Sparkes, 2007). In the words of Pelias (2005), as cited by Sparkes (2007), performative writing has the power to "expand notions of what constitutes disciplinary knowledge, . . . feature lived experiences that call forth the complexities of human life, . . . and rest on the belief that the world is not given but constructed" (p. 540). Consequently, writing informed fictionalized tales would seem to be an appropriate means to examine coaching, not only because both can be interpreted as "performances" but also because such writing can better explore "the liminal spaces between experience and language" where issues of improvisation, struggle, and negotiation come to the fore (Spry, 2001, p. 726). In this respect, such work can serve as a means of bringing the unconscious, or internal conversations, to the surface, thus allowing more detailed reflection and examination of action.

A PERSONALIZED STORY:
THE SOCIAL RULES OF COACHING PRACTICE

The players' training is over. The players, in various stages of undress, mingle in the body-warmed dressing room. Some sip hot sweet tea from polystyrene cups; others are already making mobile calls. Still others, seated, wipe mud from their boots with their socks. The talk is of beer and girls. The steam from the showers invades the communal space.

Sam: I'm pissed off with him—pissed off!

Scott: Who, mate?

Sam: Who'd ya think, dummy? The Big Dog. Calls himself a coach? What a joke!

Scott: (Says nothing)

Sam: It's OK for you, he picks you. Bastard doesn't even see me. Doesn't tell me nothing!

Scott: Hmm. . . . Maybe he wants you to work things out for yourself.

Sam: What the fuck does that mean, Einstein? All that "work things out for yourself stuff" is bollocks, that is. Oh, yes (now looking directly at Scott), I forgot. You're one of his boys, aren't you?

Scott: Don't be an idiot; take a day off, mate! Anyway, maybe you're right. To be fair, though, it's hard to change things after three wins on the bounce.

Sam: That's the only thing keepin' me from bangin' his door down. I'm tellin' ya, though, if things don't change soon I'll be in to see him. All I want is a bit of honesty, just to know where I stand. I'm pissed off being on the bench! I'm 30 next month. It's no good me not playing now, not with my maintenance payments.

Scott looks up for some help to deflect the conversation, finds none, keeps wiping his boots. Tom, a younger player, limps across to join them.

Scott: What's up, mate? Got a knock?

Tom: It's OK.

Sam: You need to get that seen, Tom. I don't think you'll be right for Saturday with that.

Tom: No, really, I'll be fine . . .

Sam (Sensing an opening): You play on Saturday and you'll make that worse; you could be out a while. I've seen a few of those; could be out a while if you mess with that.

Scott: If it's bothering you, better get it checked out, fella.

Tom stares straight ahead, takes a few sips of his tea, and says nothing. Sam starts again: "Looks nasty, that . . ." Tom gets up and walks away.

Sam: See that, cheeky bastard just walked away; anyway (more perky now), looks like I may be in the frame on Saturday after all.

I walk in, pick up a cup, notice Sam and Scott together—one demanding attention, the other a reluctant witness, one player who's on the team and one who's not. Maybe they've talked long enough. I stroll toward them. Both busy themselves as the conversation stops. I consider the face I want to present: open, yet decisive; friendly, yet focused.

Me: All right, lads?

Scott: Yeah, fine, boss (keeps wiping his boots).

Me: You OK, Sam?

Sam: Yup, great, just great.

Me: Good. You looked sharp out there this morning; good to see you coming back to form.

Scott gets up, grabs his towel, and makes his way through the steam into the showers. I stand above Sam, maintaining an aura of authority.

Sam: (looks up; his features soften) Yeah, I enjoyed that. It's what I need, a good blowout and get some touches again.

Me: (I return his gaze and hold the silence, using the space between us). I've been meaning to catch you for a couple of days; no great drama.

Sam: (A little confused) Oh, yeah, boss, what about?

Me: (I turn to leave.) Let's do it in private, when you have a minute. (Now in a slightly hardened voice, so others can hear) See you in my office. Tomorrow 11:30, OK.

I leave Sam, looking slightly apprehensive, alone as he resumes wiping the mud from his boots.

The Assistant

Phil, the assistant coach, and "Phys," the physio, are in the latter's room, "the sanctuary." The space is small, cramped by a large treatment table in the middle. Phil sits on a plastic chair, leaning against the back wall, while the aging Phys busies himself around the room, tidying, rearranging, stocking:

Phil: He's too soft with 'em, far too soft.

Phys: Who?

Phil: Who do ya think, Mensa brain? The Boss, of course!

Phys (Raising a disdainful eyebrow): Oh, yeah, why d'ya say that?

Phil: The way they played the other night, they were crap. I wanted to really hammer them, but he wouldn't let me.

Phys: (Still busy around the room) What do you mean?

Phil: Well, he gives it, "Let me handle this, OK." I says, "OK," thinking he'd lay into them before letting me off the leash but then he just sits them down and starts asking, "What went wrong?" and "Why?" What's all that about?

Phys: How did they take it?

Phil: I could see a few of them wonderin', "What's goin' on here then?" He should have given them what they deserved and expected, a right old bollocking! This isn't little boys' football. It's all shit, that questioning stuff is.

Phys: Hmm . . . yeah (still stocking his kit bag).

Phil: Don't get me wrong. I like the Boss and all, but I just don't understand him sometimes.

Phys: Maybe he likes to keep people guessing, keepin' them on their toes and stuff.

Phil: (Laughing) Don't you start, old fella; I've got enough questions in my head already. What I need are answers!

Phys: Hmm . . . yeah . . . OK.

Phil: (Rocks upwards to a standing position) Got to go. Can't sit here all day gassin' to you. Got a session to get ready for, a real hard one for the boys (rubs his hands together). It's gonna sort out a few, let me tell ya! See ya later.

Phys: Yeah, bye. See ya.

Phys smiles to himself. His bag is restocked. He'd like a cigarette but settles for another cup of tea.

The Chairman

It's two hours since the game finished. Bob, the chairman, now alone, is picking over the remnants of the buffet laid out for the opposing team's dignitaries. Half-eaten chicken drumsticks and ham sandwiches litter the table. He stares out over the muddy pitch. It's still raining. The central heating is turned high, irritating him. He shifts his weight to avoid growing sciatic pain. John, the club secretary, appears.

John: You comin' for a drink downstairs then, Bob?

Bob: Yes, yes, in a minute. . . . How many were here today, John? What's the takings? (Nibbles what's left of a drumstick)

John: Not many, I'm afraid. Not enough to pay the wages. We'll have to dip into the bar takings a bit more this week.

Bob: (Resorting to mild bluster) Bloody not good enough, John. I keep dippin' into my own pocket for this club and what do I get back? A shit performance like that, that's what.

John: Yeah . . . not good enough.

Bob: You're damn right not good enough.

John: Hmm . . . yeah, I know (picks out a remaining ham sandwich).

Bob: So . . . what do you think I should do then, John?

John: (Suddenly aware that he's on the spot with half a sandwich in his mouth) Oh . . . well . . . maybe talk to Rob, the coach, see what he thinks (swallows hard).

Bob: I know what he'll say to that. (In a sarcastic voice) "No money to spend; what do you expect?"

John: Suppose you're right. (Thinks for a second) We do have some money, though: the extra that we held back from him at the start of the season, remember?

Bob: (Belches loudly) Bloody 'ell, John. We need some money held back; he'd only spend it on more rubbish players anyway. I'm not spending my Saturdays watching that crap.

John: Hmm . . . OK . . . and my halftime tea was cold, too!

Thoughts and Strategies: A Coach's Dilemmas

I'm finally home. The rest of the family has gone to bed. I sit, nursing a glass of scotch. The day has yet to leave me. I do my best for the club; I'm honest in that. I'm pretty sincere with the players. I try my best for them, but sometimes they just don't get it. Is it me? Am I not making the difference I claim? No, I do have meaning here, but I have to have control. I know what's good for them. I can't be too honest, though, and tell them what I think (I smirk at the possible scenario of doing so). I have to play politics to realize my ambitions for them. On the other hand, if I'm constantly manipulative, how can that make me a "good" person, fit to lead and employ others? It is my enduring dilemma, my constant challenge. I turn to specific reflections in search of guidance.

I know my departing comment to Sam was overheard. It'll be common knowledge by now that Sam's been called in. I imagine the circulating rumors. It was a calculated display of power, and it will occupy Sam's thoughts 'till he sees me ("Is he going to let me go?"). It will cause him stress and concern. Still, he deserves to suffer a bit; he can't get away with constantly challenging my authority. Some players hate me, some love me. It depends on whether they're picked; that's the way it is. I'll need Sam later in the season so I can't alienate him too much, but for now he has to behave (the way I want him to) in a collective; he has to know that I hold some power. What's more important is that the other players must know that too. Sam must be the example—an example to the others—that I am approachable and sincere yet ruthless if need be.

Thoughts turn to Phil. Football's a small, insecure world. Old physios with their time-honored methods, their sponges, and their loyalty are to be valued. Their rooms, where they heal tired, injured bodies, are confessionals. Phys hears it all. I listen to him. He talks in generalities, in questions ("What did the players think of that?"), which make me instantly reflective. I like Phil; he's a good foil for me. Phil knows the subculture of football dressing rooms. He's also a good analyst of a game, though the vocabulary is sometimes limited. Phys had nodded: "Yeah, you're right there. . . . Take care with him, though; he's being challenged on a number of fronts. You're not all he expected, which (laughing) is not a bad thing." I smile. I'm all for pushing people out of their comfort zones but resolve to take care not to give Phil too much too quickly. That would only bring resistance. I need to allow him into some of my thoughts and strategies, to be more open and honest as a way of better managing him. It'll bring him closer while still keeping him fixed within my desired structure. I need him to think more of me.

Then there's Bob. My conversations with Bob have become increasingly strained. He wants success on a shoestring. I knew that when I took the job. Bet he's holding money back, tight bastard. Still, I can't fight him. If I did, I know I'd lose. Maybe I'll cut the wage bill myself by releasing Ted, who wants to go anyway. Fair enough; he's a fringe player, so no great loss. It'll show Bob that I'm aware of his interests. If we could only win the next two games, both at home against lesser teams, we'll be in touching distance of the playoffs. That'll give me the kudos to talk to Bob about signing a (better) replacement. I suppose I should think about his idea of doing more "community work," get the players to visit local schools, perhaps hold a social night at the club to generate more revenue—even a question-and-answer with the manager, as he put it. My stomach turns at the thought (too much of a performance even for me?). But it'll show the supporters that he's in touch with them, and it'll give me more time; that's just what I need, a little more time.

I drain the glass, philosophical that relationships aren't always complementary, an equal exchange. I'm playing the game, all right, maybe even playing it well. But for how much longer can I keep up the charade;

when will the mask become too heavy to carry? Is it all too much of a compromise? I smile inwardly, still performing (just for myself). I'd better get to bed; there's training tomorrow.

DEALING WITH THE COMPLEXITY: AN APPLIED PSYCHOLOGY APPROACH

One striking feature of the scenario just presented is the sheer complexity of the layered issues at hand. It is apparent from the coach's reflections regarding the composite relationships he has to manage that tensions exist between his need to manipulate the environment (to retain control) and the tendencies of his caring (moral) self. He is also cognizant of the value of the supportive relationships he has, while indirectly using trusted others as conduits for his (less explicit) communications, all within a context that traditionally values honest assessment and "straight talking." In this respect, he seems to be a Machiavellian-like actor in a morality play—an apparent contradiction in terms.

The remit given (within the context of the book) was to provide the coach with some direction in terms of managing the various relationships and roles he has. A traditional sport psychological approach would involve addressing the scenario by means of a single theoretical perspective—for example, self-determination theory. Recommendations would then be made in terms of how the coach's interactions could be modified to make his relationships with the players, staff, and chairman more motivationally adaptive and subsequently functional. Doing so would undoubtedly tie things up very neatly, but it would also leave us open to accusations of reductionism, of oversimplifying the complex social world. It would also put us at odds with previous positions, wherein rigid adherence to given constructs and linear models involving a series of arrows and boxes has been roundly criticized (Jones, 2007; McFee, 2005). Indeed, McFee's (2005) appraisal of sport psychology texts is illuminating here. McFee accuses such work of ineffectually engaging with the work of Freud, one of modern psychology's founding fathers, insofar as it bears little relation to Freud's appreciation that individuals cannot and should not be viewed discretely but are part of a surrounding cultural landscape that influences behavior, morality, and sense of self (McFee, 2005; Jones, Potrac, Hussain, & Cushion, 2006). Jones and Wallace (2005, 2006) took this critique a step further in claiming that such positivistic reductionism often leaves us with an unbridgeable gap or pathos within the process of applying sport psychological theory to practice.

This is not to say that reductionist logic per se is a bad thing; its essence marks a genuine attempt to strip away conceptual ambiguity. The problem is the almost total decontextualization both of the notions used and of the social actors under study. There is no wish to do that here. Hence, the theories and notions presented in addressing the scenario are given as a framework to think with—a guide not to unproblematically follow but to help question, challenge, and generally scaffold thought. Adhering to the spirit of the book, then, we acknowledge that context is critical, that sometimes the best we can do is muddle though and "satisfice" (Simon, 1981) in terms of situated outcomes, taking account of circumstance as best we can. The call here is for a pragmatic approach—to use the theory as a structure on which to peg ongoing reflections and decision making. Such a position supports the view that in any consultancy role, much of our action is based on "structured improvisation" (Bourdieu, 1977) derived from implicit sources of social encounters and working with others.

OUTLINING A FRAMEWORK: A MULTITHEORETICAL PERSPECTIVE

The purpose of this section is to highlight some of the key relational issues that arise from the scenario as perceived by the coach and to provide some directions that a sport psychologist might suggest based on a multitheoretical approach. We accept the criticism that some may level at us here—that we are fitting "reality" to theory rather than adopting a theoretical position on which to evaluate reality. However, as stated previously, the intention is to adopt a pragmatic approach to illustrate how a variety of theoretical positions can be used to guide and channel thought. The implication is that we should not be constrained to a single theoretical position but can draw on experiences and knowledge of differing, complementary, and contradictory positions to peg ongoing reflections and inform contextual decision making.

• **The players.** Sam is a disillusioned individual. He's frustrated because he perceives that he has been given no direction to "right the wrongs" that have led to his being out of favor. He seeks answers to questions: "Where am I going wrong?" "What do I need to do?" "Where do I stand?" On the face of it, his frustrations are a reflection of his nonselection. Sam is also demanding attention and an acknowledgment of his position by Scott, a colleague; he wants an ear, to be heard by anyone who will listen and validate his case for perceived unfair treatment. Several theoretical positions might "fit" with the issues here. However, the salience of these theories may depend on whether we (as sport psychologists) want to intervene with Sam indirectly, by modifying the coach's behavior toward him, or directly, by helping Sam reappraise the situation.

In the first case, using self-determination theory (SDT), a principal framework related to motivational processes (Weiss & Ferrer-Caja, 2002), could enable us to work on the interactions of coach and player with a view to making the relationship more motivationally efficacious. SDT (Deci & Ryan, 1985; Ryan & Deci, 2000) posits three fundamental psychological needs that are important in energizing volitional (or self-determined) human behavior: competence, autonomy, and relatedness. Satisfaction of these needs determines the effect of social-contextual events on motivation (Vallerand & Losier, 1999): if they are satisfied the social milieu can support feelings of integration and coherence with the environment and promote self-determination. One of the implications of using SDT in this context would be an acknowledgment of Sam's feelings and grievances by the coach (Mageau & Vallerand, 2003). Doing so would increase Sam's feelings of autonomy, an objective that could also be satisfied by explaining to Sam why he is not currently on the team. Sam could also be given feedback that, rather than controlling his behavior, would give him some choice of strategies and options. Following this line of thinking, the key is to help Sam see what he needs to do and then for him to take some ownership over that process.

One might alternatively adopt an attributions standpoint. According to Vallerand's (1987) intuitive-reflective appraisal model, intuitive appraisal invokes far stronger emotional reactions than does reflective appraisal. Sam, who appears to display a strong emotional response to being dropped from the team, could be encouraged to restructure his appraisal of the situation in order to diminish the emotional reaction. This approach to developing internal attributions for his lack of selection might also reduce any perceptions of incompetence since they would allow for the possibility of future success following his perceived failure (Weiner, 1986).

The coach's response to Sam's initial sarcasm—and their brief interaction in which he asks Sam to report to his office the following day—highlights the complexity of the social milieu and illustrates nicely the Machiavellian bent adopted by the coach. The coach views the short-term sacrificing of Sam as acceptable and necessary, given his wider objective of maintaining control over the dressing room. He is exerting power where he knows it will have an effect but also in a manner that ultimately will not damage his position. Based on Rahim and colleagues' (Rahim, 2002) theory of the contingency approach to conflict management (cf. LaVoi, 2007), this evidence of a dominating leadership style reflects (on the face of it) a concern for the self as opposed to others. The coach could be made to recognize such a strategy and then be questioned about what he hopes to achieve by it. This is not to say that such "strong" leadership should not be engaged with, and one could argue that the needs of the collective always outweigh those of the individual. The message here, however, is that motives and potential consequences need to be thoroughly explored and justified from several perspectives before action is taken.

- **The assistant coach.** It is clear from Phil's conversation with the physio that he too is frustrated; essentially, he does not fully understand the coach's methods, which are seemingly at odds with his beliefs about what is required. He feels challenged and insecure about his standing in the modern game. The coach is aware of this situation and considers bringing Phil into the fold by sharing with him some thoughts and strategies. Nevertheless, he is reluctant to rush the process. The challenge for the coach, therefore, is to help Phil recognize and understand his role and the value of his position while retaining control to ensure that his (i.e., the coach's) general ethos is supported.

One possible approach would be to alleviate Phil's concerns by enhancing his role efficacy. Empirically distinct from collective efficacy, role efficacy represents a person's confidence in his or her capability to carry out formal interdependent responsibilities within a group (Bray, Brawley, & Carron, 2002). It is apparent from Phil's discussion with the physio that he is unsure of his role with respect to the coach's "new" approach to dealing with the players, and this ambiguity undermines his role efficacy. That efficacy could likely be enhanced by clarifying Phil's roles and responsibilities. Furthermore, adopting a self-determination perspective, providing Phil with a clear rationale for the methods employed, and engaging him in a discussion of the relative merits and potential costs could improve Phil's perceptions of his competence and autonomy.

In professional football, the physiotherapist's room is something of a sanctuary for players—a place where they can air their views and know that the conversation will be kept confidential. The coach's relationship with the physio enables him to indirectly convey messages to the players and others using the physio as a conduit. Here, issues of manipulation and morality come to the fore. Far from being a simplistic dualism or contradiction, however, morality is positioned in the story not as residing within or above us but as created by our strategic performances, which, in turn, are "designed to affirm human dignity" (Branaman, 1997, p. xlvi). Such strategic action on behalf of the coach, then, need not necessarily be viewed as underhanded scheming. To the contrary, the coach could have carefully considered his options and chosen this indirect route as the least threatening method of giving his message to the intended recipient. In this way, potential conflict is avoided, and no one loses face. Research by Buchanan and Badham (2004) confirms that such actions are not uncommon in functioning organizations where "self-interest, deceit, subterfuge and cunning" coexist with "the pursuit of moral ideals and high aspirations" (p. 2). Such apparently scheming behaviors are motivated by the desire to preserve the collective dignity; they are designed to maintain face—"our own face and that of others" (Branaman, 1997, p. xlvi). By engaging in such manipulation, individuals commit themselves to the wider social order, ensuring that social relationships work. Such actions, it could be argued, are done for the greater good, while also supporting both the physio's sense of responsibility and that of players who may perceive that they arrived at behavioral change largely of their own volition (or certainly not in response to a coach's direct dictate).

- **The chairman.** In the narrative presented, Bob seems unsettled, even fearful of failure. He has beliefs about team selection that appear to be at odds with those of the coach. He believes that recent signings have had little positive impact and, consequently, is withholding financial support for further transfers. The coach knows that he has the most to lose from a poor relationship with Bob and so is willing to compromise in order to retain what strength he can. Giving the chairman a player to sell, or at least giving him the option to do so, is likely to promote in Bob a perception of control. Furthermore, if the coach is seen to agree with Bob's approach, he might inadvertently increase Bob's commitment to the coach's broader objectives, since Bob will perceive ownership of a plan of action with regard to playing staff. As in the dealing with players and staff, by using SDT, the coach could ensure greater buy-in and support for his working agenda.

COMPLEXITY THEORY AND ORCHESTRATION: RECOGNIZING AND MANIPULATING CONTEXT

In dealing with human problems, it is vital to embrace rather than downgrade the complexity of context. Hence, although adopting a multitheoretical approach goes some way toward addressing the host of issues evident in the given scenario, the analysis is still open to accusations of viewing the coach's actions and dilemmas in a decontextualized, behaviorally episodic fashion. Alternatively, complexity or chaos theory has been increasingly recognized as a more realistic perspective from which to examine and understand the microdynamics that underlie social processes such as coaching (Bowes & Jones, 2006; Puddifoot, 2000). This position critiques the assumption of construct or causal linearity that is embedded in much social scientific and psychological research, questioning how a social process can be defined and differentiated from activities that are nonsocial or nonprocessual in nature (Puddifoot). It is based on a view that individual thoughts and feelings are inherently dynamic and in flux (Vallacher & Nowak, 1997) and that coaching is a nonlinear, complex, and often chaotic activity. The coaching context, then, can be considered as one of bounded instability at the edge of chaos—that is, in a state of paradox between cooperation and competition, between order and disorder. Coaching is also conceptualized as an adaptive system in which learning emerges from local interactions between agents trying to improve their payoffs (Sonsino & Moore, 2001). Work by Cushion and Jones (2006); d'Arripe-Longueville, Fournier, and Dubois (1998); and Purdy et al. (2008), among others, clearly portrays coaching as an activity in which any coherent behavior arises from negotiation, struggle, and collaboration between the agents who participate. What is advocated here is a recognition that operating within a dynamic, complex social context such as coaching demands an appreciation of the interaction and interconnectivity of events; that overall behavior cannot be explained as the sum of individual parts; and that best practice emerges from a combination of structure and chaos. The often-cited example of this interconnectivity is the "butterfly effect" (Lorenz, 1979), whereby the action of a butterfly's wings in Brazil could make the difference that leads to a tornado in Texas. Thus a seemingly minor event may have the potential to result in considerable, and significantly different, outcomes. The message is that small things matter, an issue brought to the fore by Jones' (2009) autoethnography of (not) caring within coaching practice.

Such attention to detail and fine distinction is based on the premise that small things are seen in the first place. Indeed, this aspect of coaching practice—"noticing"—has yet to be truly engaged. Although it is a relatively underdeveloped field, it has been argued that noticing is vital to conscious learning (Skehan, 1998). Similarly, the need to see and be sensitive to context and to others' experience has been considered as central to caring professions such as pedagogy. Noticing is based on the prior concept of consciousness raising and refers to the drawing of attention to formal properties or phenomena (Cross, 2002). What is noticed subsequently becomes grist for learning. The question for coaches (and for assisting sport psychologists), however, is what to look for and notice. For us, the answer lies in the nuances of context—athletes' and coaches' relationships with each other; the dilemmas, joys, and paranoias suffered by both parties; the in- and out-groups established; and the conflicting agendas of the various stakeholders. Being sensitive to these factors holds greater promise than presenting presupposed symptoms for uncovering underlying causes of malaise, dysfunction, and performance. Mason (2002), writing about "the discipline of noticing," argues that we need to "increase the range and decrease the grain size" (p. xi) of what we notice as fundamental precursors to developing professional practice. He says that "at the heart of all practice lies noticing: noticing an opportunity to act appropriately" (p. 1).

We are not advocating an absence of theory and a resort to total relativism—that is, just reacting to what is seen. To the contrary, coaching is both proactive and reactive. What guides the noticing here in terms of reading the social landscape is the agenda of the coach. For example, in the scenario discussed in this chapter, the coach intends to establish positive working relationships with players, to improve them as football players, and to maintain power to ensure their compliance, all under the umbrella of winning games. The coach is thus aware of the often political nature of the job and how that reality manifests itself in his everyday practice. He is also concerned that his basic moral standing as a "good person," one who has the interests of his players at heart, is not overly compromised by his planned and considered maneuverings. These goals, dilemmas, and concerns dominate his thinking and his actions. What could also guide the coach's noticing is an increased realization of the importance of everyday practice, a sense that the minutiae of social interaction represents the essential connective tissue of human activity (Gardiner, 2000). Raising the coach's awareness of the power and influence of such intricacies could help him reflect on how to more realistically achieve his goals.

Although working with the coach to notice particular phenomena and react with social and contextual sensibilities could be an appropriate place to close this discussion, we'd like to take it a step further. We think we can offer a useful framework not only regarding raising awareness of what to look for but also regarding how coaches can better deal with the dilemmas they face and get things back on track. Here, borrowing from the work of Jones and Wallace (2005, 2006), we offer the concept of orchestration. Derived from Wallace's (2001, 2003) and Wallace and Pocklington's (2002) work on managing complex educational change, the orchestration metaphor refers to coordinated activity within set parameters expressed by coaches "to instigate, plan, organise, monitor and respond to evolving circumstances in order to bring about improvement in the individual and collective performance of those being coached" (p. 61). Orchestration implies steering, as opposed to controlling, in a complex interactive process of instigating, organizing, and maintaining oversight of an intricate array of coordinated tasks. It also involves coaching unobtrusively, engaging in much behind-the-scenes string pulling geared toward desired objectives. Orchestration, then, involves detailed oversight of the minutiae of the coaching situation. It involves constant analysis, evaluation, and scrutiny to keep things going—be they established core or new tasks. Orchestrators "attend to maintaining momentum, . . . monitor in considerable detail[,] and are ready to step in if tasks are not carried out as specified" (Jones & Wallace, 2006, p. 61). Similarly, orchestration recognizes the necessity for coaches to gather feedback in order to assist coordination and to preempt resistance; it involves a stage managing of context, thus releasing practitioners from false moral dichotomies or dilemmas in relation to "good" ethical or "dark" Machiavellian practices. The emphasis is on helping coaches develop an awareness that they need to "make the most of their limited agency without expecting to achieve strong directive control" (Jones & Wallace, 2006, p. 61). Thus the orchestration metaphor further challenges the orthodoxy of the coach as exclusive controller by positing coaching as a contested, negotiated activity. As a result, it allows coaches to invest effort where they can make a better impact for the collective good.

CONCLUSION

We do not mean to totally dismiss the field's existing theories but to highlight the drawbacks and inadequacies of monocausal reductionist diagnoses and practice. The social world is never so clean cut. What we advocate is a focus on noticing the nuances of human behavior and accepting that micropolitical activity, through orchestration (Jones & Wallace, 2006), is a part of what we do in everyday life to succeed and basically "get on" with each other. Consequently, manipulating the environment for the greater good can be viewed as worthy social practice rather than unethical conspiratorial action. In addition to using a number of theoretical frameworks to (loosely) guide action, depending on their applicability in context, our broader advice for coaches, then, should be that Machiavelli can comfortably perform (and perhaps star) in a morality play.

IDEAS FOR REFLECTION AND DEBATE

1. This essay offers a number of theoretical and philosophical explanations and observations. What might an appreciation of views from other disciplines mean for the efficacy and certainty of applied sport psychology practice?

2. What is the applied training value of material that tells a story through the medium of scripted narrative? What might be the weaknesses of this approach?

3. Consider the theoretical explanations offered for key themes in the story told here and reflect on the following statement: "Such interpretations risk making tidy and neat something that is essentially complex and untidy." What questions and issues might emerge from this suggestion?

4. Reflect on the following statement: "When ethnographic research raises questions, theory will always provide a convenient answer."

5. Consider research without theory. Is such a thing possible?

6. If single theories reduce the interpretive scope of research, what approach would broaden interpretation and offer greater possibilities for applied understanding?

REFERENCES

Bowes, I., & Jones, R.L. (2006). Working at the edge of chaos: Understanding coaching as a complex, interpersonal system. *The Sport Psychologist, 20*(2), 235-245.

Branaman, A. (1997). Goffman's social theory. In C. Lemert & A. Branaman (Eds.), *The Goffman reader* (pp. xlv–lxxxii). Oxford, England: Blackwell.

Bray, S.R., Brawley, L.R., & Carron, A.V. (2002). Efficacy for interdependent role functions: Evidence from the sport domain. *Small Group Research, 33*, 644–666.

Bourdieu, P. (1977). *Outline of a theory of practice.* Cambridge, England: Cambridge University Press.

Buchanan, D., & Badham, R. (2004). *Power, politics, and organizational change.* Newbury Park, CA: Sage.

Cross, J. (2002). "Noticing" in SLA: Is it a valid concept? *Teaching English as a Second or Foreign Language-EJ, 6*(3). http://writing.berkeley.edu/TESL-EJ/ej23/a2.html.

Cushion, C., & Jones, R.L. (2006). Power, discourse, and symbolic violence in professional youth soccer: The case of Albion F.C. *Sociology of Sport Journal, 23*, 142–161.

d'Arripe-Longueville, R., Fournier, J.F., & Dubois, A. (1998). The perceived effectiveness of interactions between expert French judo coaches and elite female athletes. *The Sport Psychologist, 12*, 317–332.

Deci, E.L., & Ryan, R.M. (1985). *Intrinsic motivation and self-determination in human behaviour.* New York: Plenum Press.

Denison, J. (2007). Social theory for coaches: A Foucauldian reading of one athlete's poor performance. *International Journal of Sports Science & Coaching, 2*, 369–383.

Denzin, N. (2003). *Performance ethnography: Critical pedagogy and the politics of culture.* London: Sage.

Fasching, D. (1992). *Narrative theology after Auschwitz: From alienation to ethics.* Augsburg: Fortress Press.

Gardiner, M.E. (2000). *Critiques of everyday life.* London: Routledge.

Gilbourne, D., & Llewellyn, D. (2007, June). *Self narrative: Illustrations of different genre and explorations of the underlying rationale for writing.* Presentation at the quadrennial FEPSAC Congress, Kallithea, Greece.

Goffman, E. (1959). *The presentation of self in everyday life.* Garden City, NY: Doubleday.

Jones, R.L. (2006). Dilemmas, maintaining "face" and paranoia: An average coaching life. *Qualitative Inquiry, 12*, 1012–1021.

Jones, R.L. (2007). Coaching redefined: An everyday pedagogical endeavour. *Sport, Education and Society, 12*, 159–174.

Jones, R.L. (2009). Coaching as caring ("The smiling gallery"): Accessing hidden knowledge. *Physical Education and Sport Pedagogy, 14*(4), 377–390.

Jones, R.L., Armour, K.M., & Potrac, P. (2004). *Sports coaching cultures: From practice to theory.* London: Routledge.

Jones, R.L., Potrac, P., Hussain, H., & Cushion, C. (2006). Exposure by association: Maintaining anonymity in autoethnographical research. In S. Fleming & F. Jordan (Eds.), *Ethical issues in leisure research* (pp. 45–62). Eastbourne, England: Leisure Studies Association.

Jones, R.L., & Wallace, M. (2005). Another bad day at the training ground: Coping with ambiguity in the coaching context. *Sport, Education and Society, 10,* 119–134.

Jones, R.L., & Wallace, M. (2006). The coach as orchestrator. In R.L. Jones (Ed.), *The sports coach as educator: Re-conceptualising sports coaching* (pp. 51–64). London: Routledge.

LaVoi, N.M. (2007). Interpersonal communication and conflict in the coach–athlete relationship. In S. Jowett & D. Lavallee (Eds.), *Social psychology of sport* (pp. 29–40). Champaign, IL: Human Kinetics.

Lorenz, E. (1979). *Does the flap of a butterfly's wings in Brazil set off a tornado in Texas?* Address at the annual meeting of the American Association for the Advancement of Science, Dallas, Texas.

McFee, G. (2005). Why doesn't sport psychology consider Freud? In M. McNamee (Ed.), *Philosophy and the sciences of exercise, health and sport: Critical perspectives on research methods* (pp. 85–116). London: Routledge.

Mageau, G.A., & Vallerand, R.J. (2003). The coach–athlete relationship: A motivational model. *Journal of Sport Sciences, 21,* 883–904.

Mason, J. (2002). *Researching your own practice: The discipline of noticing.* London: Routledge.

Pelias, R. (2005). Performative writing as scholarship: An apology, an argument, an anecdote. *Cultural Studies and Critical Methodologies, 5,* 415–424.

Puddifoot, J. (2000). Some problems and possibilities in the study of dynamical social processes. *Journal for the Theory of Social Behaviour 30*(1), 7997.

Purdy, L., Potrac, P., & Jones, R.L. (2008). Power, consent and resistance: An auto-ethnography of competitive rowing. *Sport, Education and Society, 13,* 319–336.

Rahim, M. (2002). Toward a theory of managing organizational conflict. *International Journal of Conflict Management, 13*(3), 206–235.

Ryan, R.M., & Deci, E.L. (2000). Self-determination theory and the facilitation of intrinsic motivation, social development, and well-being. *American Psychologist, 55,* 68–78.

Schön, D.A. (1987). *Educating the reflective practitioner: Toward a new design for teaching and learning in the professions.* San Francisco: Jossey-Bass.

Simon, H. (1981). *The sciences of the artificial* (2nd ed.). Cambridge, MA: MIT Press.

Skehan, P. (1998). *A cognitive approach to language learning.* Oxford, England: Oxford University Press.

Sonsino, S., & Moore, J. (2001). *Only connect: Teaching and learning at the edge of chaos.* Paper presented at the ITP Conference, New York University, New York.

Sparkes, A.C. (2002). *Telling tales in sport and physical activity: A qualitative journey.* Champaign, IL: Human Kinetics.

Sparkes, A.C. (2007). Embodiment, academics, and the audit culture: A story seeking consideration. *Qualitative Research, 7,* 521–550.

Spry, T. (2001). Performing autoethnography. *Qualitative Inquiry, 7,* 706–732.

Striff, E. (2003). Introduction: Locating performance studies. In E. Striff (Ed.), *Performance studies* (pp. 1–13). London: Macmillan.

Vallacher, R.R., & Nowak, A. (1997). The emergence of dynamical social psychology. *Psychological Inquiry, 8,* 152–159.

Vallerand, R.J. (1987). Antecedents of self-related affects in sport: Preliminary evidence on the intuitive-reflective appraisal model. *Journal of Sport Psychology, 9,* 161–182.

Vallerand, R.J., & Losier, G.F. (1999). An integrative analysis of intrinsic and extrinsic motivation in sport. *Journal of Applied Sport Psychology, 11,* 142–169.

Wallace, M. (2001). Sharing leadership of schools through teamwork: A justifiable risk? *Educational Management and Administration, 29,* 153–167.

Wallace, M. (2003). Managing the unmanageable? Coping with complex educational change [Inaugural professorial lecture, University of Bath]. *Educational Management and Administration, 31,* 9–29.

Wallace, M., & Pocklington, K. (2002). *Managing complex educational change: Large scale reorganisation of schools.* London: Routledge.

Weiner, B. (1986). *An attributional theory of achievement motivation and emotion.* New York: Springer-Verlag.

Weiss, M.R., & Ferrer-Caja, E. (2002). Motivational orientations and sport behavior. In T.S. Horn (Ed.), *Advances in sport psychology* (2nd ed., pp. 101–183). Champaign, IL: Human Kinetics.

INDEX

A

abuse. *See* sexual abuse, of children and youth
The Abyss: Exploring Depression Through a Narrative of the Self (Smith) 80
achievement goal theory 222-223
acquisitiveness 96-97
action research 221-223
active forgetting 113
Affluenza (James) 97
Agamemnon (Aeschylus) 25
alternative erotic lifestyles 132-135
alternative narratives 10-15, 17-19
American Anthropological Association 146
anatta 178
anxiety, competitive 185-187, 244-245
anxiety, existential 238-239, 240, 244-245
applied practice. *See also* sport and exercise psychology
    Buddhism in 183-185
    child abuse implications for 260-262
    multitheoretical approach to 278-282
    playful deviance in 136-137
arts-based research methodologies 26-27. *See also* ethnodrama
Association for Applied Sport Psychology 196, 204
asylum, political and humanitarian 114-115, 121, 124
attachment
    about 173, 175, 179-180, 181
    metaphors 96-97
attribution theory 224
Australian horse racing study 43-56
Australian Psychological Society 197
authenticity 239
autoethnography. *See also* ethnodrama
    about 74-75, 84
    of BDSM activities 132-135
    of coaching experiences 270-278
    deviance of 131-132
    emergence of 78-80
    illustrations and selections of 80-83
    informed fiction 270
    presentation of 34-35
    rejection of 220
    topics in 79
autonomy 279
avoidance 256

B

BDSM, autoethnographic research 132-135
Beck, Aaron 208
behavioral rehearsal 163
being and doing 183-184
biography, personal. *See* autoethnography; narrative inquiry
biopsychosocial model 253-255. *See also* collaborative practice
Black Watch (Burke) 25

blame casting 160-161
boundary situations
    about 234, 246
    existential psychology and 238-241
    human development theory and 238
    narrative inquiry into 241-245
    transition and identity 236-238
Bourke, A. 235
Buddhism
    about 174-175, 188-189
    and applied practice 183-185
    clinical narratives 185-188
    ego development 181-183
    four noble truths 178-181
    metaphors 88, 96-97
    mindfulness 176-178, 184-185
    no-self 177-178
    role in sport psychology 175-185
    therapeutic alliance 184-185
Burke, Gregory 25
bystander effect 258-259, 262

C

career transitions. *See* boundary situations
case study research 40, 42
Cathy Come Home (Sandford) 26
certification, and supervision 168-169, 203-205
change 180
child and youth athletes, protecting
    applied practice implications 260-262
    biopsychosocial model 253-255
    bystander effect 258-259
    identification training 260-261
    safeguarding issues 252-253
    sexual abuse 255-260
clinging (attachment) 173, 175, 179-180, 181
coaches/coaching
    abusive practices 257-260
    autoethnographical perspective 270-278
    complexity theory and context 282-284
    multitheoretical approach 278-282
    noticing 283-284
    orchestration 284
    as performance 268-270
    and performance narratives 12
    and sport psychology 268
Coaches Training Institute 136
co-active model 136-137
cognitive-behavioral supervision 163-164
collaborative practice. *See also* biopsychosocial model
    about 107-112, 254
    conclusions 124-125
    psychotherapy support 112-120
    sport psychology support 120-124
commitment 99
communication, and cultural norms 147-149, 154-155
competence 279

complexity theory 282-284
conflict management 280
context 226, 278, 282-284
Convention on the Rights of the Child 253
countertransference 164-165, 201
creative nonfiction 78, 83
criminal offenders 138-139
critical social science commentary 62, 63-65, 68
Crosset, Todd 4-5
Crouching Tiger, Hidden Dragon (film) 94-95
culture
    communication and 147-149, 154-155
    cultural awareness 146-150
    cultural immersion 152-153
    cultural loss 114
    cultural membership 146
    developing cultural awareness 151-154
    microculture 150-151
    stereotyping 145-146

D
Davies, Hunter 234
Denzin, Norman 3-4
depression 6, 16, 223
desire 173, 179-180, 181
deviance, playful
    about 129-130, 140
    in applied practice 136-137
    BDSM lessons 132-135
    labeling 139-140
    learning from criminal offenders 137-139
    in qualitative research 130-132
discovery narrative 8-10
dissociation 256
documentary drama 26
Douglas, K. 81-82
drama 24-29. *See also* ethnodrama
dreams 90
dukkha 177, 178-179, 181

E
Edna the Inebriate Woman (Sandford) 26
education, sport psychology. *See* professional training programs
efficacy, role 280
ego 177-178, 180-183, 222-223
Einstein, Albert 40
Ellis, Albert 208
emancipation 63
emotional engagement 227-228
empathy 185, 225
empowerment 63
enculturation 149-150
English Premier League football 234-235
Ensler, Eve 25
Erikson, Erik 237-238, 246
erotic transference 201
ethics
    knowledge, and dilemmas of 5
    in transitions 240
ethnicity 146
ethnodrama. *See also* autoethnography
    about 24-29, 36

autoethnography 34-35
    narratives as script 30-32
    scenography in 28, 30-34
    sport-based examples 30-35
    storytelling as monologue 34-35
    subtext in 27-28, 30-32
ethnography. *See* autoethnography; ethnodrama
Ethnography in the Performing Arts: A Student Guide (Kruger) 27
existential psychology 238-241
eye contact 148

F
facilitative anxiety 239
failure. *See* performance failure
fan experience 29-35
Fates, Mates and Moments (Gilbourne) 24
female athletes
    homogenization of 4-5
    relational narratives of 13
    sexual and physical abuse 255-262
    silencing of narratives of 13
film, and metaphor 93-95
flotation tank therapy 92-93
flow 176
folktales. *See* metaphors and folktales
football fan experiences 29-35
Frank, A. 79
free association 100
Freud, Sigmund 161-162, 176, 180, 188, 277

G
Gallipoli (film) 93-94
Gallwey, Timothy 176
Gilbourne, David 24, 60, 83
Gilligan, Carol 13
greetings 148
grief 117

H
Habermas, J. 62, 63, 64
hardship 238
hearing and listening 99-101
Helen Bamber Foundation 108, 113
hero narrative 7
horse racing 43-56
human development 238
humanistic psychology 238, 239

I
identity
    anxiety and 239
    female homogenization 4-5
    transition and 236-238
If You Meet the Buddha on the Road, Kill Him (Kopp) 175
illness narratives 7
illumination 67
imagery. *See* metaphors and folktales
individualism 244-245
informed fiction 270
injury 4
International Olympic Committee 253
interpersonal space 148

interview methodology 14
introspection 158-161
intuitive-reflective appraisal model 279

J
James, Oliver 97
jockey study, Australian 43-56
judgment 225-226

K
knowledge generation 67, 158
Knowles, Zoe 60
Korzinski, Michael 108, 112-120
Kruger, S. 27

L
labeling 139-140
language, in sport psychology xxi-xxiii, 42-43
learning 283
Lebenswelt 245
Levine, Harold 130
licensure, and supervision 168-169, 203-205
Lindsay, P. 64
listening 99-101, 220, 223
Lysistrata (Aristophanes) 25

M
manipulation 281
Martin, David 160
masculinity 4, 235
Maslow, A. 239
McCullough, Dearbhla 108, 120-124
McFee, G. 277
McGuiness, Jim 34-35
media, and metaphor 93-95
memories 90-91
mental toughness xxi-xxii
mental training techniques. *See* psychological
        skills training (PST)
metaphors and folktales
    about 88, 101-102
    attachment metaphors 96-97
    hearing and listening 99-101
    Nasruddin, the wise fool 91-93
    in popular media 93-95
    power of 88-91
    self-protection metaphor 97-99
microculture 150-151
A Midsummer Night's Dream (Shakespeare)
        25
mindfulness 174-175, 176-178, 184-185, 188-189
modeling 163
monologue 34-35
morality 281
Morley, C. 63-64
multicultural practice. *See under* culture
multidisciplinary support. *See* collaborative practice
multitheoretical approach 278-284

N
narrative inquiry. *See also* ethnodrama; metaphors
        and folktales
    about 5
    alternative narratives in sport 10-15, 17-19

autoethnography 34-35
of boundary situations 241-245
discovery narrative 8-10
identifying sport narratives 8-10
implications of 17-19
narrative analysis 90
performance narrative 8-10, 15-16
potential of 6-8
reflective writing 65-68
relational narrative 8-10, 13
Nasruddin, Mullah 91-92
National Strength and Conditioning Association
        196
negative experiences, psychology of 238-241
Niven, Ailsa 60
noble truths, four 178-181
norms, cultural
    awareness of 147-149
    and microcultures 150-151
no-self 177-178
noticing 283-284

O
objects relation theory 164
Ogilvie, Bruce 178
"On Transience" (Freud) 180
orchestration 284
"othering" 140

P
parenting 182-183
Parker, A. 234-235
performance enhancement, overemphasis on xix,
        xvii, xx-xxi, 220-221
performance failure 218
performance fluctuations 15-16
performance narrative 8-19
personality xxi
PETTLEP (physical, environment, task, timing,
        learning, emotion, perspective) ap-
        proach 89-90
playwriting 25-26
Poetics (Aristotle) 25
postpositivism 65-66, 219
post-traumatic stress disorder (PTSD) 113
practitioners. *See* sport psychologists
probabilities 40-41
professional training programs. *See also* supervi-
        sion, therapeutic
    academic staff disconnection 206-209
    accreditation 209
    departmental affiliation 196, 203
    future of 209-210
    limitations of 237
    origins of 195
    process-oriented training 200-203
    PST overemphasis xiv, 194, 198-200
    reflection and refraction in 159
    supervision 161-169, 203-206
    theoretical gaps in 199-200
prompts 163
psychodynamic supervision models 164-165
psychological skills training (PST) model xiv, 194,
        197, 198-200

The Psychology of Enhancing Human Perfor-
mance: The Mindfulness-Acceptance-
Commitment Approach (Gardner and
Moore) 177
psychosocial theory 220
psychotherapy
in collaborative practice 112-120
free association 100
hearing and listening 99-101
narratives of 92, 95
for practitioners 202-203
Publication Manual of the American Psycho-
logical Association (APA) 77-78

Q
qualitative research
arts-based research methodologies 26-27
case study research 40, 42
certainty and 40
criticism of 42-43
disciplinary associations 219
effecting change with 39
emergence of 75-77
ethnography 26-27, 36
language ambiguities in 42-43
playful deviance in 130-132
postpositivist influences 65-66, 67-68, 76
realist tale 76-78
theory-led 221-223
Qualitative Research in Sport and Exercise
(journal) 77
quantitative research
about 40-43
arbitrary metrics in 41-42
Australian horse racing study 43-56
certainty in 40-41
effecting change with 56
generalization to population 52
self-report measures 41
and sport stakeholders 41, 52-53, 54

R
race 146
racism 146-147
realist tale 76-78
reflective practice
about 59-62, 68-69, 157-158
Buddhist lessons for 183-185, 188-189
cultural awareness 152-153
current studies in 62-65
knowledge generation 67, 158
and psychodynamic supervision models 164-165
self-reflection 158-161, 165-167
supervision and 161-169
victim-blaming 160
writing reflectively 65-68
relatedness 279
relational narrative 8-10, 13
religion 154
research methodologies. *See also* qualitative
research; quantitative research
arts-based 26-27
autoethnography as emerging 78-80
ethnography as qualitative inquiry 26-27, 36

intractability of 74
subjective experience in 74
restitution narrative 6-7
retirement
and performance narratives 9
transition research on 236
Richardson, D. 83
Roberts, Glyn 131
Rogers, Carl 183, 184-185, 188
role efficacy 280
role plays 163
Running Man (Stone) 81

S
sacrifice 238
Salter, D. 240
Sandford, Jeremy 26
Scanlan, Tara 130
scientific revolutions 135
scientific tale 77
self-determination theory 279, 282
self-knowledge 147, 239, 240. *See also* identity
self-management 163
self narratives 4
self-protection metaphor 97-99
self-reflection, in practice 158-161, 165-167, 169
self-talk 154-155
sense making 67
sexual abuse, of children and youth 255-260
sexuality and eroticism 134
sexual offenders 138-139
Shakespeare, William 25
Smith, B. 80
social gerontology 237
social work, generalist approach of 137-138
somatics 136-137
Sparkes, Andrew 4, 76, 77-78
spiritual materialism 177, 189
sport
goodness of xv-xvi
microcultures in 150-151
negative aspects of xv, xvii-xviii
sexual abuse in 255-260, 262
sport and exercise psychology. *See also* professional training programs
critical theory in 63
critique of xiii-xiv
current state of practice 196-198
educational and clinical separation 207-209
effects of poor supervision on 166-167
embracing complexity of 18-19
employment 196-197
full spectrum of xvii-xviii
importance xiii
language in xxi-xxiii
multitheoretical approach 278-282
performance enhancement overemphasis xvii,
xix, xx-xxi
positivistic reductionism in 277-278
process-oriented issues 200-203
PST overemphasis xiv, 194, 198-200
sexual abuse research 260-262
supervision and certification 168-169, 203-205
theory in xiv-xv, 221-223, 226-227, 229-230

unruly growth of 194-195
Sport Performance Assessment and Rehabilitation Centre (SPARC) 120
sport psychologists. *See also* professional training programs
    Buddhism and 183-185
    communication and culture 147-149, 154-155
    cultural awareness of 146-150, 151-154
    emotional engagement of 227-228
    hearing and listening 99-101
    motives for 202
    personal psychotherapy for 202-203
    Rogerian characteristics 183, 184-185
    self-reflection 158-161
    themes associated with role of 61
    therapeutic metaphor 101-102
stakeholders, sport 41, 52-53, 54
Stanford Prison Experiment 138
stereotyping 145-146
Stone, B. 81
Storying Myself (Douglas) 81-82
story/stories. *See* narrative inquiry
storytelling. *See also* autoethnography; ethnodrama; metaphors and folktales
    emotional control and 89
    as monologue 34-35
    research as 219
Strean, William 130
Strozzi Institute 136
subjective experience, in research 74
subtext 27-28, 30-32
suffering 173, 177, 178-179, 181, 182, 187, 238
suicide 44-45, 116-119
sukha 177
supervision, therapeutic
    about 161, 169
    after training programs 205-206
    clinical narrative 187-188
    cognitive-behavioral supervision 163-164
    future of 167-169
    history of 161-162
    models of 162-165
    psychodynamic models of 164-165
    versus self-reflection 165-167
    training in 168
    in training programs 203-205
Supervision Interest Network 168

T
Tales From the Field (Gilbourne and Richardson) 83
Telling Tales in Sport and Physical Activity (Sparkes) 77-78

The Tempest (Shakespeare) 25
thanatological studies 237
theater 24-29. *See also* ethnodrama
therapeutic alliance 95, 118-119, 122-124, 184-185, 200-203, 261
therapeutic boundaries 123-124
toughness xxi-xxii
training. *See* professional training programs
training and education. *See* professional training programs
transference 164-165, 201
transition situations
    about 234, 246
    existential psychology and 238-241
    human development theory and 238
    and identity 236-238
    narrative inquiry into 241-245
traumatic history 109-112
travel, cultural immersion of 152-153
trust 95, 118-119, 122-124

U
unconditionality 220, 225-226
UNICEF 253
Unprotected (Wilson) 25

V
The Vagina Monologues (Ensler) 25
Van Maanen, J. 78
victim-blaming 160-161

W
The War Game (Watkins) 26
Watkins, Peter 26
winning, in performance narratives 15-16
women athletes. *See* female athletes
writing. *See also* autoethnography; ethnodrama
    in reflective practice 65-68, 74
    styles, in research writing 76

Y
Your Breath in the Air (Gilbourne *et al.*) 29-35
youth athletes. *See* child and youth athletes, protecting

Z
Zen in the Art of Archery (Herrigel) 176
Zen in the Martial Arts (Hyams) 176

ABOUT THE EDITORS

Photo courtesy of David Gilbourne and Mark B. Andersen

Mark Andersen & David Gilbourne

David Gilbourne, PhD, is a professor of qualitative research in sport at the University of Wales Institute Cardiff and teaches in the Cardiff School of Sport. He cofounded and codirected the first and second International Conferences on Qualitative Research in Sport and Exercise (2004 and 2006) and acted as external advisor to the third conference at Roehampton University, UK, in 2009. David also cofounded *Qualitative Research in Sport and Exercise,* the first peer-reviewed journal dedicated to disseminating qualitative research from all sport-based disciplines.

David speaks internationally on the topics of sport-oriented social science and qualitative research, and in 2010 he acted as visiting professor at Copenhagen University. His writing focuses on issues of qualitative methodology. Alongside colleagues, he has commented frequently on the topic of action research and reflective practice in applied sport psychology. His current work explores a range of autoethnographic communications with particular emphasis on storytelling through creative short-story writing, drama, and poetry.

Mark B. Andersen, PhD, is a professor in the School of Sport and Exercise Science and the Institute for Sport, Exercise, and Active Living at Victoria University in Melbourne, Australia. He also coordinates the master and doctoral degrees in applied psychology in the School of Social Science and Psychology. He received his PhD in psychology with a doctoral minor in exercise and sport sciences from the University of Arizona at Tucson in 1988.

In 1994 Mark received the Dorothy V. Harris Memorial Award for excellence as a young scholar and practitioner in applied sport psychology from the Association for Applied Sport Psychology. He has been a keynote speaker at 10 international and national conferences and has published more than 60 articles in refereed journals and more than 75 book chapters and proceedings. He has edited three other Human Kinetics books: *Doing Sport Psychology, Sport Psychology in Practice,* and *Overtraining Athletes: Personal Journeys in Sport.* Mark is a member of the Australian Psychological Society (APS) and APS College of Sport and Exercise Psychology. In addition to his academic duties, he maintains a small psychotherapy practice in Melbourne.